THE ELUSIVE QUEST FOR GROWTH
IN ARGENTINA

Other Books by Daniel Chudnovsky

Empresas Multinacionales y Ganancias Monopólicas en una Economía Latinoamericana.

Capital Goods Production in the Third World. An Economic Study of Technology Acquisition.

Las Economías de Argentina e Italia. Situación actual y perspectivas de asociación.

Transnational Corporations and Industrialization.

¿Por qué Sucedió? Las causas económicas de la reciente crisis argentina.

El Desafío de Integrarse para Crecer. Balance y perspectivas del MERCOSUR en su primera década.

Other Books by Daniel Chudnovsky and Andrés López

Los Transgénicos en la Agricultura Argentina. Una historia con final abierto.

La Transnacionalización de la Economía Argentina.

El Boom de Inversión Extranjera Directa en el MERCOSUR.

Investimentos Externos no MELCOSUL.

Las Multinacionales Latinoamericanas. Sus estrategias en el mundo globalizado.

Auge y Ocaso del Capitalismo Asistido. La industria petroquímica latinoamericana.

Los Límites de la Apertura. Liberalización, reestructuración productiva y medio ambiente.

THE ELUSIVE QUEST FOR GROWTH IN ARGENTINA

Daniel Chudnovsky
and
Andrés López

THE ELUSIVE QUEST FOR GROWTH IN ARGENTINA

First published in 2007 by
PALGRAVE MACMILLAN™
175 Fifth Avenue, New York, N.Y. 10010 and
Houndmills, Basingstoke, Hampshire, England RG21 6XS
Companies and representatives throughout the world.

PALGRAVE MACMILLAN is the global academic imprint of the Palgrave Macmillan division of St. Martin's Press, LLC and of Palgrave Macmillan Ltd. Macmillan® is a registered trademark in the United States, United Kingdom and other countries. Palgrave is a registered trademark in the European Union and other countries.

ISBN-13: 978–1–4039–7789–2
ISBN-10: 1–4039–7789–5

Library of Congress Cataloging-in-Publication Data is available from the Library of Congress.

A catalogue record for this book is available from the British Library.

Design by Newgen Imaging Systems (P) Ltd., Chennai, India.

First edition: May 2007

10 9 8 7 6 5 4 3 2 1

Printed in the United States of America.

CONTENTS

LIST OF TABLES

LIST OF FIGURES

LIST OF ABBREVIATIONS

TRIPs	Agreement on Trade-Related Intellectual Property Rights
FONTAR	Fondo Tecnológico Argentino [Argentine Technological Fund]
ADEFA	Asociación de Fábricas de Automotores de Argentina [Automobile Makers Association]
BITs	Bilateral Investment Treaties
CP	Clean Production
CET	Common External Tariff
ECLAC	Economic Commission for Latin America and the Caribbean
EOP	End-of-pipe
EMA	Environmental Management Activities
CIS	European Community Innovation Services
FDI	Foreign Direct Investment
FOMEC	Fondo para el Mejoramiento de la Calidad Universitaria [Fund for the Improvement of University Quality]
GATT	General Agreement on Tariffs and Trade
GMOs	Genetically Modified Organisms
GACTEC	Gabinete Científico y Tecnológico [Government's Science and Technology Cabinet]
GDP	Gross Domestic Product
ISI	Import-substitution Industrialization
ICSID	International Centre for Settlement of Investment Disputes
IDRC	International Development Research Centre
IMF	International Monetary Fund
ISO	International Standard Organization
BICE	Banco de Inversión y Comercio Exterior [Investment and Foreign Trade Bank]
FIEL	Fundación de Investigaciones Económicas Latinoamericanas [Latin American Economic Research Foundation.]
MIT	Massachusetts Institute of Technology

M&A	Mergers and Acquisitions
MAI	Multilateral Agreement on Investment
BANADE	Banco Nacional de Desarrollo [National Bank of Development]
CNEA	Comisión Nacional de Energía Atómica [National Commission of Atomic Energy]
CONICET	Consejo Nacional de Investigaciones Científicas y Técnicas [National Council of Scientific and Technological Research]
INTA	Instituto Nacional de Tecnología Agropecuaria [National Institute of Agricultural Technology]
INPI	Instituto Nacional de la Propiedad Industrial [National Institute of Industrial Property]
INTI	Instituto Nacional de Tecnología Industrial [National Institute of Industrial Technology]
INDEC	Instituto Nacional de Estadísticas y Censos [National Institute of Statistics and Census]
OECD	Organization for Economic Cooperation and Development
PWDC	Postwar Development Consensus
UPOV	Protection of New Varieties of Plants
PPP	Purchasing Power Parity
REER	Real Effective Exchange Rate
RER	Real Exchange Rate
R&D	Research and Development
CENIT	Centro de Investigaciones para la Transformación [Research Center for Transformation]
S&T	Science and Technology
FONCYT	Fondo para la Investigación Científica y Tecnológica [Scientific and Technological Research Fund]
SMEs	Small and Medium Enterprises
MERCOSUR	Mercado Común del Sur [Southern Common Market]
TFP	Total Factor Productivity
TNCs	Transnational Corporations
UNDP	United Nations Development Program
UNESCO	United Nations Educational, Scientific and Cultural Organization
VAT	Value Added Tax
WC	Washington Consensus
WTO	World Trade Organization

PREFACE

Despite the rich availability of natural resources and ample base of human capital, in the past 40 years Argentina has shown a poor growth performance when compared to most other countries, except for the group of low income developing economies in Africa, Asia and Latin America. Key development indicators such as unemployment, poverty, and income inequality have also severely worsened during this period. This performance by itself makes Argentina an intriguing puzzle for any analyst of development economics. It challenges easy explanations that aim at finding single causes—that is, the role of Peronism, the domestic "oligarchy" or of neoliberalism the influence of the International Monetary Fund, corruption, the curse of "natural resources."

Furthermore, the country has not been on a permanent stagnation like many other developing countries. Two growth episodes took place during this period, in 1964–1974 and in 1991–1998. These growth episodes took place under two different paradigms in development thinking: the Postwar Development Consensus and the Washington Consensus. A peculiarity of the policies applied in Argentina, inspired in those paradigms, was that they actually led to significant growth of the economy and to a remarkable learning process at firm level that contributed to important productivity gains.

In both occasions, unfortunately, growth was only temporary since it was followed by extremely severe institutional and economic crisis. These crises, along with long recessionary periods such as the 1980s, dissipated all the gains that were attained during the growth episodes. The last crisis that ended with the Convertibility currency board scheme attracted worldwide attention not only by its severity, but also because of the fact that it was part of the series of systemic crises that affected emergent markets under the Washington Consensus.

This book attempts to shed light on the complex set of key determinants of the economic and social performance of Argentina since the early 1960s to the current economic recovery from the 2001–2002 depression.

In contrast to other contributions that focus almost exclusively on macroeconomic variables, in this book we pay due attention, on the one hand, to institutional variables and, on the other hand, to firms' strategies and performances under different macroeconomic and policy settings.

Hence, combining an institutional and historical approach with rigorous economic analysis this book offers a timely, comprehensive and distinctive contribution to the elucidation of the Argentina's development puzzle.

Chapter 1 surveys the main issues that have attracted development thinking since the end of World War II to the present days and hence situates the Argentine puzzle into the wider development debate. While it is largely focused on the rise and fall of both the Postwar Development Consensus and the Washington Consensus, it also provides an insight of the progress made in the academic literature to deal with the role of institutions and firms in the process of economic development.

The key long-term economic, social, and institutional features of Argentina's history, especially in the period under study, are described in chapter 2. Chapter 3 deals with the growth episode that took place under the import substitution industrialization strategy in 1964–1974, discussing the macroeconomic and institutional setting, the evolution of the production structure, and the nature and determinants of private firms' learning processes in that context. The early attempt to apply a neoliberal policy experiment by a military dictatorship in 1976–1981 and the long recession of the 1980s that followed the episode are analyzed in chapter 4.

The specific way in which the structural reforms suggested in the Washington Consensus were applied by Menem's administration in the 1990s is discussed in detail in chapter 5. This chapter also discusses the lack of effective complementary policies aimed at dealing with the negative effects of those reforms. The uneven impacts of the reforms on the macroeconomic, sectoral, and social evolution during the growth period of 1991–1998 are analyzed in chapter 6.

Chapter 7 aims at analyzing the key features of the "microeconomics" of the 1990s. First, it presents an overview of manufacturing firms' strategies and performance during that period. Second, relying on a unique data base at manufacturing firm level, it discusses the main findings of several econometric studies we have recently completed on innovation, trade, foreign direct investment, and environmental management issues during the Convertibility period.

Chapter 8 analyzes the external shocks and domestic determinants that led to the 2001–2002 crisis and gives a stylized account of the management of the crisis after the default in the external debt and the huge peso devaluation as well as of the key features of the current recovery since 2003.

The last chapter summarizes the main conclusions and policy implications of the whole book. It ends with a brief reflection, based on the current debates after the failure of the Washington Consensus reforms; on the so far successful evolution of the Argentine economy after the crisis with the aim of highlighting the challenges it faces to transform the present recovery into a sustainable growth and development process.

ACKNOWLEDGMENTS

We have been working together on several research projects related to the topics of this book at the Centro de Investigaciones para la Transformación (CENIT) in Buenos Aires for the past 15 years. The International Development Research Centre (IDRC) of Canada, through various programs and networks, has been the main source of financial support for our work on key themes of the book such as industrial restructuring, technological change and innovation, environmental management, and foreign direct investment. The National Agency for Scientific and Technological Promotion of Argentina cofinanced some of those studies.

The United Nations Industrial Development Organization (UNIDO) Research Program requested us, in 2005, to prepare a report that analyzed the long run determinants of productivity growth in Argentina. That report has been largely revised to transform it into several chapters of this book. The main findings of the book were discussed at a seminar in the Latin American Centre at Oxford University in May 2005.

Materials used for writing chapters 6 and 7 were discussed at seminars at the Universities of San Andrés and Di Tella in Argentina, at the Globelics International Conferences held at Rio de Janeiro, Beijing and Pretoria in 2003, 2004, and 2005, respectively, at the sixth Global Development Conference held at Dakar in January 2005, at the Bellagio Conference organized by the Harvard JFK School of Government in May 2005, and at the 2005 LACEA Conference in Paris. We would like to thank Research Policy for releasing the copyrights of material used in chapter 7 and which was published by us in that journal in 2006.

Chapter 8 on Argentina's 2001–2002 crisis is largely based on the findings of a project financed by the United Nations Development Program and the Ministry of Foreign Affairs of Argentina.

Several junior colleagues at CENIT participated in this work in an outstanding way. Germán Pupato has been the coauthor of two of the materials we used in chapter 7 and of an early version of chapter 8. Gastón Rossi and Eugenia Orlicki have also coauthored some of the materials that were used in chapter 7.

In the preparation of the manuscript of this book we have benefited from the excellent research assistance of Mara Pedrazzoli, Ariana Sacroisky, and Verónica Gutman, as well as from some translations into English made by Giselle Cohen and Verónica Gutman.

We have benefited a lot from the work and discussions with several colleagues, as well as from the findings of many of their studies (as reflected in the quotes and bibliography of this book). In that connection, we would especially like to thank Roberto Bisang, Juan Carlos Del Bello, José Fanelli, Roberto Frenkel, Sebastián Galiani, Pablo Gerchunoff, Daniel Heymann, Jorge Katz, Bernardo Kosacoff, Gustavo Lugones, Fernando Porta, Mariano Tommasi, and Gabriel Yoguel. Needless to say, neither they nor our colleagues at CENIT are responsible for any of our views or mistakes. We thank Pablo Gerchunoff and Juan J. Llach for making available the database required for graph 2.2, and José M. Fanelli for graph 2.7.

CHAPTER 1

INTRODUCTION: THE END OF PANACEAS; FROM THE POSTWAR CONSENSUS TO THE POST–WASHINGTON CONSENSUS

The Postwar Development Consensus and the Import–Substitution Industrialization Stage

The early Postwar Development Consensus (PWDC) was based on a few theoretical contributions (like Rosenstein-Rodan, 1943 on the "Big Push")[1] and mostly on "big ideas," like the government being the driving force behind development and the importance of capital accumulation. This was stressed by authors such as Nurkse (1952) and Lindauer and Pritchett (2002).

These ideas spread in a scenario when the "Keynesian revolution" had given a rationale to active macroeconomic policies in order to achieve employment objectives and overcome recessions. Keynesian ideas had also given place to the first "growth models," such as those of Harrod and Domar, which suggested the key role of savings and investment in the growth processes—although those models were not meant to "explain" why countries grow, they were used later for that purpose (Easterly, 2001).

Moreover, the apparent successes of the Soviet economy contributed to consolidate the idea that physical capital accumulation was the key for growth and also stressed the need of State planning as the way to achieve resources mobilization required to attain investment objectives. The experience of World War II in countries such as the United Kingdom was also influential in shaping the early thoughts on the role of State indicative planning to coordinate the large (and mostly public) investments required for the "Big Push" in developing countries.[2]

The power of these ideas was so intense that even international financial institutions like the World Bank endorsed the need of high investment rates and allowed a large role for the State (see Easterly, 2001). The World Bank adopted a saving-investment gap approach to estimate the need of foreign financial aid for developing countries in order to meet growth objectives.

When the so-called structuralist school of thought appeared, it emphasized the fact that developing countries had distinct structural problems that could not be properly addressed using conventional economic theories. Albert Hirschman and Raul Prebisch[3] were among the pioneers of this school, which helped shape the import-substitution industrialization process (ISI)—although the ISI itself had began spontaneously after the 1930 crisis in many developing countries, prompted by foreign currency scarcity and trade restrictions, structuralist economists advocated for the need of "industrial programming" as a way to achieve industrialization goals (Oman and Wignaraja, 1991).

The Hirschman (1958) thesis of "unbalanced growth" suggested the need to identify growth "poles" that could pull the rest of the economy and hence attain high growth. This thesis implied a "picking winners" strategy through an active industrial policy (Singer, 1997). The "picking winners" strategy was also fostered by the growing consensus on the idea that industrialization was heavy industrialization—as it had happened in the Soviet experience.

At the same time, authors such as Singer (1950) and Prebisch (1950) found that the terms of trade between primary products and manufactured goods tended to deteriorate over time. Hence, developing countries, exporting primary commodities, would find that a certain level of exports would afford gradually decreasing import levels. This thesis also stressed the need of developing countries to industrialize, an objective that could be attained through protectionist policies. It is no surprise then that the ISI strategy was heavily inward-oriented, a fact reinforced by the "export pessimism" that was widely shared among development economists and policymakers at the time.[4]

Criticisms of the ISI strategy were already published in the 1950s, but it was in the late 1960s and early 1970s that they began to attract attention. Those criticisms asserted that beyond distorting natural specialization patterns— in detriment of economic efficiency—ISI policies had other negative consequences, such as the "anti-export" bias generated by high levels of effective protection rates (Little et al., 1970; Balassa, 1971). The inward-oriented ISI strategy was soon to be confronted with the export-led growth processes that, according to neoclassical thinkers, had been taking place in East Asia, giving way to more dynamic and stable growth trajectories vis-à-vis those taking place in Latin American countries (Balassa et al., 1982).

Another point of criticism toward the PWDC and the ISI process related to the role of the State. As stated by Singer (1997), proponents of State intervention in the industrialization process considered government failures less relevant (or more easily tractable) than market failures.[5] However, the assumption of a benevolent government was soon to be put into question as well as the idea that government intervention was not a costless process since government failures significantly outweighed market failures in many cases (Krueger, 1990).[6]

State intervention did not only lead to traditional deadweight (efficiency) losses but also carried costs when private agents divert resources from productive activities toward "rent seeking" activities in order to capture rents generated by State intervention. Krueger (1974) was among the first economists to stress these costs studying the consequences of import quotas in developing countries.

Inflation was another cause of debate at the time. While the PWDC regarded inflation control as a desirable object but subordinated to employment creation, and the structuralist approach deemed inflation as a price to pay for maintaining growth and overcoming structural disequilibria, the "orthodox" opinion—which was behind the stabilization policies suggested by the International Monetary Fund (IMF)—stressed the need to reduce inflation through contractive fiscal and monetary instruments.

Since the late 1960s a new and very relevant kind of criticism to the ISI process and the PWDC emerged, on the basis of the evidence of growing income distribution inequality and widening dualism in many developing countries. Even in countries with a good growth record like Brazil, income distribution—which was already quite unequal in 1960—worsened further (Fishlow, 1972). It thus became clear that more than a decade of rapid growth in developing countries was of little or no benefit to perhaps a third of their population (Chenery et al., 1974).[7]

Seers (1969) and Myrdal (1972) were among the first to question the idea that development was merely Gross Domestic Product (GDP) growth and called for urgent action on poverty, inequality, and employment issues. All this meant that the PWDC ideas on growth and income distribution that were largely inspired on the Kuznets (1955) inverted-U hypothesis— which suggested that growth may initially cause inequality but later on it would reduce it—began to be rejected.

The difficulties in reducing inequality under the PWDC growth process were at the origin of the studies on basic needs (Streeten et al., 1981) and then on entitlements and capabilities. These papers made the important point that economic growth was no more than a means to some other key development objectives like life expectancy, literacy, higher education, health, and freedom (Sen, 1983, 1999).[8] Although this literature had little influence on economic development policies at that time, they contributed to the erosion of the PWDC that, as seen before, had started to be criticized from other quarters.

Finally, environmental problems that had been ignored so far were highlighted by the famous "Limits to Growth" report of the Club of Rome, which stated that industrial expansion threatened to deplete natural resources and cause unsustainable pollution levels that would finally lead to economic and social catastrophes (see Oman and Wignaraja, 1991).

The end of the PWDC was prompted by a series of different events including, among others: (1) the rise of inflation in developed countries, which put into question the Keynesian approach to macroeconomic policies; (2) the decline of the Soviet economy, which eroded the faith in State planning; (3) the failures of the aid policies based on the saving-investment gap approach; (4) the growing macroeconomic problems faced by Latin American countries that had embarked upon ISI strategies.

As mentioned before, the ISI[9] process in Latin America began after the 1930 crisis, prompted by the collapse of primary commodities prices and the upsurge of export pessimism throughout the world (see Waterbury, 1999). The ISI began with the production of final goods that were formerly imported but since the late 1950s a drive toward heavy industrialization took place in the largest countries, such as Argentina, Brazil, and Mexico.

The set of public policies commonly employed during the ISI included foreign exchange controls, high import tariffs, import licenses and quotas, credit rationing, and fiscal and financial incentives to foster investments in infant manufacturing industries. In contrast, science and technology (S&T) policies were less relevant. Resources devoted to research and development (R&D) activities in Latin America were much lower than in industrialized countries and even some high-growth Asian developing countries devoted more resources to R&D than the largest Latin American countries.

While State-owned companies provided public services and produced intermediate—for example, steel, petrochemicals, and so on—and defense—related goods, transnational corporations (TNCs) affiliates often had a leading role in the production of consumer durables and capital goods. However, small and medium enterprises (SMEs) contributed to the bulk of employment creation in manufacturing industries during those years and had a strong presence not only in light industries such as textiles, but also in the production of chemical products and capital goods.

Although R&D efforts were mostly carried out in public firms, public technology institutes, and universities, a significant learning process took place also in the private sector (though hardly reflected in the R&D or patents statistics). Many SMEs were able to develop technological and engineering capabilities that allowed them to obtain productivity gains by improving their plant layout, product design engineering, and production organization technologies. At the same time, the subsidiaries of TNCs introduced new products and production technologies but had to adapt them to the specific features of the local environment by creating engineering departments and technical assistance activities to suppliers and clients (Katz, 1987).

The ISI model was rather successful in generating growth (average real per capita GDP nearly doubled between 1950 and 1970) and employment, although it worked better in countries like Brazil or Mexico vis-à-vis Argentina or Chile. Large productivity gains were achieved through capital goods imports, foreign direct investment (FDI) and the learning processes that took place at the microeconomic level. This, jointly with some policies aimed at relieving the above mentioned anti-export bias, led, at least in the largest countries, not only to significant increases in exports but also to the enhancement of the technological content of the latter (Katz, 1998).

However, a number of problems eroded the sustainability of the ISI model in many countries, including growing macroeconomic and institutional instability, price distortions, and the failure to attain high competitiveness levels in many protected industrial sectors. This failure was the result, among other causes, of the lack of quid pro quo mechanisms aimed at fostering firms to improve their productivity and efficiency in exchange for the subsidies and protection they received, jointly with the lack of sound technology policies, the excessively high levels of protection, and the failure to gradually reduce tariffs in infant industries, which made the latter "eternal" infants.[10]

The Emergence of the Washington Consensus

The demise of the "Keynesian" era and the declining faith in ISI policies paved the way for the resurgence of the neoclassical orthodoxy, which would later converge in what was called the "Washington Consensus" (WC).

While Keynesian economics was replaced by monetarism in the design of macroeconomic policies in the industrialized world, the literature that had been sharply criticizing the outcome of import-substitution policies gained growing popularity.[11] At the same time, the neoclassical interpretation of the East Asian successful experience of export-led growth[12] gave additional support to the heavy criticism to the already moribund early development consensus.

In this scenario, the debt crisis triggered the need for reforms in Latin American countries. It must be noted that the debt crisis also took place in countries that had already made early attempts to introduce orthodox reforms as it were the cases of Chile (since 1973) and Argentina (1976–1981)—in both cases reforms were carried out under military governments. In both countries simultaneous deep financial and trade reforms with macroeconomic arrangements involving preset exchange rates to try and curb price inflation in a context of plentiful external funding led to large external debts and substantial current-account deficits in the late 1970s.

When the United States began to adopt a contractive monetary policy through interest rates increases since late 1979, foreign exchange and financial crisis broke out shortly afterwards in the highly debted Latin American countries, and finally led to the Mexican debt moratorium in 1982.

The crisis initiated the so-called lost decade of the 1980s in which little if any growth was achieved in most Latin American countries. Inflation soared and domestic currencies depreciated in a context in which external financing was rationed and the substantial debt services had to be permanently negotiated with international financial organizations and private debtors. Within these critical conditions the concerns about inequality, poverty, education, and health issues remained at the periphery of the policy agenda.

But, at the same time, democratic governments replaced military dictatorships in Argentina, Uruguay, Brazil, and finally Chile. These emerging democracies had to start a complex institutional learning process while coping with very demanding civil societies (after years of lack of freedom under military dictatorships) in very bad economic times.

After several failed attempts to deal with the consequences of the debt crisis, the policy of structural adjustment initiated by the U.S. Secretary of the Treasury James Baker in 1985 became the key policy approach followed by the IMF and the World Bank and paved the way to the emergence of the WC.

The collapse of the Soviet Union and other socialist countries in 1989 strengthened the popularity of the WC recommendations among policymakers in Latin America. Nevertheless, it was the debt crisis of the 1980s, and its devastating impact that created a very favorable environment for its eventual triumph.[13]

The recommendations of the WC were aimed not only at achieving price stabilization in high inflation countries but also at promoting deep structural reforms like import liberalization, domestic financial reform, opening the capital account, privatization, tax reform, and deregulation.[14] The WC, hence, did not include only macroeconomic goals (low inflation and high growth), but also microeconomic ones (more competitive and efficient firms and productive sectors).

Despite the apparent universality of the ten famous recommendations of the WC (see Williamson, 1990, 1997), the initial conditions, the policy instruments actually used, the pace and sequence and the outcomes of the reforms varied in each country (Fanelli and Mc Mahon, 2006).

In Latin America, Chile and Mexico were early adopters of the WC recommendations, although they applied them partially and gradually. Later on, Argentina (with Peru) became "the poster child" for the implementation of the WC in a big-bang manner. In contrast, reforms in Brazil proceeded more slowly and with pragmatism (Castelar Pinheiro et al., 2004).[15]

Reforms in Latin America were generally successful in reducing inflation and restoring growth after the "lost decade." These outcomes took place in a context of ample international financial resources aimed at investing in the so called "emerging markets," which favored the application of what was then called the "first generation" reforms.

These reforms were mainly aimed at dismantling the previous regulatory regime, introducing new macroeconomic rules, and reducing the size and scope of the State. They included drastic budget cuts and tax reforms, price and markets deregulations, trade, financial, and foreign investment liberalization and privatizations. Although reforms were naturally carried out by local authorities, they were strongly supported by the World Bank and the IMF—who also helped in their design in many cases—and the international financial establishment (Naim, 1994).

The reduction of inflation and the increase in budget discipline were certainly the main achievements of the first generation reforms. However, the impact of such reforms on economic growth was not as high as originally expected by the reformers and was probably temporary (Loayza et al., 2005; Forteza and Tommasi, 2005). While growth performance certainly improved with respect to the 1980s, in most countries it was disappointing as compared with the Latin American performance during the ISI period as well as vis-à-vis East Asian developing countries.[16]

Moreover, deep systemic crisis occurred in many countries after reforms were implemented. The WC was cautious on the foreign exchange rate policy[17] and said nothing on currency and financial crisis prevention. This was probably due to the fact that the prospect of a crisis in countries with good fundamentals and no budget deficits—as it was advised by the WC—was simply dismissed.

Budget deficits—combined with an overvalued exchange rate and huge current account deficits—had been present in the Argentine 1980–1982 crisis, which hence could be thought as a typical "first generation crisis"—as they are called in the specialized literature. The WC approach implicitly assumed that this kind of crisis would not recur once good fundamentals were in place.

However, it is striking that the WC did not take into account the lessons of the Chilean crisis in 1981–1983, a country that had good fundamentals, no budget deficit, and had made several of the reforms later incorporated in the WC. In fact, according to studies on the sequencing of the reforms in the Southern Cone countries in late 1970s, it was argued that the crises in Argentina and Chile had been caused by premature financial liberalization. The resulting policy recommendation was that capital markets should be opened only when the economy has been stabilized, opened to international trade, and had a robust financial system (Frenkel, 2003).[18] This key lesson was ignored by the WC, a fact that may be explained by the globalization euphoria in which it emerged.[19]

Unfortunately, the optimism of the WC proved wrong. Several systemic crises took place in the 1990s and 2000s,[20] and they began in Mexico and the East Asian countries, which did not have budget deficits and that had taken significant steps toward financial and trade liberalization.

Argentina's crisis of 2001–2002 was the worst of these episodes. It took place in a context in which there was already a critical examination at the original WC recommendations, as well as to the management of the IMF of the previous crises. In turn, the severity of the Argentine crisis reinforced those criticisms. In any case, the experience of Latin America after the reforms shows that macroeconomic stability was a goal far more difficult to achieve than that envisaged by the WC (Ocampo, 2004).

In a context of relatively low growth and systemic crisis, regional poverty rates (using a US$2 purchasing power parity [PPP] a day poverty line) may have fallen by almost 4 percent between the early and mid-1990s, but increased by almost 3 percent between the mid-1990s and early 2000. As a result, poverty rates at the beginning of 2000 were nearly the same as in the early 1990s—around 25 percent—while the number of poor people increased from 106 million to 124 million in the same period. However, the evolution of poverty rates was heterogeneous within the region. While poverty incidence fell in countries such as Bolivia, Chile, and Brazil, it had significant increases in Venezuela, Argentina, and Colombia (World Bank, 2006).

In a region that features the most inegalitarian income distribution in the world, inequality increased in South America and remained stable in Central America and the Caribbean during the 1990s. Brazil, that had the most unequal inegalitarian income distribution in the region, experienced a small reduction in inequality (the same happened in Mexico). In contrast, Argentina suffered a sharp rise in income inequality. Inequality also increased in other South American countries, such as Chile, Uruguay, and Venezuela (World Bank, 2004).

Although there is no agreement in the literature about the impact of the reforms on inequality, it appears that reforms have been neither a curse nor a cure for income inequality (Morley, 2000; Stallings and Peres, 2000; World Bank, 2004; see a summary in Forteza and Tommasi, 2005). Although there are many variables at stake, on balance the evidence suggests that reforms may have had mild unequalizing effects. The principal hypothesis that explains the growing inequality is that skill biased technical change brought by trade liberalization increased the demand for tertiary educated workers and resulted in more wage inequality (World Bank, 2004).

The existence of a committed group of reformers was identified as a key condition for the initiation of reforms. However, reform capture has been a very frequent phenomenon. Reformers have often used the window of opportunity to reshape institutions and implement policies that favored them, their cronies, and/or allied political groups. In these conditions, it is hardly surprising that distributive conflicts were the primary determinants of the content and path of reforms (Fanelli and McMahon, 2006).

As for investment patterns, in a context of high capital mobility, fixed (or quasi fixed) exchange rates in many countries and attractive privatization schemes, the region was successful in attracting large FDI flows. In the case of South America, these flows were more geared to nontradable activities than to expand capacity in tradable goods. Nonetheless, it was assumed that FDI would have positive effects on the efficiency and competitiveness in tradable sectors not only due to the introduction of modern technologies and managerial methods, but also due to enhanced access to international markets and significant improvements in domestic infrastructure—as a result of privatization.

Exports certainly increased. Between 1990 and 2003 the average annual increase in merchandise exports amounted to 7.8 percent in terms of volume, the fastest rates of growth in the region's history (Ocampo, 2004).

However, the reforms were clearly less successful in fostering investment increases and productivity growth. Investment rates in the 1990s never recovered the 1970s levels. In turn, the weighted total factor productivity (TFP) of the 10 largest Latin American countries grew at only 0.2 percent a year in 1990–2002 versus 2.1 percent in 1950–1980 (Ocampo, 2004).

With regard to export performance within the Latin American continent, it was found that while South America lost share in world markets, Mexico and the Caribbean had increased their shares. Moreover, South America reinforced its specialization pattern in natural resources based activities, while Mexico and the Caribbean managed to significantly increase their exports of textiles, automobiles, and electronic products. In other words, while South America tended to specialize in low growth activities, Mexico and the Caribbean gained presence in some of the most dynamic world markets (Mortimore et al., 2001).

This divergent specialization pattern is to a large extent the outcome of the different types of FDI attracted by each region. However, even in the case of Mexico and the Caribbean, successful integration in expanding world markets had impacts mostly on employment, but, given the low levels of integration of export activities with the local economy (i.e., innovation, suppliers, and customers development, and so on), did not become a growth engine for the countries as a whole.

The failures of the first generation reforms made them very unpopular in the region—see Lora et al. (2004) for evidence on the "reform fatigue" and Forteza and Tommasi (2005) for information about the changing attitudes of citizens on reforms. While mainstream economists called for second generation reforms that were supposedly aimed at dealing with the undesirable social outcomes of the early reforms and at building better institutional settings in Latin American countries—bad institutions were blamed, for instance, for the shortcomings of privatizations[21]—other economists pointed toward more basic problems of the reformist approach.[22]

As stated by Ocampo (2004), besides a narrow conception of macro-economic stability and a lack of proper understanding of the relations between economic and social policies, the reforms underrated the need for adopting policy interventions in the productive area aimed at promoting investment, productivity, growth, and technological development.

As mentioned earlier, in spite of the shortcomings of the ISI strategy, in many Latin American countries a significant learning process had taken place such that, especially since the late 1960s, significant productivity and export gains had been attained. However, the promoters of the WC based reforms often saw the ISI industries as uniformly inefficient and industrial policies as a tool for creating rent-seekers rather than an instrument that fostered competitiveness and innovation.

Hence, it comes as no surprise that instead of a gradualist approach aimed at preserving the capabilities accumulated during the ISI process while progressively opening the economy to push protected firms and sectors to improve their efficiency, in many countries sweeping reforms were adopted with little or no concern for the need of helping those firms and sectors to adapt to the new rules of the game. In other words, a creative destruction process was supposed to take place, with the demise of old inefficient industries and the expansion of competitive activities; the problem was that there was seemingly more destruction than creation, with the above mentioned negative outcomes.

This flaw of the reformist thinking had its roots in the way conventional neoclassical theory analyzes firms' behavior and technological change. For conventional or textbook microeconomic theory, the center of analysis is the "representative" firm, a completely rational agent that responds only to factor and product price market signals. Knowledge is assumed to be a codified free good to which the firm has instant and easy access. Learning to produce goods in an efficient manner thus becomes entirely predictable once the market forces work and the right prices are in place.

This stylized picture has been sharply questioned by evolutionary and other non-neoclassical scholars (Dosi et al., 1988; Fagerberg et al., 2005; Nelson, 2005). Technological knowledge is not only codified but also mainly tacit. Moreover, as it is partly proprietary it cannot be assumed to be a free good. Even in firms that are not at the technological frontier, as is mostly the case in developing countries, knowledge has to be acquired through experimentation, research, trial and error, and the accumulation of endogenous capabilities, along with the access to external sources such as licensing and consulting agreements and/or FDI (Katz, 1987; Kim and Nelson, 2000).

The literature on National Systems of Innovation (see Edquist, 1997, for a survey) has stressed the interdependent, socially embedded and systemic nature of the processes that are related to the acquisition, modification, and generation of knowledge. Hence, this literature suggests that firms do not innovate in isolation, but that technological change is a process in which different agents interact under specific rules of the game that prevail in the nation, region, sector, and so on in which they move.

In fact, firms' behavior is shaped not only by price signals, but also by the institutional and macroeconomic environments in which the firms conduct their businesses. In developing countries there is often a high degree of macroeconomic volatility and institutional instability. As investments in physical capital and innovation are activities that by themselves are subject to a high degree of uncertainty (this is specially the case of innovation), they are adversely affected by that kind of environment.

In the same vein, in developing countries market and coordination failures are usually stronger than in industrialized nations. Market failures in financial markets, for instance, may be an obstacle for domestic firms—especially SMEs—wishing to invest or to undertake technological change processes.

Furthermore, all firms do not react in the same way to the signals coming from the environment in which they act. On the contrary, firms differ in their competences and structures; hence they adopt different strategies even in the presence of the same rules of the game. At the same time, a firms' behavior is strongly path-dependent, which means that firms need time to adapt their strategies to changes in the institutional and/or macroeconomic setting.

The WC promoters certainly expected that firms and sectors would behave in a heterogeneous way after reforms were implemented. That heterogeneity was assumed to reflect the relative levels of "efficiency" of each firm or sector. However, the arguments stated above strongly suggest that many more variables were at stake. Hence, the pattern of "winners" and "losers" after the reforms process was strongly shaped by the previous competences and skills possessed by firms, but also by the presence of wide-spread market and coordination failures, by path-dependent effects and by the not always clear signals emerging from the macroeconomic and institutional settings of Latin American countries even after reforms were made.

A proper understanding of the determinants of firms' behavior and technological change processes would have called for policies aimed not only at helping firms to adapt to the new rules of the game and at solving market and coordination failures, but also at actively promoting innovation activities as well as at promoting better productive and export specialization patterns.[23]

These kinds of policies had a significant role in the East Asian experience, as it has been interpreted by non-neoclassical authors (Amsden, 1989; Wade, 1990; Evans, 1995; Lall and Teubal, 1998; Lall, 2000). However, while the instruments of the old industrial policy of the ISI were mostly abandoned in Latin America during the 1990s, they were hardly replaced by new tools aimed at tackling the above mentioned objectives without falling into the vices of the ISI regime—Brazil was probably the only country that managed to keep some kind of industrial policy even after the reforms, although with mixed success. This flaw may help us understand some of the key failures of the WC in Latin America.

A Post–Washington Consensus?
The End of Development Panaceas

Although at the end of the 1990s some papers suggested that the world was heading toward a "post–Washington Consensus" (Stiglitz, 1998), as aptly suggested by the title of a recent Dani Rodrik's paper what has happened is that we have moved from the Washington Consensus to a "Washington Confusion" (2006). This is not only the result of the shortcomings of the WC based policies, but also of a more wide acknowledgment of the fact that we know very little about what explains long-run economic development.

Easterly (2001) criticizes the previous "development panaceas" that were tried at different times since the end of World War II. Lindauer and Pritchett (2002) do the same with what they call the "big ideas" about development. No wonder then that a recent book by Helpman (2004) is titled "The Mystery of Economic Growth." Furthermore, there is a growing consensus about the fact that universal and "one size fits all" policy advises must be abandoned in favor of a case-by-case approach.

For instance, studies that posit that countries open to international trade flows grew faster than countries that were closed—and hence provided strong support to the original WC policy recommendations in this field— have been subject to serious criticism (Rodriguez and Rodrik, 2000). More generally, there is a widespread skepticism about the possibility of finding universal policy recommendations through traditional cross-country studies, since policies are usually too complex to be represented by a single index, may have different impacts on different types of countries and may not be exogenous (see also Rodrik, 2005).

The recent literature on growth and development suggests that human capital may play a role in explaining differences in per capita income and growth rates. Technological change, in turn, also explains a large part of those differences, although at present most economists conceived it not as an exogenous "manna"—as in the Solow type models—but as mainly endogenous. Many theories also acknowledge the existence of tacit components in knowledge generation and diffusion, as well as the fact that innovations developed in industrialized countries may not always be used without adaptations in developing countries. However, after accounting for both physical and human capital accumulation and for the effects of technological change, substantial variation in the levels and growth rate of income per capita remains unexplained.

Most economists doing research on growth and development are now convinced that institutions may be the key to decipher the mystery. Institutions, understood as a set of formal and informal rules that structure human interaction (North, 1990), play a key role since they may (or may not) foster coordination and cooperation among economic agents, and shape the incentives structure faced by those agents. Hence, institutions define the extent to which individuals and firms undertake innovation activities, accumulate human and physical capital, and engage in trade. "For these reasons institutions are more fundamental determinants of economic growth than R&D or capital accumulation, physical or human" (Helpman, 2004, p. 139).

But institutions have also a strong impact on the distribution of the outcomes of growth (Acemoglu et al., 2005). Since political power has a large influence on institutions and the State is the locus of power, it is very difficult to separate changes in the balance of political power from institutional change. As it is rightly pointed out in the studies on market reforms processes in the 1990s, the dilemma of institution building is that those who benefit from their current configuration are frequently the ones that are implementing the reforms (Fanelli and McMahon, 2006).

The rediscovery of institutions by economists, and the efforts made to analyze their influence on growth and development, and to face the challenge of implementing the institutional reforms required for developing countries is certainly good news. Once their key role is acknowledged, a number of issues have to be addressed, including the following:

- Which institutions matter for development?
- How can we analyze their impact in terms of growth and distribution?
- How can poor countries get the "right" institutions?
- Can "good" institutions be imported?

Unfortunately, so far we have made little progress in answering these questions (see Helpman, 2004 and Shirley, 2005 for good reviews). Interesting historical studies have been made, but general lessons may hardly be extracted from them. Case study findings are sui generis and hence not easy to compare, especially considering the influence of norms and customs and the characteristics of the polity that are highly particular to local circumstances (see Bates et al., 1998; Fanelli and McMahon, 2006).

In turn, the introduction of institutional variables in cross-country growth regressions has been so far the preferred approach, but this procedure is also not exempt of criticisms (Aron, 2000; Shirley, 2005). First, many of the explanatory variables are not institutions but outcomes (i.e., secure property rights, socioeconomic conditions and ethnic fragmentation) or the results of economic policies (i.e., inflation, trade barriers, and black market premiums). Second, typically the institutional variables are broad aggregates. Third, it is not clear how institutions interact with specific country characteristics. Finally, institutions cannot be considered as exogenous variables, since they are endogenous to income levels.[24]

Anyway, it is possible that the combination of many case as well as country studies along with more refined econometric work can improve our knowledge about the relations between institutions and economic growth. So far, we only know that "whatever these institutional variables are measuring, they typically explain a sizeable fraction of economic growth" (Shirley, 2005, p. 627), but few if any general policy recommendations can be made for developing countries to improve their institutional settings.

This is very important considering that beyond the awareness of the fact that no general blueprints are available for development policy, there is nowadays a new attitude toward the roles of States and markets, which perhaps stands some way between that prevalent during the ISI and that advised by the WC.

The fact that development problems call for a more active role of the State than as envisaged by the WC, but mainly as a complement and not as a substitute of markets, is increasingly accepted within the economics profession. Public opinion and politicians in developing countries, as a result of the disappointment with market-oriented reforms, also favor a stronger presence of the State.

The first problem in this regard is that agreements are harder to obtain when discussing the exact role the State must fulfill. More important, it seems difficult that the State might be able to deal with pervasive market and coordination failures, design adequate policies in the productive and innovation areas, and provide crucial public goods without attacking the serious problem of institutional feebleness that is endemic in most developing countries (see Acuña and Tommasi, 1999). Only very general guidelines are available in this regard, and this makes the task even more difficult.

To end with this section, it must be noted that at present it is clear that growth per se must not be the goal of development strategies. Instead, human sustainable development objectives should be pursued. This means not only that equity and poverty problems are important by themselves but that we should not expect them to be solved merely by GDP growth (World Bank, 2000 and 2006; Cornia, 2004).

Furthermore, it has been shown that inequality may adversely affect growth. For instance, inequality may lead to dynamic inefficiency when credit markets do not exist or are imperfect. In that case, individuals with low wealth may not be able to take advantage of profitable opportunities be these in the form of skill acquisition, occupational advantages, or investment projects (see Ray, 1998).

The same happens with regard to the environment. Although growth and environment protection need not be incompatible, the idea of an environmental Kuznets curve (in which growth first leads to an increase in pollution levels but, after a turning point, becomes environment-friendly) has been severely criticized (Stern et al., 1996; Borghesi, 1999). In turn, environmental degradation not only affects individuals' welfare, but also may imply a constraint on future growth, since it often translates into a lower availability of resources for future generations.

Hard debates exist on the specific goals to be targeted and the nature of the policies that should be followed to attain human sustainable development. However, as discussed earlier, nowadays there is a wide consensus on the need of adopting specific instruments and strategies in those areas, since growth per se may lead to increasing inequality and environmental pollution, and the latter, in turn, may adversely affect growth rates. In this regard, it seems worthwhile to take into account that to some extent the type of policies aimed at equity and environmental objectives overlap with those relevant in the growth area. For instance, equity and income distribution problems are strongly related to access to education. In turn, to make growth compatible with environmental protection innovation policies are crucial.

Our Research Approach

The disappointment with the results obtained through cross-country growth regressions (Lindauer and Pritchett, 2002, call for an "obituary to growth regressions") and the methodological weaknesses of traditional country case studies have moved economists and other social scientists to search for other ways to analyze the unsolved questions about why countries differ in their growth rates and income and welfare levels.

One avenue has been explored in a book edited by Rodrik (2003), containing national studies based on an "analytic narratives" approach. These studies aim at explaining growth patterns through exploring the respective roles of microeconomic and macroeconomic policies, institutions, political economy, and initial conditions at a country level. Hence, they are an attempt to connect specific country experiences with growth theory and cross-national empirics.

A second avenue is based on the analysis of firm level data. Fortunately, in recent years the availability of firm level data has increased in many developed as well as developing countries. This has allowed exploring issues related to trade, FDI, innovation, and other key variables at a microeconomic level, instead of relying only on cross-country or cross-section studies as was the case earlier. Several papers on different subjects have recently encouraged researchers to research that area, as is the case of Hallak and Levinsohn (2004) and Rodriguez and Rodrik (2000)—both on trade and growth—and Moran et al. (2005)—on FDI and development.

Our research is mainly inspired on the analytic narrative approach. We have written a long essay that takes explicitly into account the evolution of the institutional and political context in Argentina and aims at analyzing the key macroeconomic and microeconomic policies that were adopted by different governments during the period under analysis (from the early 1960s to the present) with the goal of assessing what went right or wrong with those policies according to their impact on growth and development.

At the same time, we have also undertaken microeconometric research based on a rich firm level data set representative of the manufacturing industry during the Convertibility Plan. This allowed us to have a deeper understanding of the determinants of firms' technological behavior and productivity performance in the context of the WC based reforms.

We think that the combination of the analytic narrative approach with the findings of microeconometric research allows us to gain a deeper understanding of what happened in Argentina during the period under analysis and why sustainable growth has been so elusive. This is the subject to which the rest of this book is devoted.

CHAPTER 2

ARGENTINA'S ECONOMY IN A LONG-TERM VIEW*

The Main Trends

Until World War I, Argentina enjoyed a great economic expansion based largely on its exports of agricultural products. The country took advantage of trade opportunities opened by the growing demand of these products in industrialized countries, especially in Great Britain, a fact that was also helped by some key innovations in maritime transport and refrigeration techniques that allowed exporting chilled and canned meat to Europe.

The population in Argentina increased from 1.8 to 7.8 million between 1869 and 1914—fueled by the large inflows of European immigrants—and the average annual growth of GDP per capita was 3.9 percent in 1875–1912 (Cortés Conde, 1997). Between 1890 and 1913, the Argentine per capita income vis-à-vis that of a group of advanced countries increased from 87 to 95 percent (see graph 2.1)[1] and Argentina was, by 1929, the eleventh country in the world in the per capita income ranking (Maddison, 1995).

Furthermore, wages in Argentina were relatively high and income distribution (measured as the proportion of wages in per capita income) was fairly equal—when compared with developed countries such as Great Britain—(Williamson, 1999; Gerchunoff and Llach, 2003). However, this did not prevent the emergence of social tensions, especially in the rural zones with export activities as well as in major urban centers.

As seen in graph 2.2, Argentina was a very open economy in the past, as reflected in the high share of exports and imports in tradable production.[2] Exports were mostly concentrated in agricultural products (beef, wheat, corn, wool, leather)—which is why historians have named this period as the "agro export model"—and most imports were manufactured goods. However, although agriculture was the leading economic activity, a rapid process of industrialization took place, and a modern services sector developed.

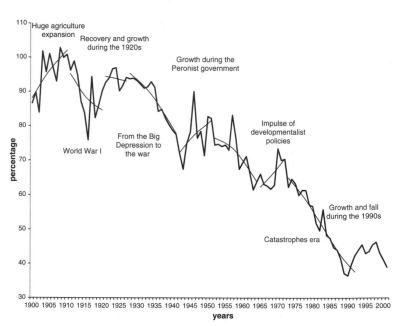

Graph 2.1 Evolution of Argentine GDP per capita as a percentage of the average GDP per capita of the United States, United Kingdom, France Germany, Italy, Japan, Canada, Australia, and New Zealand, 1900–2001

Source: Own elaboration on the basis of data from Gerchunoff and Llach (2003) and from Maddison (2003).

Graph 2.2 Argentina's foreign trade as a percentage of domestic tradable production, 1891–1999, in 1993 constant prices

Source: Gerchunoff and Llach (2003).

Table 2.1   Employment sectoral distribution, 1895–2001, percentages

	1895	1914	1947	1960	1970	1991	2001
Primary sector	34.9	26.8	27.2	20.3	16.7	11.5	8.7
Secondary sector	29.8	35.6	29.7	35.4	33.8	25.1	18.1
Manufacturing	27.1	31.3	25.0	27.8	23.9	17.5	11.4
Tertiary (services) sector	35.4	37.6	43.1	44.3	49.5	63.3	73.2

Source: Galiani and Gerchunoff (2003) for 1895–1991 and authors' estimates based on census for 2001.

The importance of industry and services in the economy during this era is clearly shown in table 2.1.

At the same time, universal education received government priority. The illiteracy rate was reduced from 54 percent in 1895 to 35 percent in 1914, and to 12 percent in 1930. Enrollment in primary education increased from 30 to 59 percent between 1895 and 1930 (Veganzones and Winograd, 1997). Secondary and university education were also promoted during those years.

Foreign investment played a significant role during this period. British investment was particularly relevant (between 1880 and 1913, British capital in Argentina increased twentyfold; see Romero, 2002). Foreign investment went to trade, banking, utilities, transport—specially railroads—and to the growing industrial sector—meatpacking, for instance, was dominated by foreign firms.

The arrival of FDI and immigrants—who were the bulk of industrial entrepreneurs—was the main channel of technology transfer, along with the import of capital goods, for the Argentine economy during that phase.

Key transformations occurred during this period in the institutional arena. The rule of law was guaranteed by the gradual emergence of a modern State and the enactment of a number of laws aiming at protecting property rights and at providing the infrastructure needed for productive investments and exports. Although it was not until 1916 that free and clean elections were held, governments were appointed through electoral processes.

As shown in graph 2.1, the successful catching-up process stopped after 1930—in that same year the first coup d'etat of modern Argentine history took place, marking the beginning of more than 50 years of alternation between civil and military governments. From then on, with fluctuations, a clear and steady "falling behind" trajectory was observed.

Between 1962 and 2002 the average compound per capita GDP growth rate was very low (1 percent per year), in a country with an annual population growth of only 1.5 percent.[3] In 1990, GDP per capita in constant pesos was below that of 1965, after a fall of 23 percent in comparison with that of 1975.

In turn, GDP per capita in 2002 was 5 percent lower than that of 1992 and 11 percent lower than in 1974 (see table 2.2). Productivity performance was also weak, as shown in table 2.3. Argentina's labor productivity fell in relative terms compared with developed

Table 2.2   Argentina's GDP per capita, 1962–2005 (thousand 1993 pesos)

Year	Per capita GDP (thousand 1993 Pesos)	Growth rate (%)	Year	Per capita GDP (thousand 1993 Pesos)	Growth rate (%)
1962	4989	−3.1	1984	6600	0.3
1963	4795	−3.9	1985	6067	−8.1
1964	5209	8.6	1986	6403	5.5
1965	5601	7.5	1987	6500	1.5
1966	5556	−0.8	1988	6270	−3.5
1967	5622	1.2	1989	5749	−8.3
1968	5782	2.8	1990	5537	−3.7
1969	6185	7.0	1991	6138	10.9
1970	6420	3.8	1992	6744	9.9
1971	6618	3.1	1993	7106	5.4
1972	6711	1.4	1994	7445	4.8
1973	6998	4.3	1995	7161	−3.8
1974	7247	3.6	1996	7481	4.5
1975	7068	−2.5	1997	8007	7.0
1976	6840	−3.2	1998	8231	2.8
1977	7070	3.4	1999	7873	−4.4
1978	6726	−4.9	2000	7732	−1.8
1979	7187	6.9	2001	7280	−5.8
1980	7305	1.6	2002	6422	−11.8
1981	6868	−6.0	2003	6919	7.7
1982	6463	−5.9	2004	7440	7.5
1983	6577	1.8	2005	8015	7.7

Source: Authors' calculations on the basis of national accounts data.

Table 2.3   Argentina's labor productivity—GDP per hour worked—as a percentage of labor productivity in other countries, 1950–1998

Argentina as a percentage of	1950	1973	1990	1998
Weighted average West Europe★	111	66	40	47
Australia	64	62	43	50
Canada	60	54	41	52
United States	49	45	32	39
Brazil	248	185	137	171
Chile	132	120	101	102
Japan	296	92	51	60

★ Austria, Belgium, Denmark, Finland, France, Germany, Italy, Netherlands, Norway, Sweden, Switzerland and United Kingdom.

Source: Authors' elaboration on data from Maddison (2001).

countries as well as vis-à-vis Latin American nations such as Brazil and Chile both between growth periods (1950–1973) and stagnation ones (1973–1990). A growth trend was apparent until 1998, but was far from being strong enough as to restore the relative productivity levels of 1950.

However, this long stage of low growth was, in fact, the result of the combination of growth episodes with deep crisis and recessionary periods in which all the gains attained during those episodes (listed below) were dissipated (see graph 2.3). The first growth episode was from 1962 to 1974, and GDP growth reached an annual 4.4 percent. The second took place between 1991 and 1998—in the middle of it there was a crisis year, 1995, because of the Tequila effect—and GDP growth was 5 percent a year (see table 2.4).

Between both growth periods, GDP increase averaged merely 0.1 percent from 1975 to 1990.[4] In turn, from 1999 to 2002, the accumulated real GDP fall amounted to more than 18 percent, ending with the bigger economic and social crisis in the country's history.

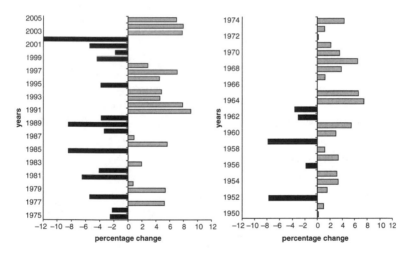

Graph 2.3   Real GDP per capita, 1950–2005 (annual percentage changes)

Source: ECLAC.

Table 2.4   Productivity and GDP growth, 1962–1998, annual percentage rates

Period	TFP growth	GDP growth	Capital growth	Employment growth
1962–1974	2.3	4.4	3.3	1.1
1975–1990	−1.6	0.1	1.5	2.0
1991–1998	3.2	5.0	1.7	1.6

Source: Authors' estimates based on Maia and Kweitel (2003).

Productivity evolution, naturally, being one of the key determinants of economic growth, closely matched GDP per capita trends. The TFP—which measures the part of GDP growth not attributable to factor accumulation[5]— exhibited a growing trend from the beginning of the 1960s until the mid-1970s (2.3 percent on annual average). However, the main source of growth during that period was capital deepening.

Since 1975 and until 1990—a period in which the economy experienced what some authors describe as *The Argentine Great Depression*[6]—TFP growth was negative (−1.6 percent a year). In turn, capital stock grew slower than employment.

When the economy resumed growth in the 1990s, TFP again showed a good performance—it increased at an annual average of 3.2 percent between 1991 and 1998 (table 2.2 and graphs 2.4 and 2.5). In fact, TFP was the main source of growth, since both capital stock and employment augmented at relatively low rates.

As shown in graph 2.6, the poor growth performance during this period of economic history in Argentina went along with high volatility in terms of GDP per capita evolution (see also table 2.2), due to recurrent episodes of crisis associated with political and institutional instability, macroeconomic, and financial turmoil and/or sharp modifications in the economic policy regimes.

In this not very prosperous context, two important structural changes took place during the period under analysis. First, after decades of being a relatively closed economy, Argentina's openness to trade significantly increased

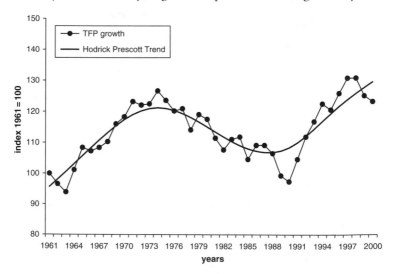

Graph 2.4   TFP growth, 1961–2000, index numbers (1961 = 100)

Source: Authors' estimates based on Maia and Kweitel (2003).

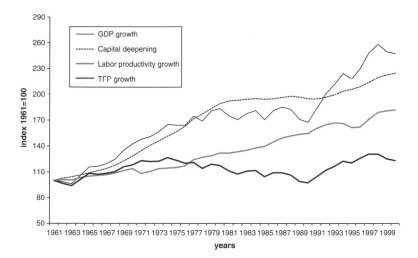

Graph 2.5   Sources of growth, 1961–2000, index numbers (1961 = 100)

Source: Authors' estimates based on Maia and Kweitel (2003).

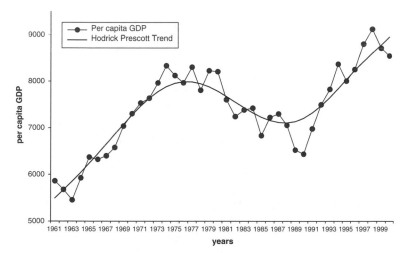

Graph 2.6   Per capita GDP, 1990 international Geary-Khamis dollars, 1961–2000

Source: Authors' calculations based on data from Maddison (2003).

in the 1990s (see graph 2.2). Second, the share of the primary and secondary sectors in total employment declined throughout the past century, while services became the leading source of employment, a trend that accelerated since the 1970s. Hence, by 2001, the manufacturing sector accounted only for 18 percent and services for 73 percent of total employment— against less than 50 percent in 1970—(table 2.4).

This "reversal of fortune" story has been extensively analyzed in the received literature, and the poor performance of the Argentine economy in the post–World War II era is one of the big puzzles for historians and economists. This book aims at shedding light on this puzzle by analyzing not only macroeconomic trends and institutional settings, but also microeconomic behavior. For the reader to have a global background of what happened during the period under study, in what follows we highlight the main trends in the political, institutional, economic, and social areas.

Political Instability

In the 38 years between 1962 and 2000, Argentina had 18 presidents—16 of whom took office between 1962 and 1988—and 37 ministers of economy. In contrast, in the 36 years between 1928 and 1962, the country had 12 presidents (the same number as in the 48 years between 1880 and 1928). Hence, it is apparent that (growing) political instability has been the norm rather than the exception in Argentina, a factor that is quite apparent in the frequent military coups that took place up to 1983.

As the reader may guess, instability and frequent changes were not limited to the presidency and the Ministry of Economy. A high rotation level was also observed at the ministerial and other high-level positions in all State areas. The changes in the number, names, and incumbencies of ministries, secretaries and undersecretaries have also been high (Spiller and Tommasi, 2003).

In 1955, in the middle of President Perón's second term, a coup d'etat took place. A new election was held in 1958, but the participation of the Peronist Party was banned. The leader of the so-called *desarrollismo* (developmentalism) movement, Arturo Frondizi, won the election, but was deposed by a new military coup in 1962.

In 1963, a new democratic president was elected but he was also forced out by the Armed Forces in 1966. Three military presidents took office between 1966 and 1973, when the Peronist Party returned to power. After the death of Perón in 1974, his wife succeeded him and was deposed in 1976.

The 1976 military coup paved the way for the bloodiest dictatorship in Argentina's history. After General Videla's presidency from 1976 to 1981, three military presidents took office in less than two years. A new democratic government led by Raúl Alfonsín took office at the end of 1983. Having faced several military rebellions during his presidency, Alfonsín finally resigned a few months before the end of his mandate amidst hyperinflation and a severe social crisis (which included massive looting in many large cities).

The Peronist Party won the 1989 polls and Carlos Menem was elected. The ten years during which Menem was president (following a reform in the constitution that allowed his reelection in 1995) and the five years in which Domingo Cavallo was minister of economy—1991 to 1996—were clearly an exception in the long history of political instability in Argentina. However, it must be noted that Menem also suffered a military rebellion during his presidency, his government is perceived as one of the most corrupt in Argentina's history and that, at the end of his second mandate, he tried to force a new constitutional reform to allow his reelection yet again. All these factors were signs that Argentina was far from having attained political stability.

The next president, Fernando De la Rúa, resigned in 2001, two years before his mandate and in the middle of the deepest economic, financial, and institutional crisis in the country's history. In 2000, his vice president had already resigned—in disagreement with the government's attitude toward a corruption scandal—and during De la Rúa's mandate there were three ministers of economy, none of whom was able to prevent the final collapse of the Convertibility Plan, which had been implemented in 1991 in order to attain price stabilization after two hyperinflation crisis.

Three persons were appointed as presidents by the parliament between 21 December 2001 and 2 January 2002, and, finally, President Duhalde took office. He was able to keep his post amidst a turbulent economic and social scenario and called for a new election that was held in 2003, when current President Kirchner was appointed.

Institutional Fragility

Not only is Argentina's economy volatile but so also are its economic policies. "In a ranking of countries by the volatility of the 'economic freedom index' published by the Fraser Institute for the period 1970–1999, Argentina shows up as the seventh most volatile case in a sample of 106 countries" (Spiller and Tommasi, 2003, p. 284).

This is a symptom of a more general problem regarding the weak institutional foundations of the policymaking process in Argentina. In fact, the country has a long history of institutional instability, a problem that has worsened over the past decade. Public policies lack credibility, stability, and coherence and their implementation is often poor. According to Spiller and Tommasi (2003), the following are the main factors underlying this situation.

First, the intertemporal linkages among political actors lead to shortsighted behavior not conducive to self-enforcement of cooperative arrangements.

Alternative enforcement mechanisms, whether by judicial means or bureaucratic delegation, have been relatively weak.

Second, key government officials, legislators, and judges have all usually had short-term horizons. The shortness of horizons in Argentine polity is a consequence not only of past institutional instability but also of the electoral mechanisms and executive powers that work against having a congress populated by long-term legislators.

Third, the country does not have a professional bureaucracy with a long-term principal. In these conditions, the bureaucracy[7] faces weak long-term incentives facilitating shirking and requiring intrusive administrative controls to avoid corruption. Each new executive unable to motivate (or to fire) the permanent bureaucracy has nominated large numbers of political appointees creating a "parallel bureaucracy." The frequent rotation at ministerial and secretarial levels implies rotation in the "parallel bureaucracy," limiting the accumulation of organizational knowledge. The lack of a system of meritocratic recruitment of public officials has also been detrimental for the quality of policymaking (see Sikkink, 1993).

Finally, a Supreme Court with justices with very short periods of tenure has tended to be politically aligned with the president and has failed to be an important enforcer of political agreements over the past several decades.

In the opinion of the international business community, these features of public policies are quite costly for the operation of the private sector. This accounts for Argentina's position of the sixty-first place in a ranking of 75 countries in this respect and its position of the seventieth place concerning tax evasion. The private sector perception with regard to the competence of public officials is also negative and, in this regard, Argentina is ranked in the seventy-first place among the 75 countries (Spiller, Stein, and Tommasi, 2003).

With regard to the private sector perception with respect to corruption in Argentina, table 2.5 shows that in the 1980s the country was in a relatively good position vis-à-vis the other Latin American countries considered and

Table 2.5   Trends in perceived corruption, 1980–2001

Country	1980–85	1988–92	1995	1996	1997	1998	1999	2000	2001	2002	2003	2004	2005
Mexico	1.9	2.2	3.2	3.3	2.7	3.3	3.4	3.3	3.7	3.6	3.6	3.6	3.5
Brazil	4.5	3.5	2.7	3.0	3.6	4.0	4.1	3.9	4.0	4.0	3.9	3.9	3.7
Argentina	4.9	5.9	5.2	3.4	2.8	3.0	3.0	3.5	3.5	2.8	2.5	2.5	2.8
Chile	6.5	5.5	7.9	6.8	6.1	6.8	6.9	7.4	7.5	7.5	7.4	7.4	7.3

Source: Transparency International, "Historical Comparisons" (1996) and rankings for 1995, 1996, 1997, 1998, 1999, and 2000, *Corruption Perception Index* (taken from Nef, 2003 and Transparency International). The index refers to the perception of the private sector and ranges between 10 (highly clean) and 0 (highly corrupt).

had the best performance in 1988–1992. The ranking noticeably worsens in the 1990s and since 1996 Argentina is in a worse position than Brazil and, with the exception of 1988–1992, Chile shows a better performance than Argentina for the whole period.

Economic Volatility

As mentioned earlier, volatility has been a key feature of the Argentine economy, deeply influencing every aspect of the society, and, in particular, the actions and the investment decisions of private economic agents. More specifically, long-term decisions have been particularly affected by the uncertainty about the future levels of key economic indicators (growth rate, exchange rate, relative prices, and so on) and the instability of the "rules of the game" (policy regimes, regulatory norms, property rights enforcement, and so on).

Major events due to external shocks—such as the debt crisis in the early 1980s—or across-the-board shifts in the policy regime—the package of structural reforms and the currency board adopted in the early 1990s—are very frequent in Argentina and induce sharp fluctuations in the level of economic activity and discontinuous jumps in the growth rate.

Severe foreign exchange crises occurred in 1975, 1981, 1982, 1989, and 2001. The recurrence of systemic financial crisis leading to violation of property rights and the breach of private contracts has also been a feature of the Argentine economy over the past 30 years. Large income transfers among different groups of the society have been one of the consequences of these crises, as well as huge wealth windfall gains or losses for economic agents.

In this scenario, it comes as no surprise to find that the frequency of growth downturns in Argentina is well above the developing country's average. The 1975 crisis represents a breaking point concerning instability. Between 1950 and 1974, the probability of a downturn was more or less in line with that of developing countries (21 percent). In 1975–2001 this probability increased to 52 percent. This means that GDP per capita fell in more years than it grew and that volatility has been increasing in Argentina (Fanelli, 2002).

The variations in the real exchange rate (RER) and the inflationary tax are also good examples of the volatility of the Argentine economy (graph 2.7). Both sets of variations have a similar trend and their peaks are associated with periods of macroeconomic adjustment. It seems that both instruments were used for income and wealth redistribution to deal with the consequences of the several crises that have taken place in the country (Fanelli, 2004).

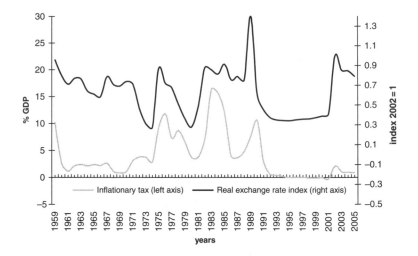

Graph 2.7 Inflationary tax on the monetary base and real exchange rate index
Argentina–United States, 1959–2005
Source: Fanelli (2003).

Social Indicators

Argentina has a relatively good position in the human development index
elaborated by the United Nations Development Program (UNDP). In 2002,
the country was ranked 34 out of 177 countries. Life expectancy at birth is
74 years—vis-à-vis a world average of 67 years—and the adult literacy rate
reached 97 percent—very close to developed country standards.

While enrollment rates in primary education are almost 100 percent since
the 1960s, substantial increases are apparent in enrollment rates in secondary
education (from 23 in 1960 to 77 percent in 1996) and in tertiary education
(from 14 in 1965 to 42 percent in 1996). However, desertion rates are very
high and the quality of education has been deteriorating (see chapter 6).

On the other hand, there are other less encouraging trends in income
distribution, poverty, and unemployment. Regarding income distribution,
the labor share in national income prior to the 1940s was about 40 percent.
During the first Peronist government (1946–1952), it reached 50.9 percent,
but after 1954 fell again. The share increased again during the 1960s
and early 1970s, but dropped sharply in 1976, reaching a minimal level as a
consequence of the repressive wages policy imposed by the military
government. Since then, it has fluctuated, often considerably, around
35 percent.

Income distribution among workers remained almost unchanged until the mid-1970s, but strongly worsened after 1974. This is apparent in a comparison of the wage distribution in 1974 and the late 1990s: almost all the population deciles (population is divided in ten deciles, according to the level of income of the inhabitants, when analyzing income distribution) lost, except those workers in the ninth and tenth deciles, an indication that high-wage workers have gained at the expense of the rest of the labor force (Galiani and Gerchunoff, 2003).

Inequality and poverty have been consistently measured since 1974, when the first Household Permanent Survey was carried out in Greater Buenos Aires, to be later extended to cover all the urban population of the country.

The Gini coefficient in Greater Buenos Aires increased from 34.2 in 1974 to 47.4 in 1999. Inequality strongly increased during the second half of the 1970s and the early 1980s in a context of trade liberalization, civil liberties and labor union repression, and macroeconomic crisis. Income distribution remained quite stable since the return of democracy in 1983, but hyperinflation at the end of the 1980s dramatically worsened it (graph 2.8).

With the implementation of the Convertibility Plan, and as a result of price stabilization, an improvement in income distribution was apparent. However, since 1993 the country returned to a pattern of growing inequality that, by the end of the 1990s, had reached levels similar to those experienced during the hyperinflationary peak (Bebczuk and Gasparini, 2001).

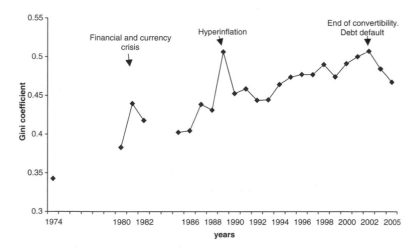

Graph 2.8   Income distribution in Greater Buenos Aires (Gini coefficient), 1974–2005

Source: Authors' elaboration on the basis of data estimated by Fundación de Investigaciones Latinoamericanas (FIEL).

With regard to poverty, its evolution is similar to that described in the case of inequality. It increased strongly during the 1980s, especially during the hyperinflationary peak, to later fall after macroeconomic stabilization in 1991. However, from 1994 to 1996 it grew again and then stabilized at very high levels until 2000 (graph 2.9).

The recession that began in late 1998 and ended in the aforementioned severe crisis in 2001 and 2002 brought poverty and inequality indices in Argentina to unprecedented levels in the country's history: 29.3 percent of the population was below the poverty line in Greater Buenos Aires in 2000, a figure that escalated to a historic peak of 52 percent in 2002 (Household Permanent Survey, INDEC). In turn, the Gini coefficient in Greater Buenos Aires increased from 47.4 in 1999 to 49.1 percent in 2000 and 50.7 percent in 2002.

When considering the evolution of unemployment in the early 1960s it affected around 8 percent of the working population (Galiani and Gerchunoff, 2003). Later on, it decreased to below 5 percent until the late 1980s, when it surpassed 7 percent (graph 2.10). This shows that, despite all the economic and political fluctuations in Argentina during that period, unemployment always remained at relatively low levels.

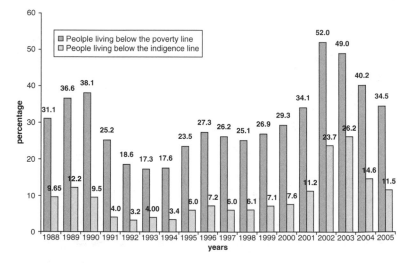

Graph 2.9   Poverty and indigence levels in Greater Buenos Aires (percentage), 1988–2005

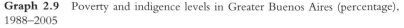

Source: Authors' elaboration on the basis of INDEC's data.

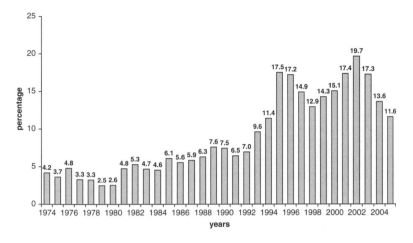

Graph 2.10   Urban unemployment rate (percentage), 1974–2005

Source: Authors' elaboration on the basis of INDEC's data.

In the mid-1990s it increased to two-digit levels and remained in these proportions ever since. The dramatic increase in unemployment during the 1990s was due to a combination of macroeconomic shocks, the consequences of structural reforms and labor shedding in the manufacturing sector (Galiani and Gerchunoff, 2003) as discussed in chapter 6.

CHAPTER 3

THE IMPORT-SUBSTITUTION INDUSTRIALIZATION, 1962–1974

The Macroeconomic and Political Evolution

Although Argentina's growth performance during the ISI was relatively weak in the international comparison, between 1964 and 1974 the economy experienced 11 years of positive GDP growth in a row. However, even during those years recurrent balance of payments and institutional crises and growing social unrest were present.

The model developed by Braun and Joy (1968) is very useful to understanding the dynamics (and the dual character) of the Argentine economy during this period. On one hand, there was a competitive sector, agriculture, which was the main source of foreign exchange and supplied key wage goods. On the other hand, there was the manufacturing sector, which produced, almost, exclusively for the domestic market and was protected by high tariffs (see table 3.1). This sector relied on imported inputs and capital goods. Hence, its growth depended on the foreign currency generated by agricultural exports. This was the rationale for promoting import substitution in intermediate and capital goods, a strategy that was explicitly followed by the government from the late 1950s.

During the periods of economic expansion, the high elasticity of imports in the manufacturing sector led to a situation in which the foreign currency generated by the agricultural sector was not sufficient to pay for growing imports. As a result, a balance of payments crisis set in which was solved by devaluing the domestic currency. The devaluation was supposed to increase—with a certain lag—agricultural output and exports, but it immediately restrained imports. Inflation was another outcome of the crisis. Since wage goods were also the main export items, their prices tended to rise.

This also applied to industrial products with high import content. Naturally, real wages declined as the consequence of inflation and this led

Table 3.1   Legal tariff rates, 1959–1997, percentages

	1959	1969	1976	1988	1991	1993	1997
Non-durable consumer goods	197	142	200	53	25	30	23
Durable consumer goods	198	142	149	63	21	20	19
Intermediate goods	118	102	86	44	17	20	14
Machinery	147	93	87	57	22	8	14
Transport equipment	188	124	132	57	27	9	21
Weighted average	141	107	99	48	19	17	16
Mean (unweighted average)	145	103	97	52	19	17	15
Standard deviation	56	42	41	16	5	8	5
Dispersion (percent)	38	41	42	30	27	44	30

Source: Berlinski (2003).

to a fall in consumption that, together with the reductions in imports that affected manufacturing production, resulted in a decline in economic activity. Stabilization policies exacerbated the fall in aggregate demand by reducing money supply. The ensuing recession led to a temporary improvement in the balance of payments, which was the objective of the devaluation.

Although the growth in manufactured exports since the early 1960s and the launching of incomes policies not based on the reduction in real wages in late 1960s (see below) softened to a certain extent this "stop and go" cycle, the frequent fluctuations in the level of economic activity and the distributive conflicts between capital and labor and between agriculture and industry were key features of the period under review.

The roots of this dynamics are to be found in the course taken by the Argentine economy since 1930. The dislocation in world markets that followed the 1929 crisis had a strong impact on Argentina's agricultural exports. The ensuing currency shortage faced by the country forced the government to adopt measures aimed at restricting imports. Hence, import substitution transpired to meet local demand of goods that were previously supplied from abroad.

After World War II, the Peronist government deliberately stimulated the deepening of the import substitution process, linking it to an economic policy that had the goal of redistributing incomes in favor of the working class. Light industries producing nondurable consumption goods, such as textiles, were the leading sectors during this period (1945–1955), protected by high trade barriers.

Trade barriers were the only way to promote industrialization in a context of growing wages plus technical backwardness of the bulk of the industrial sector. In this context, it is not surprising to find that the growth between 1930 and 1955 was based mostly on factor accumulation (especially labor) while technological progress and increasing returns to scale were weak (Katz, 1969). Industrial exports, which had been growing until 1943, were discouraged by the Peronist government. Agricultural exports were also affected, due to a combination of stagnating productivity and public policies that transferred part of the export rents of the agricultural sector to the industry, for example, in the form of cheap credit.

President Frondizi's *desarrollista* (developmentalist) government took office in 1958 and launched an ambitious industrialization project aimed at "deepening" import substitution by promoting (mainly foreign and public) investment in the intermediate, consumption durables, and capital goods industries. The final objective of this project was to reduce industry dependence on imports, hence eliminating what was perceived as the main obstacle to sustained growth in Argentina, since local production of consumption goods had not reduced import needs, but merely transformed its structure (from final to intermediate and capital goods).

An investment boom took place in the wake of the government's strategy. However, the *desarrollista* project was implemented while dealing with balance of payments crises and huge devaluations, stabilization measures negotiated with the IMF, an increasing incidence of strikes (see table 3.2) and growing discontent among the Armed Forces. The latter ultimately led to a military coup in 1962, when a temporary civilian government was appointed. Although import substitution policies were also pursued by the subsequent governments, the *desarrollista* project aimed at almost complete self-sufficiency was never fulfilled.

A civilian government led by President Illía took office in 1963 with only 25.4 percent of the votes in national elections in which the Peronist

Table 3.2   Indicators of socio-political protest, 1956–1972

Year	Strikes	Revolutionary "direct action"*	Year	Strikes	Revolutionary "direct action"*
1956	37	107	1965	291	173
1957	118	158	1966	263	158
1958	124	73	1967	68	146
1959	206	347	1968	50	84
1960	134	223	1969	93	341
1961	215	169	1970	116	447
1962	181	309	1971	237	608
1963	143	87	1972	187	737
1964	265	215			

*Includes bombings, all assassination attempts (whether successful or not), kidnappings, "armed propaganda" and other acts.

Source: Archive on Socio-Political Protest in Argentina, 1956–1974 from Smith (1991).

Party was proscribed. The new government had to deal with the 1962–1963 recession, which was overcome by applying expansionary monetary and fiscal policies and by promoting exports.[1] The sharp increase in agricultural output and exports and the maturation of several of the import substitution investment projects launched in the late 1950s also helped to restore growth.

The fact that the press operated without restrictions, labor unions were free from State intervention, and civil liberties and political rights were respected strengthened the Argentine democracy. However, the context in which Illía won the election, its moderate nationalism (as reflected in the cancellation of contracts with foreign oil companies) and weak political management created growing social tensions within the labor unions, the large corporations and the wealthy businessmen, and the Armed Forces.

In June 1966, the military removed President Illía, dissolved the Congress and the political parties, and appointed General Onganía as President. Its authoritarian bias was clearly reflected in many measures taken by the government such as the removal of all judges from the Supreme Court, the imposition of severe limitations on judicial autonomy, the violation of university autonomy and the sacking of leading professors.

The first economic team of the new government was replaced in December 1966 when Krieger Vasena was appointed minister of economy. Although Onganía's government preserved the import-substitution strategy, it also stressed the need to foster efficiency improvements in the industrial sector—an increasingly widespread concern among local economists. To attain this objective, tariffs were reduced (see table 3.1) and industrial exports were promoted—although estimates by Berlinski and Schidlowsky (1982) still showed a strong anti-export bias in the 1969 tariff structure. Furthermore, the new economic team favored large domestic and foreign firms in order to stimulate a new investment boom in the country.

On the macroeconomic front, Krieger Vasena attempted to stabilize wages and prices on the basis of a freeze in the real income distribution of 1966. This income policy, together with an unorthodox monetary policy, substantially reduced the inflation rate and favored economic recovery. A devaluation of the exchange rate by 40 percent was also implemented. For traditional (agricultural) exports, the devaluation was almost offset by a tax, while subsidies for nontraditional exports were removed. On the import side, reductions in tariffs did not fully offset the devaluation. Inflationary cost increases in 1968 and 1969 were offset by a reduction of the export taxes and the reintroduction of the export subsidies (Berlinski and Schidlowsky, 1982).

While agricultural producers were critical of the policies followed by Krieger and his team (due to the export taxes), large manufacturing and services enterprises were predominantly in favor of them. By contrast, local small and medium enterprises (SMEs), which were almost exclusively oriented toward the internal market, criticized the orientation of the economic team toward large businesses and its overtures to foreign capital. The GDP annual cumulative growth rate reached 5.2 percent between 1966 and 1970, due to a significant increase in gross domestic investment. Unemployment remained very low and the total number of salaried workers increased during the same period. The main issues for the working class opposition to the military regime were political rather than economic: workers' demands were met with repression and the political unity of the labor movement was shattered (see Smith, 1991 for further details on the Krieger policies).

The drastic decline in strikes in 1967 and 1968 was reversed in 1969, the year in which the *Cordobazo* (a large popular and working class revolt that took place in the city of Córdoba) took place (see table 3.2). This was a mass uprising against the Onganía regime and the Krieger economic policies, led by militant labor unions mostly in the motorcar factories. The social explosion expressed in the *Cordobazo* not only forced Krieger's resignation but also contributed to the emergence of strong revolutionary movements dedicated to guerrilla warfare.

Although revolutionary "direct" action was not new (see table 3.2), it increased dramatically from 1969 onward. Most of the kidnappings, bombings, and assassinations carried out by guerrilla organizations were aimed at managers and owners of large firms, although military installations were also regular targets (Smith, 1991). Paramilitary repression started in those years and sharply expanded in 1974–1975.

Until a new civilian government led by Perón took office in 1973, several changes took place in the leadership of the military government and in the economic policy framework. Successive devaluations of the peso created a race between the exchange rate and nominal wages, which fueled inflation. At the same time, measures were taken to promote exports and control imports (including technology transfer payments). The deepening of the ISI process was fostered through special policy regimes that favored investments in intermediate goods.

When Ferrer was appointed minister of economy in 1970 by Onganía's successor, Levingston, several measures to favor locally owned firms were announced, especially in the credit system, and through the so-called Buy National Law. Local firms were also favored to undertake large investment projects promoted by the government (this is what Schvarzer, 1996, calls the "silent bet" for local capital).

However, the policy agenda was dominated by the politics of the transition from the military to a civilian government that was managed by

General Lanusse, Levingston's successor, in an increasingly turbulent social and political climate. In March 1973, a democratic election was held and a new President, Héctor Campora, was appointed. He called for a new election in September 1973, which was won by Juan Perón, whose participation in the previous election had been forbidden by the military.

The Peronist government was initially favored by the rise in world prices that fostered exports. The government took advantage of the improved balance of payments position to expand demand and raise real wages. The new economic policy was at odds with that implemented by Krieger, since it clearly favored local capital (mostly SMEs) and introduced several restrictions on foreign investment. Strong quantitative import restrictions were reintroduced together with foreign exchange controls. At the same time, generous promotion schemes were put in place for nontraditional exports jointly with the taxation of traditional exports.

The economic boom lasted only until the trading conditions began to turn against Argentina in mid-1974 in an increasingly difficult fiscal and political situation (aggravated by the death of Perón in July 1974 and the appointment of his widow Isabel Martinez de Perón as president). In 1975, a severe economic crisis set in and against the background of a huge fiscal deficit, the peso was drastically devaluated (called *Rodrigazo*, after Celestino Rodrigo the then minister of economy). This gave rise to pressures from labor unions to achieve an increase in nominal wages larger than the peso devaluation. The outcome was an acceleration of inflation to (at the time) unknown levels for the country.

The impaired economic situation, coupled with the weak government and the increasingly violent political and social scenario, paved the way for the 1976 military coup that marked the beginning of the end of the ISI process in Argentina.

Investment, Knowledge, and Productivity Growth in the Industrialization Process

The Investment Drive and Productivity Growth

The *desarrollista* investment drive was fostered by two key legal instruments: Law No. 14,780 on FDI and Law No. 14,781 on industrial promotion.[2] They jointly defined the incentives regime through which significant physical investments in new plants making chemicals, petrochemicals, motor vehicles, and other metal products were made. Furthermore, tariff protection against imported goods was very high (see table 3.1) and provided significant incentives for the domestic production of consumption and intermediate goods.

Table 3.3   Annual growth rates of physical volume of production, number of workers and labor productivity in the manufacturing industry, 1962–1998

	Physical volume of production	Number of workers	Labor productivity
1962–1974	6.1	2.8	3.2
1975–1990	−1.3	−3.9	2.7
1991–1998	4.0	−2.7	6.9

Source: Authors' calculations based on data from INDEC and BCRA.

Industrial production grew at an annual rate of 6.1 percent between 1962 and 1974. The figures for employment and labor productivity were 2.8 and 3.2 percent respectively (see table 3.3). In turn, industrial exports grew from US$100 million in 1969 to US$800 million in 1974, representing 20 percent of total exports in the latter year.[3] Total manufacturing exports (including agricultural-based products) surpassed US$2,300 million in 1974, accounting for almost 60 percent of total exports (Bisang and Kosacoff, 1995).

Furthermore, by the end of the ISI period, significant technology exports were flowing to other Latin American countries—for example, "turnkey" plants, licenses, technical services, and so on (Katz and Ablin, 1985)—and several local firms were engaged in internationalization processes through FDI in neighboring countries (Katz and Kosacoff, 1983). In both cases, the key intangible assets of local firms were product and process technologies designed and/or adapted to the conditions of the countries in the region.

The leading sectors during this phase of the ISI were automobiles, chemicals, metallurgy, and electrical machinery and equipment, while food and textiles lagged behind. Capital deepening (an increase in the capital stock per worker) took place in most industrial sectors, but it was more intense in chemicals, metallurgy, and electrical machinery and equipment. As shown by Katz (1972), technical progress (measured as the "residual" of the production function), accounted for almost 70 percent of industrial production growth in the 1960s. The same three aforementioned sectors were those that enjoyed the highest impact of technical progress.

The maturation of investments made since the late 1950s, together with the progressive accumulation of technological capabilities in many firms, allowed the manufacturing sector to gradually increase productivity (see graph 3.1). As shown in table 3.3, in this period the increase in productivity took place jointly with rising employment (see also graph 3.2).

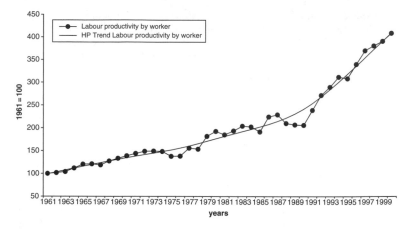

Graph 3.1   Manufacturing industry: Labor productivity by worker, 1961–2000, index numbers (1961 = 100)

Source: Authors' calculations based on data from INDEC and BCRA.

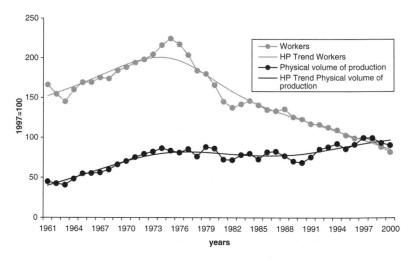

Graph 3.2   Physical volume of production and number of workers, 1961–2000, index numbers (1997 = 100)

Source: Authors' calculations based on data from INDEC and BCRA.

As mentioned before, TNCs were a key agent of this stage of the ISI process. Between 1958 and 1963, 200 foreign companies made greenfield investments in the country. By the early 1970s, TNCs' share in industrial production had reached 33 percent (Kosacoff and Bezchinsky, 1993).

Production by affiliates of TNCs grew at an annual rate of 8.8 percent between 1955 and 1973, while the respective figure for local firms was 4.3 percent. In contrast, employment in such affiliates grew only at 0.94 percent during the same period, compared with 1.2 percent in domestic firms (Sourrouille et al., 1985).

Though many TNCs brought secondhand machinery into Argentina, they also transferred modern product and process technologies, quality control techniques, and subcontracting practices to their subsidiaries (Katz and Kosacoff, 2000). This, together with the use of less labor-intensive techniques and the TNCs propensity to locate in capital-intensive sectors, ensured higher labor productivity levels in affiliates of TNCs than in local firms.

Data from the National Economic Census revealed that, in 1963, labor productivity in affiliates of TNCs was around 185 percent higher than that of domestic firms in the manufacturing sector. Between 1955 and 1973, labor productivity in foreign firms grew at an annual rate of 7.7 percent, vis-à-vis only 3 percent in domestic firms (Sourrouille et al., 1985).

The massive inflows of foreign investment and the establishment of some large State plants in sectors such as steel and petrochemicals paved the way for a more modern industrial structure. This process meant an increase in the level of concentration of the manufacturing sector. The rise of oligopolistic structures was a consequence of the expansion of capital-intensive industries and the quest for economies of scale that substantially increased the previously low levels of manufacturing productivity (Katz, 1969; Gerchunoff and J. Llach, 1975).

However, in spite of this substantial transformation of the manufacturing industry, the plants established during this period of the ISI, including TNCs affiliates, generally fell short of international standards in terms of competitiveness. They were less automated and more vertically integrated than their counterparts in developed countries. A key issue was that most of them had been established to sell almost exclusively in the domestic market, which was not large enough to permit efficient operations and adequate economies of scale.

Summarizing the findings of several studies on the subject, Katz and Kosacoff (1998) list the following five basic features of what they call "the microeconomics of the ISI," which would allow us to understand why the static efficiency levels and the dynamic learning path of that model were flawed.

1. The size of industrial plants was much smaller than the average in developed countries (the standard ratio was 1 to 10).
2. The layout of the plants and the organization of the work processes were much less sophisticated, both because of their adaptation to the

different relative production factor prices and the lack of adequate information, equipment, and organizational expertise.

3. Capital goods, especially in SMEs, were frequently secondhand or home made.

4. The degree of vertical integration was very high—given the flaws in the production structure and the lack of independent suppliers of spare parts[4]—and the internalization of scale economies was much lower than that observed in developed countries.

5. The level of diversification of the production mix was often higher than that observed in specialized plants in advanced nations, which resulted in short runs of many different products, limiting the attainment of specialization and scale economies.

In turn, R&D expenditures were very low (see next section) and the technological efforts of the industry were not oriented to reach the best practices frontier, but rather to solve mainly adaptive and individual problems (Nochteff, 1994a and 1994b). The relatively small domestic market size and the prevalence of affiliates of TNCs in many modern industrial sectors were among the factors that explained the pattern of innovation activities in Argentina's industry as previously described.

It is also important to bear in mind some additional factors that constrained the performance of industrial enterprises. Among these were the low levels of financial development, which was the main obstacle to access to investment capital and frequently even to working capital. Given the high levels of economic and institutional volatility, it is no wonder that the ratio of bank deposits to GDP fell from the mid-1940s until the early 1960s. At that point in time they resumed a growth trend, but fell far short of the prewar levels. Financial repression in the form of negative interest rates also contributed to the observed low levels of financial intermediation. In this scenario, and considering also the existence of pervasive market failures in the financial system, it is easy to understand that access to long-term finance was hardly an option for domestic firms, especially for SMEs (Fanelli 2004; Veganzones and Winograd, 1997).

Regarding human capital, the inadequate supply of qualified workers, technicians, engineers, and administrators, vis-à-vis the level of economic development of the country, was pointed out in several studies undertaken at the time (ECLAC, 1958; OECD, 1967).[5] Furthermore, cooperation linkages between the educational system and the productive sector hardly existed. Educational organizations—with few exceptions—tended to autonomously establish their strategies when defining their curricula and career opportunities, without taking into account objectives related to the technological and productive development needs of the country.

Hence, the balance of this experience throws both shadows and lights. Orthodox economists mostly tend to stress the shadows, deeming the whole ISI process a big mistake. This diagnostics would back the sweeping reforms adopted by the military government that took office in 1976 (see chapter 4), as well as the later adoption of the WC-based program in the 1990s (see chapter 5).

However, other authors (such as Katz and Kosacoff, 1989) argue that, in spite of the weaknesses of the ISI model, a learning process had been taking place within the manufacturing industry, which had led to a gradual closing of the productivity and competitiveness gap with the industrialized world. Llach (2002) states that by the early 1970s the manufacturing sector was ready to start a self-sustained growth process that, according to Llach, was unfortunately frustrated by macroeconomic instability and political violence.

At that time reforms were certainly needed, not with the aim of drastically changing the ISI rules of the game, but rather of improving the efficiency of the manufacturing sector through a gradual process of trade liberalization and the removal of the above mentioned obstacles faced by industrial firms. This stance emphasized on preserving the accumulated productive and technological capabilities in a large part of the manufacturing sector, and on the relevance of the process of knowledge diffusion and creation at enterprise level that had been taking place and had a significant impact on productivity growth. The following section surveys the determinants and nature of this process.

A Technological Learning Process

R&D activities were far from being the main source of technological innovation during the ISI period. Katz (1972), surveying a number of large industrial firms, showed that while they expended 0.35 percent of their gross production value in R&D activities,[6] the payments for technology transfer—including patents, know-how agreements, trademarks, and so on reached 1.3 percent of the surveyed firms' sales.

Chudnovsky et al. (1974), analyzing a pool of firms that had signed technology transfer contracts, found similar results (the relation between payments for imported technology and R&D expenditures was more than 3 to 1). The firms surveyed by Chudnovsky allocated 0.55 percent of their sales to R&D activities.[7] It must be noted that these estimates did not take into account imports of capital goods that would have rendered the balance between local and foreign technology even more favorable for the latter.

However, R&D expenditures seemed to have had a positive impact on the observed rate of technical progress in the manufacturing industry—and hence on productivity growth—although this impact was lower than that estimated for the U.S. industry for a similar period (Katz, 1972). In contrast, no association was found between technology transfer payments and technical progress in the Argentine manufacturing industry.

In order to deal with this apparent lack of impact of technology imports on domestic productivity, Katz (1972) observed that the amounts involved in payments for technology contracts did not actually reflect a real knowledge transfer in all cases, since they included trademark payments and the prices charged had a strong monopolistic component.[8]

Chudnovsky et al. (1974), in turn, stated that in many cases, domestic buyers had weak technological competencies—which would have led to underutilization of the imported technology and to very high prices for the transferred items. The authors also indicated that technology transfer contracts often included limitations or prohibitions for the buyer in terms of exporting the products based on the acquired technology.

Capital goods—a large part of which were of foreign origin—were naturally the key sources of technological modernization during the ISI. In spite of the fact that investment promotion regimes allowed duty free imports of those goods, domestic production was also important in different segments such as machine tools, equipment for the food and beverages industry and others.

Informal innovation activities were also very relevant for the learning process in the manufacturing industry. Katz and Kosacoff (1998) show that many firms engaged in technological efforts aimed at sequentially improving product design, production and process engineering, and labor organization (time and motion studies, lay-outs, and so on). These activities led to significant productivity gains. A large number of firms created departments or ad hoc groups for R&D, technical assistance, engineering, and so on, that engaged in different types of innovative activities.

Affiliates of TNCs had to undertake substantial efforts to make technological adaptations. Gradually, activities such as product engineering and design, then production and methods, and finally, organization and planning were undertaken in a systematic manner and consolidated the accumulation of an internal technological capacity. This capacity was not only specific to each firm, but also generated positive spillovers for the rest of the industrial sector.

The process of technological learning in local industry reached peaks in some R&D–intensive sectors: the metalworking industry (machine tools, in particular, where reverse engineering was common), pharmaceuticals (where many local firms benefited from the lack of patent legislation in this sector by copying recently discovered molecules and entering the domestic market with specialties under their trademarks),[9] and electronics (where one local firm—FATE—advanced from the production of calculating machines to planning the eventual production of computers[10]). Those sectors showed the highest ratio between R&D expenditures and sales within Argentine industry, although they were also those where the gap with the same ratio in the U.S. industry was larger (Katz, 1972).[11]

Firms' Behavior, Strategy, and Performance

A usual criticism to the ISI process is that it generated a rent-seeking behavior in firms protected by high tariffs, subject to a diverse array of State regulations and able to lobby for government subsidies. In Argentina, a number of authors have expressed similar arguments, making a link from State interventionism to rent-seeking strategies in the private sector (Llach, 1997; C. Rodríguez, 1988). Furthermore, even authors who do not make such a link also depict Argentine entrepreneurs as extremely averse to invest resources in long-term investment and innovation activities and are prone to count on State aid to survive and expand in their businesses (Sábato, 1988; Schvarzer, 1996).

While it is true that rent-seeking strategies spread during the ISI, the fact is that State interventionism was, as discussed in chapter 1, not an Argentinean curiosity but a key part of the PWDC. The problem, hence, is to explain why the Argentinean version of the ISI generated more rent-seeking and less "Schumpeterian" behaviors than socially desirable.

A number of factors may contribute to explain this outcome, including: (1) macroeconomic and institutional instability; (2) high level of uncertainty about the continuity of public policies; (3) the excessively inward-oriented nature of the ISI regime as it was adopted in Argentina; (4) strong distributional conflicts in a context of growing political violence; (5) the weak linkages between education, science, technology and production; (6) the low level of financial development; (7) the deficiencies in the formulation and implementation of the pro-industrialization policies (see below).

However, in spite of the structural limits for "Schumpeterian" strategies during the ISI stage, it is clear from the remarks made in previous sections that not all entrepreneurial activities were rent-seeking. The behavior and performance of the different segments of firms during that period were determined both by a combination of their size, sector and origin of capital and their different capacities and strategies.

The massive arrival of TNCs in the late 1950s and early 1960s had a substantial impact on Argentine industry well beyond that derived from the installation of new plants. Many of those firms created engineering departments and supplier development programs. They trained their labor force, introduced their personnel to the technological and entrepreneurial culture of their parent companies, and diffused the use of quality norms as part of the routine industrial practices. In some cases, they even played a role in the transfer of engineering services within the corporation to affiliates operating in similar environments (Katz, 1999a).

Even though TNCs did not invest in Argentina with the explicit intention of developing a local technological capacity—and, in fact, their expenditures in R&D were usually low—in practice they often contributed to such development. In view of the idiosyncratic characteristics of the host country, it was often necessary for the affiliates to allocate resources to innovative adaptive activities in order to be able to apply product and processes technologies developed in their respective parent companies.[12]

As TNCs invested in Argentina with market-seeking strategies,[13] exports played a marginal role in their activities. They often used product and process technologies that fell well short of international practices and operated plants with strong diseconomies of scale. However, the aforementioned technological learning process contributed over time to increased export flows.[14] These flows were mostly—but not exclusively—destined to Latin America (Katz and Ablin, 1977).[15] When these exports were part of the corporations' intrafirm trade within Latin America, Argentine affiliates tended to specialize in the more technologically complex business segments.

With regard to family-owned SMEs, most of them were set up with disordered organizational and productive structures, secondhand or self-manufactured machinery, and scant technological knowledge. However, many of them were able to grow and create technical and engineering teams to launch new products and production processes, train their personnel, and advance along their own particular learning path. This process took place largely without external support by copying imported technologies and/or relying on the skills of their owners (often immigrants), which naturally involved frequent risks.

The learning curve of these firms generally started by copying relatively old products. At the beginning of the ISI period, their main objective was to produce in a protected and undersupplied market, without deference to costs, quality, delivery times, or efficiency. It was only when the conditions of the market started to stabilize that their technological efforts were oriented to designing more sophisticated products better adapted to international standards. It was during this phase that management and planning activities, improved company structures, quality, and export-marketing initiatives gained momentum (Katz, 1999a).[16] However, these firms seldom developed "genuine" innovations (i.e., new products or process for world markets).

Finally, there were a significant number of mainly family-controlled domestic conglomerates.[17] Large stand-alone local firms—especially those in family ownership—were also important. Both groups of firms generally made highly standardized products and their level of technological capabilities laid mainly in machinery and equipment. Hence, their innovative performance was largely dependent on their linkages with the capital goods producers.

Several of those firms created engineering departments to improve their production processes. They gradually accumulated technological capacities that allowed them to both reach dominant positions in the local market and, in some cases as previously mentioned, to export technology and invest abroad. However, few of these firms seriously tried to move toward more technologically complex segments—which would have implied systematic R&D activities—and they rarely contributed to create knowledge in scientific disciplines related to their activities (Katz, 1999a).[18]

Institutional and Policy Weaknesses

Although the industrialization strategy started in 1958 was termed "developmentalist," the Argentine State was far from being what Evans (1995) calls a "developmental state" (Japan, Korea, or Taiwan) or even an "intermediate state" (Brazil or India). Whereas in the case of Brazil an "isolated high level bureaucracy" was crucial in implementing the ISI strategy, this bureaucracy was absent in Argentina. In fact, according to Sikkink (1993), Frondizi "was forced to elude the bureaucracy to formulate and instrument his policies" (authors' translation, p. 545).

The frequent changes in ministries, secretaries, and other government departments naturally led to rotations in the bureaucrats, since it was common that the newly appointed officials distrusted the previously existing bureaucracy. This not only affected the efficacy of government action, but also impeded the formation of a stable and meritocratic bureaucracy.

In this context, it is not surprising to find that the received literature repeatedly shows failures in the design and implementation of the industrialization policies adopted at the time.

Tariff policy was erratic and was often unable to grant (and remove) protection to sectors according to their technological and efficiency gaps vis-à-vis international practices. The deepening of import substitution was also in itself an obstacle for a progressive reduction of tariffs in mature sectors. As the latter replaced the imported with local inputs, the higher costs offset the productivity gains previously obtained (Nochteff, 1994b). Furthermore, and in contrast to what happened in Asian developmental states, there was no effective capacity to discipline protected sectors and to obtain reciprocity or quid pro quo commitments regarding productivity gains, rising exports, and other objectives.

The investment promotion policies also failed to yield better results. In the case of the automobile sector, for example, in 1960, there were 21 plants operating in a market of 100 thousand vehicles per year. A few years later most of these plants had to close down when the overcapacity vis-à-vis the existing and projected local demand became evident. This clearly shows the failure of the government to design long-term sectoral strategies (Katz and Kosacoff, 1989).

In turn, projects promoted for the production of basic inputs such as steel, petrochemicals, pulp and paper, and so on, were carried out against a background of conflicts, corruption complaints, delays, and other problems that obviously implied high costs for the society as a whole (Schvarzer, 1996).[19]

In general, these regimes lacked performance requirements with regard to technology, local provision of equipment or exports, unlike the situation in Brazil or East Asia. The main criterion for success was actual import substitution. A central point to bear in mind is the influence of the Armed Forces in the definition of the promotion policies in sectors such as aluminum, iron and steel, or petrochemicals. This obviously introduced noneconomic elements in decisions on the approval of investment projects and probably disregarded microeconomic efficiency.

Regarding credit policies, in the late 1960s the government tried to reform the Industrial Bank that had been created in 1944. The objective of this reform was to have the bank assume a leading role in the promotion of medium- and long-term investments in the manufacturing sector.[20] In fact the bank had been assigned this role on its inception, but it had never fulfilled it. However, even in this new period, a substantial share of the credits was given to State suppliers or to firms that faced threats of bankruptcy (Rougier, 2004). Hence, Rougier suggests that the allocation of credits did not follow the theoretical guidelines established in respect of the type of firms to be supported and the sectors to be promoted. The performance of the Bank was also impaired by institutional instability[21] and by the volatility of the macroeconomic environment.

In the area of S&T, no initiatives were adopted during this period to foster R&D or innovative activities in private firms through fiscal, financial or other types of incentives. This was in contrast with what was the practice in other countries. On the contrary, inspired on the ideas of the so-called linear model of innovation (see Kline and Rosenberg, 1986), the government focused on the creation of public S&T institutions (and research departments in some State firms, as in the case of the oil company YPF). This approach by the government was based on the assumption that the private enterprises would eventually be "users" of their services.

Key institutions created in the late 1950s under this approach did not generally play a relevant role in the technological development of the manufacturing industry. This is particularly true of the National Council of Scientific and Technological Research (CONICET) headed up by the winner of the Nobel Prize for Medicine in (1947), Houssay, whose main aim was to foster basic scientific research.

The National Institute of Industrial Technology (INTI) was rarely involved in R&D or technological development activities, and its main goal was to provide routine services (e.g., metrology, tests).[22] Only the National Commission of Atomic Energy (CNEA) had an impact on certain segments of the manufacturing industry on account of its technological capabilities in metallurgy and its development programs for suppliers.

The creation of the above mentioned public S&T institutions led to an increase in R&D expenditures in relation to GDP. This ratio grew from 0.1 percent in 1954 to about 0.4 percent by the mid-1970s. However, considering this indicator and others such as the number of scientists and engineers dedicated to R&D activities and the expenditures in R&D per researcher, Argentina was clearly lagging behind in any international comparison.

Besides the creation of these public institutions, no effective S&T policies existed during the ISI. The INTI started to register and control technology transfer contracts in the early 1970s, but without an explicit policy of fostering private indigenous innovative activities. Other measures were taken to regulate technology imports and promote the development of local technologies, especially in State firms and organizations. However, given the increasingly unstable institutional and economic context in which these measures were applied, they had little or no impact.

Notwithstanding the flaws and failures of the industrial and trade policies of the time, most of them had a theoretical rationale, provided that one accepts the idea that Argentina needed to promote industrialization. For example, the investment promotion policies were probably the only way of fostering a massive investment program in an environment in which private banks did not offer long-term financing for the industrial sector, the capital markets were clearly underdeveloped and a high level of economic and institutional uncertainty prevailed. This also applies to the National Bank of Development (BANADE). Tariff protection for new sectors finds a rationale in the traditional "infant industry" argument although the latter calls for selective and temporal protection, two features that were notably absent in Argentina. In any case, it seems that the aforementioned institutional, political, and macroeconomic problems, and the failures in their design and implementation led these policies to have fewer benefits and more costs than originally expected. It is also plausible to argue that the excessively inward-oriented nature of Argentina's industrialization strategy and the lack of sound technology policies also contributed to the relative failure of industrial policies, in contrast to the situation in East Asian countries that adopted more outward-oriented development patterns and paid more attention to technology policies.

Technological Modernization in the Agriculture Sector

As shown in graph 3.3, after a long period of decline, agricultural production started to grow since the late 1950s. As a result of outdated technologies in use in Argentina, yields had been stagnating or falling since the 1940s and showed a huge gap vis-à-vis U.S. yields (see graphs 3.4 and 3.5). The need to foster agricultural output and exports was widely accepted at that time, since the latter were the main source of foreign currency, hence placing a limit on industrial growth, as we saw earlier.

The main economic advisor of the *Revolución Libertadora* that overthrew the first Perón government in 1955, Raúl Prebisch, emphasized the need to increase agricultural exports. Among his recommendations were the creation of a public institute dedicated to technology diffusion and the modernization of infrastructure in agriculture.

The call for pro-agricultural policies was accepted. A process of technological modernization took place and enabled production to recover and exports to expand. In contrast to what happened in the manufacturing sector with INTI, the role of the National Institute of Agricultural Technology (INTA), created in 1956, and the CREA groups[23] in this process

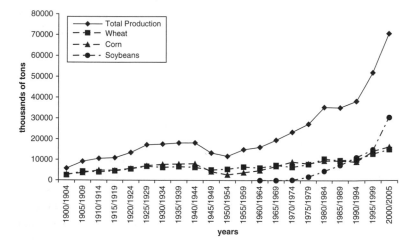

Graph 3.3   Agricultural production in Argentina, thousand of tons, 1900–2005

Source: Own elaboration of the basis of SAGPyA data and Barsky et al. (1988).

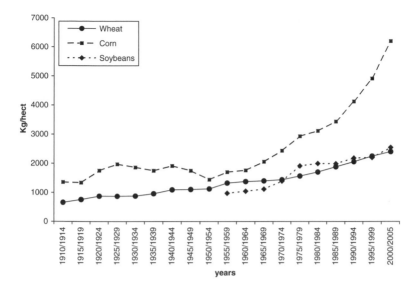

Graph 3.4 Agricultural yields, kilogram/hectare, 1900–2005

Source: Own elaboration of the basis of SAGPyA data and Barsky et al. (1988).

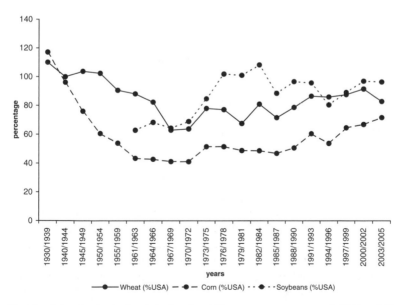

Graph 3.5 Argentina's agricultural yields as a percentage of U.S. yields, 1930–2005

Source: Own elaboration of the basis of USDA and SAGPyA data and Diaz Alejandro (1975).

was very relevant. Subsidies and cheap credits—which fostered a significant increase in the adoption of capital goods such as tractors—also favored agricultural producers during this period.

Product and process innovations were adopted from the late 1950s. Among the former, the more important was the introduction of hybrid seeds,[24] soybean and grain sorghum and improved varieties of existing seeds. There was also a significant increase in the use of tractors with improved mechanical capacities and better availability of agrochemicals and fertilizers (Obschatko et al., 1984; Barsky et al., 1992).

Furthermore, soybean demanded new types of handling and farming practices that were later transferred to other crops. Artificial insemination systems were diffused and improvements in health techniques in livestock breeding were introduced. The State played a key role in this regard, but there was also a surge in private services such as soil analysis laboratories, insemination centers, specialized machinery contractors, and so on (Becerra et al., 1997).[25]

These new "technological packages" allowed significant increases in land productivity (see graphs 3.4 and 3.5), which, since the mid-1960s, led to a gradual closing of the gap that had been steadily widening vis-à-vis U.S. agricultural yields.[26] They also made it profitable to undertake farming activities in new areas and this formed the basis that sustained the above mentioned process of agricultural expansion (Obschatko and Del Bello, 1986; Obschatko et al., 1984).

Concluding Remarks

Argentina, like many other developing countries during the period under study, engaged in an import-substitution strategy after the crisis of 1930. Although import substitution was first mostly spontaneous, it became a conscious strategy from Peron's government on. Later on, the *desarrollista* government that took office in 1958 embarked upon an ambitious industrialization project aimed at deepening import substitution toward durable goods (including automobiles) and intermediate goods (steel, petrochemicals, and so on), as well as some capital goods.

This strategy paved the way for a modernization of the industrial structure and eventually led to 11 years of positive GDP growth between 1964 and 1974. Productivity gaps with developed countries were reduced during this period, and manufacturing exports recorded significant increases since early 1960s. Even technology exports were materialized in those years. All these facts were a consequence of not only physical capital investments promoted under the *desarrollista* regime but also of the learning process that took place during that period in the manufacturing industry.

The gradual maturation of the industrial structure generated during the ISI stage was interrupted by the growing macroeconomic instability and the increasing political violence that finally paved the way for the 1976 coup. The military government that took office that year implemented a liberalization program cum exchange rate appreciation that marked the beginning of a complete restructuring of the manufacturing sector and its loss of the position of leading economic sector that had attained during the ISI (see next chapter).

As counterfactual experiments are nearly impossible in social sciences, we will never know what would have happened with the industrial sector in another policy setting. Some authors see the "glass half full." They stress the learning process and the productivity gains that had been attained during the ISI, arguing that a gradual liberalization of the economy would have allowed preserving the accumulated productive and technological capabilities while reducing the most obvious inefficiencies that existed at that moment. Those who see the "glass half empty" state that a gradual removal of trade barriers would have been impossible—due to political pressures by rent-seekers—and that inefficiencies were much more extended than acknowledged by the first group of authors.

In any case, in our judgment the ISI experiment was not an error by itself—as argued by "mainstream" economists—but, in the Argentine case at least, it was plagued with problems that mainly came from the macroeconomic and institutional settings (and this could explain why Argentina had a modest growth record during that stage and why, even during the 1964–1974 growth spurt, productivity gains did not play a major role in explaining economic growth).

Macroeconomic volatility was always present during the ISI, as it is shown by the existence of "stop and go" cycles that went along with periodical balance of payments crisis, devaluation, and high inflation. Institutional instability was also a feature during those years. This affected not only the continuity of economic policies but also progressively affected policymaking capabilities. Hence, it comes as no surprise to find that the design, implementation, and monitoring of policies in such key areas as trade or finance were plagued with deficiencies and inconsistencies. Increasingly severe distributional conflicts even hampered these negative features of the Argentine economy in those years.

Unfortunately, as it is seen in next chapters, macroeconomic and institutional problems were even further aggravated after the end of the ISI process. It is no surprise, then, that a long recession emerged between 1975 and 1990. The next chapter is devoted to its analysis.

CHAPTER 4

THE LONG RECESSION, 1975–1990

The Macroeconomic and Political Evolution

The military dictatorship that took office on March 1976 decided to fight against guerrilla movements with a kind of "dirty war," in which human rights were systematically violated. At the same time, political parties and labor unions were neutralized by the government (either through suspension of constitutional rights and changes in the labor legislation or through direct repression). It is in this context that a new economic policy was implemented, supposedly aimed at radically changing the structure and performance of the Argentine economy.

During the first months of the military government, and after the appointment of Martínez de Hoz as minister of economy, trade liberalization measures were taken together with the implementation of a stabilization plan that resulted in a drastic fall in real urban wages. At the same time, a new foreign investment law was passed[1] and a financial reform implemented that liberalized interest rates and modified the criteria for credit allocation.

Although strong reductions in import tariffs were imposed in 1976 (on average 40 percent points),[2] imports failed to rise significantly in the subsequent three years. This was due to the fact that there were loopholes in the tariffs—that is, the legal rates were not fully utilized by domestic producers (Berlinski, 2003). Furthermore, the devalued peso discouraged imports. In this context, production of durable consumer goods and capital goods entered a period of recovery.

In spite of the fact that inflation control was one of the main targets of the military government, this goal was far from being attained. Inflation rates kept at high levels (180 percent a year), in a context of high fiscal deficits. This led to a new policy package in late 1978. A preestablished schedule was adopted to steadily reduce over time the devaluation of the local currency against the U.S. dollar (the so-called *tablita cambiaria*), and, at the same time, a new round of trade liberalization was launched.[3] This policy was based on the assumption that domestic interest and inflation rates would gradually converge to the corresponding international rates.

However, convergence was not achieved. The actual inflation rates were higher than the forecasted ones, leading to an increasing overvaluation of the peso. Interest rates also failed to fall to international levels due, in part, to economic and political uncertainty and the high cost of financial intermediation. Current account deficits, in turn, grew strongly.

These problems did not have an immediate consequence on the growth performance of the economy, since the government was able to take advantage of some favorable elements of the international context. Financial liberalization allowed substantial inflows of short-term capital into the country and these offset the current account deficits. In view of the ample supply of international credit, fiscal spending increased and investment rates reached high levels.

Investment projects were mainly related to the infrastructural developments, defense sector objectives, and capacity expansion in intermediate goods such as steel, paper and pulp, and petrochemicals. Foreign indebtedness was a major source of finance for investment during those years.

In the latter case, projects were undertaken mainly by domestic conglomerates that were often partners of the State and received substantial incentives from different promotion regimes. While local conglomerates gradually became the leading actors in the Argentine economy, the role of TNCs affiliates declined. Between 1976 and 1981 most FDI inflows were directed at the oil and financial sectors, while new FDI in manufacturing was quite low. In fact, some large TNCs, especially in the automobile sector, closed their subsidiaries or scaled down their operations during those years.

By early 1980, the policy had succeeded in bringing the annual rate of inflation to below 100 percent, but at the cost of a profit squeeze for a large part of industry. At the same time, the prevailing high domestic interest rates in a period of weak supervision of the financial system led to the bankruptcy of the most important private bank in March 1980. This was the beginning of a banking crisis that continued with the closure of other banks.

In this situation, public confidence in the government program began to erode. The anticipation of future currency devaluation increased the demand for dollars and sharply reduced the reserves in the Central Bank. The government took on additional foreign debt in order to satisfy the growing demand for dollars as international interest rates started to rise in 1981.

In March 1981, in accordance with a previously stipulated schedule, a new military president took office. The economic team was also replaced. After some delays, the anticipated devaluation was decided amidst a worsening economic situation. By this time, a high level of foreign debt had been accumulated. Partly as a consequence of the Mexican default that affected all Latin American countries, Argentina suffered its own foreign debt crisis in 1982. With a huge public deficit, high inflation, continuous currency devaluations, and an external debt crisis, conditions in the country in 1981–1982 were even worse than those that had prevailed in 1975. Between 1975 and 1981, GDP per capita fell by 3 percent and real wages by 25 percent.

In mid-1982, exchange controls and import restrictions were reestablished closing the economy to competing imports. In this connection it should be noted that while protectionism in the 1960s was a main tool of the industrialization strategy, in the 1980s it was driven by macroeconomic conditions.

Relief measures were undertaken for financial institutions (and their borrowers) and the State took most of the private foreign debt through a system of exchange rate risk insurance. "This huge transfer of wealth rescued many enterprises from bankruptcy, but it was a gift to others, who, by having foreign liabilities backed by foreign assets, got rid of the former while keeping the latter. The effect was to place the private sector in a net creditor position, leaving the government as the sole debtor without means of domestic financing" (Canitrot, 1994, p. 80).

The 1982 foreign debt crisis resulted in the intensification of both the external and the fiscal structural imbalances in the Argentine economy. These two basic imbalances were complemented by the short-run dynamics of the high inflation regime. Financial fragility amplified the consequences of the measures adopted to deal with these imbalances. The high inflation regime produced self-propelling propagation schemes that resulted in volatile inflation rates (Damill et al., 1989).

At the same time, the precarious financial situation caused both by the demonetization process and the lack of external financing was one of the main obstacles to economic policy management. This produced a permanent climate of uncertainty that damaged the investment process and encouraged substantial capital flight (Kosacoff, 2000).

Following defeat in the Malvinas War in 1982, the military called for elections to reinstate a constitutional regime. The Radical Party that won the 1983 elections in which President Alfonsín was elected emphasized democracy and the defense of human rights. The military leaders were tried for their crimes during the "dirty war" in 1985. The manner in which the judicial process was conducted and the fact that the military leaders were sentenced were well-received by the public opinion.

Regarding economic policy, after a failed attempt to control inflation by a general agreement on prices and wages, the Austral Plan launched in 1985 focused on inflationary inertia and adopted a price freeze at the core of the stabilization policy. Early attempts by the Argentine government to consider the external debt as illegitimate evolved into a rollover agreement with the U.S. government in exchange for the payment of debt arrears.

The initial success of the Austral Plan in reducing inflation without a recession gave popularity to the government for a while. The price freeze was then replaced by a system of price guidelines, including the exchange rate, loosely adjusted to current inflation. Although the trend toward peso overvaluation was checked, inflation grew again and resulted in falling fiscal revenues in a context in which there was no political consensus for dealing with the sources of the fiscal deficit.[4]

A last unsuccessful attempt to stabilize the economy was made in mid-1988 with the so-called Spring Plan. Pressures on the exchange rate soon became unsustainable and faced with growing demand for dollars, the Central Bank suspended sales in early 1989. The exchange rate accumulated a substantial growth in a few weeks and inflation surged and turned rapidly into hyperinflation (Canitrot, 1994). The already high level of de facto "dollarization" of the economy increased as a result of these episodes.

Poverty and income distribution inequality increased to previously unknown levels (see graphs 2.8 and 2.9), leading to massive public protests, lootings, and widespread social unrest. In July 1989, Alfonsin resigned and Menem, the Peronist candidate who had won the presidential election held in May, had to assume the presidency before the scheduled date.

The balance of this period was clearly negative. The fall in GDP per capita amounted to 20 percent between 1981 and 1990. Between 1980 and 1990 GDP declined by 8 percent, imports by 59 percent, consumption by 16 percent, and investment by 70 percent, while unemployment doubled over the same period (see Kosacoff, 2000). GDP per capita was 22 percent lower in 1990 than in 1975 (see table 2.2). This critical situation paved the way for the introduction of the "Washington Consensus"–based reforms, which is analyzed in the next chapter.

Investment, Exports, and Productivity in the Manufacturing Sector

The manufacturing industry was particularly hit by the crisis. Between 1975 and 1990, industrial output fell by around 25 percent, industrial employment by 45 percent, and industry participation in GDP dropped from 28.3 percent to 20.7 percent. In turn, manufacturing industry's share in employment fell from 23.9 percent to 17.5 percent between 1970 and 1991 (see table 2.1). As the decline in manufacturing output was comparatively less than that of the decline in employment, productivity gains were obtained (see table 3.3). The mechanisms in force were, however, not exactly the same throughout the whole period under review.

Between 1976 and 1980, there was a drastic reduction in the number of industrial workers,[5] which was in part a response to the previous "overemployment" as a result of closed-economy conditions and strong unionization—labor unions were systematically repressed since 1976—but also of the above mentioned reduction of industrial production that particularly affected labor-intensive industries (see below).

However, the decline of the industrial sector was not a lineal process. Until 1979–1980, manufacturing production had recorded a modest increase vis-à-vis 1975–1976 levels and a technological modernization process had taken place. This process benefited mainly large firms that were able to take advantage of trade liberalization by upgrading their machinery and equipment (Kosacoff, 2000).

Overvaluation in a context of trade liberalization and high interest rates was the main reason for the large industrial crisis of 1981. Later on, the industrial sector was negatively affected not only by the stagnation and high volatility of the Argentine economy, but also by the lack of credit[6] and the high tariff and mainly nontariff barriers that made the import of industrial inputs and capital goods very expensive. In this context, it comes as no surprise to find that from 1981 to 1990, both production and employment fell and the process of technological modernization was slowed.

Within this general scenario, there were significant differences in the performance of various sectors. Basic metals, chemicals, and (to a lesser extent) paper and pulp were the fast-growing industries in the period under review. These are capital-intensive, large-scale sectors that mostly rely on natural resources.

In contrast, the machinery and equipment sector—a skill-intensive activity with major design and engineering capabilities—experienced a sharp decline (with a brief recovery in the second half of the 1980s), stimulated by the possibility of exporting to the Brazilian market after the beginning of the integration process between both countries (see below). Labor-intensive industries such as textiles were also severely affected by the long crisis. The food processing sector remained stagnant, although there was a remarkable growth in the export-oriented sector producing edible vegetable oils and a contraction in the traditional meatpacking industry.

The heterogeneous paths of the different industrial sectors were, in part, a reflection of the differences in sectoral investment performance during the period under review. In 1976–1990, the national industrial promotion program provided subsidies to about 50 projects to produce intermediate inputs in large capital-intensive plants (Kosacoff, 2000). Although these projects were justified in the early 1970s within the previous ISI model, they were largely implemented during the military government and, to a lesser extent, in the 1980s.

The investment promotion regimes also favored certain regions and firms, including the aforementioned domestic business conglomerates. In terms of regions, a special incentives scheme was established in Tierra del Fuego in the late 1970s to encourage the production of consumer electronics with little local content and engineering inputs.

During this same decade, a regime to foster investments in less developed provinces was also established and attracted projects that were mostly oriented toward the final stages of the production process in order to maximize tax deductions. These promotion schemes were criticized for their fiscal cost and lack of transparency. Performance requirements in terms of innovation, exports, labor training, and so on were also omitted. The absence of *ex ante* clear criteria to select sectors, firms and activities for promotion and the lack of any *ex post* evaluation of the promotional mechanisms were other key weakness of these industrial policy instruments.[7]

Also of relevance were two investment programs put in place in the second half of the 1980s. First, the external debt-equity swap programs that facilitated financing of US$660 million for 82 investment projects mostly undertaken by TNCs in the second half of the 1980s (Fuchs, 1990). These investments were mainly oriented toward the food, automobile, petroleum, and chemical industries. Second, the preferential credit lines granted by the Italian and Spanish governments favored the acquisition of capital goods in the same period.

It is very important to take into account the fact that virtually all the relevant investment projects undertaken during the 1980s were based on one of the aforementioned incentives schemes in place (Azpiazu et al., 1993), which is not a surprising finding in the macroeconomic scenario described.

The roots of investment retraction may be traced to the 1979–1981 period. During those years, unexpected changes in trade policy in a context of peso overvaluation led to an anti-investment bias (Nogués, 1986). Difficulties for accessing long-term credit and interest rates volatility also contributed to generate that bias.

Financial reform-cum-peso overvaluation generated attractive arbitrage opportunities (i.e., borrowing in U.S. dollars to relend the money in local pesos), which were capitalized by many firms to make short-run profits, hence further damaging productive investments (Petrei and de Melo, 1985).

During the 1980s, investment was negatively affected by macroeconomic and institutional uncertainty. In this scenario, it is no wonder to find a strong preference for liquidity and flexibility among domestic firms. The preference for the short-run in financial markets and the gradual replacement of the peso by the U.S. dollar as a store of value, in turn, had a negative impact on financial deepening, hence making credit expensive and scarce for domestic firms (Fanelli and Frenkel, 1996).

In this context, surviving firms were not necessarily those more efficient but those less affected by the hostile environment, while the only investments that were made were those benefited by State subsidies or those with short-run and secure repayment perspectives (Fanelli and Frenkel, 1996).

Given the modest investment levels, technological modernization, as mentioned, was slowed. Capital goods and intangible technology imports were low, and the same happened with FDI flows (which only augmented in late 1980s due to the above mentioned debt-equity swap program). R&D expenditures by Argentine firms were also very low. All this naturally led to an increase in the productivity gap vis-à-vis developed countries (see table 4.1; and see also table 2.3).

The only economic indicator with a positive performance during the 1980s was export trade that expanded by almost 80 percent, favored by prevailing exchange rates and the domestic recession.[8] Exports of manufactured goods (accounting for a growing proportion of total exports—see table 4.2) benefited from various types of government subsidies and also from cross-subsidization due to high prices commanded by firms operating in concentrated and protected domestic markets (Bisang, 1990). Furthermore,

Table 4.1   Argentine industrial labor productivity relative to the U.S. levels,* 1970–2000

1970	1980	1990	2000
0.52	0.58	0.55	0.80

* Estimated as the ratio between manufacturing value added (measured in U.S. constant dollars) and total employment in the manufacturing industry.

Source: Authors' estimates based on data from World Bank, OECD, and INDEC.

Table 4.2   Argentine exports, 1980–2000, current US$ million, five-year averages

	Total	%	Primary products	%	Manufactures of agricultural origin	%	Manufactures of industrial origin	%	Fuels and energy	%
1980–1984	8,147	100	3,513	43	2,857	35	1,346	17	430	5
1985–1989	8,064	100	2,399	30	3,275	41	2,112	26	279	3
1990–1994	13,104	100	3,397	26	5,065	39	3,499	27	1,144	9
1995–1999	24,189	100	5,617	23	8,395	35	7,379	30	2,799	12
2000	26,341	100	5,346	20	7,864	30	8,230	31	4,902	19

Source: Authors' calculations on the basis of INDEC data.

a program to foster cooperation and expand bilateral trade with Brazil was launched in 1986, which also had a positive impact on exports.[9]

Despite severe fiscal restrictions, the export promotion policies during the 1980s provided different fiscal and financial incentives regimes for exports of manufactured goods. Drawback and temporary admission schemes were also in place during that period. These mechanisms were adopted for different reasons in each case, but the three main underlying objectives were to compensate for the anti-export bias due to the closing of the local economy, to reimburse indirect and/or direct taxes paid internally, and to address market failures in the financial system that prevented access of local firms to export credits.

According to Bisang (1990) institutional fragmentation, instability, and lack of coherence plagued the export promotion system as its benefits were concentrated on a small number of firms and sectors. The system also lacked transparency and effective control mechanisms. It should also be noted that explicit export subsidies complemented the aforementioned mechanism of cross-subsidies between the internal and the export market. The activities that mostly benefited from the explicit promotion system were in fact often those that were in a position to subsidize their exports with the high prices obtained in the protected domestic market.[10]

In evaluating the evolution of the manufacturing industry in Argentina between 1975 and 1990, Kosacoff (2000) argues that, apart from its drastic contraction, the sector underwent radical transformations during that period. On the one hand, a "regressive restructuring" took place. The economic team that took office in 1976 did not try to improve the existing base of knowledge, skills, and equipment accumulated during the ISI, but rather initiated a rapid restructuring process aimed at the disappearance of "inefficient" sectors. This led to the destruction of capabilities that could have formed the basis for a more efficient industrialization pattern if a gradual restructuring strategy had been adopted. The chosen "shock" strategy, instead, gave rise to a new productive structure that was not able to generate more employment and was more dependent on natural resources endowments than the previous one, thus opening limited opportunities for a knowledge-based development path.

On the other hand, Kosacoff (2000) observes a growing heterogeneity within the industrial sector, both at sectoral level and at enterprise level. While a large group of firms shrank, closed down, or passed from production to import activities (SMEs were prominent within this group), a smaller group expanded, modernized their structures, and became more competitive and efficient. As indicated in the following chapters, this heterogeneity was also a feature of the 1990s.

A Brief Account of the Agricultural Sector

The process of expansion of agricultural production that had started in late 1950s continued until the 1984–1985 harvest. At that time production levels were four times those of 1950–1954 and 60 percent higher than those of 1972–1973. The dynamism of the agricultural sector was based on the increased utilization of new grains (soybean), the diffusion of new genetic traits and the ongoing process of mechanization that had been initiated in the 1950s.

However, like the manufacturing industry, a growing heterogeneity was observed during this period in the agricultural sector. While modern agricultural units were increasingly similar, in terms of technological levels, to those of developed countries (Obschatko et al., 1984), since mid-1970s the gap between those producers and the rest widened (Solá, 1986). The availability of capital was the main source of differences in terms of access to technological packages among agricultural producers.

The agricultural expansion was interrupted at mid-1980s and only in 1994–1995 production will recover the 1984–1985 levels (see graph 3.3). The new period of stagnation in the sector was the result of the high taxation levels imposed by the State (in the context of permanent fiscal crisis) and the low international prices of the main commodities exported by Argentina. Both factors led to a drastic reduction in profitability and hence in production and investment (Barsky, 1993).

Concluding Remarks

The sole data that in 1990 Argentina's GDP per capita was more than 20 percent lower than in 1975 is, in itself, strong enough to describe the magnitude of the economic disaster suffered by the country during those years. Domestic and international problems joined to produce one of the most egregious cases of "falling behind" in the international economic development history.

On the domestic side, the trade liberalization experiment initiated in 1977, which was made in a context of severe exchange rate appreciation and high real interest rates, led to a big economic and banking crisis, which was soon followed by the debt crisis in 1982. During the 1980s a continuous and finally sterile struggle against inflation was fought amidst constant pressures from the fiscal and external areas.

Among the most negative legacies of this stage—limiting ourselves to the socioeconomic area—we find, first, the impairment in income distribution. Second, the loss of technological and productive capabilities in many industrial sectors, which perhaps could have been preserved in a context of a gradual restructuring, as said in the previous chapter. Third, the consolidation of microeconomic behaviors based on a strong preference for liquidity and flexibility. Finally, an almost complete replacement of the peso by the dollar as a store of value. It was in this very unfavorable context that the WC inspired structural reforms program and the Convertibility Plan were launched. The next four chapters deal with the evolution and impacts of these reforms, from the initial high growth period to the devastating 2001–2002 crisis.

CHAPTER 5

STRUCTURAL REFORMS AND COMPLEMENTARY POLICIES DURING THE 1990s

Introduction

After entering office in 1989, Menem's administration made several unsuccessful attempts to stabilize an economy under hyperinflation (the so-called Bunge and Born Plan and others). The renewed inflationary episodes in 1990 and the resignation of two ministers of economy paved the way for the appointment of Cavallo (and his team) in the Ministry of Economy in early 1991.

Cavallo launched a currency board scheme (the so-called Convertibility Law)[1] in order to stop inflation. The currency board was an acknowledgment of the fact that the economy was dollarized de facto as a result of many years of high inflation and the hyperinflationary episodes that had taken place since the late 1980s. The adoption of the currency board went hand in hand with a complete deregulation of the capital account of the balance of payments.

Convertibility went along with a far-reaching program of structural reforms[2] that had been cautiously initiated during the last years of Alfonsín's government. By the early 1990s, the country was ahead of other Latin American countries in the areas of privatization of State enterprises, market deregulation, trade and financial liberalization, Central Bank independence, and social security reforms.

In the first part of this chapter we concentrate on three issues that, according to the architects of the reforms, were key factors for competitive restructuring and productivity improvements in the private business sector: privatization, trade liberalization, and market deregulation (which included the creation of a climate that enabled FDI and technology transfer from abroad).

In chapter 6 we briefly comment on labor, financial, and social security reforms, and discuss the impact of the complete reforms package on the macroeconomic, sectoral, and social areas during the 1990s.

While complementary policies, originally envisaged by Cavallo's team, were not aimed at facilitating the adaptation of economic agents to the new rules of the game, the difficulties faced by the firms to adjust to the new business environment led the government to introduce a number of horizontal policies to deal with those difficulties. These initiatives, jointly with some sectoral policies that were applied during the 1990s, are also examined in this chapter.

Privatizations[3]

By late 1980s, there was a broad consensus about the fact that State enterprises delivered low-quality services—although the causes of their inefficiency was disputed.[4,5] Their privatization was, therefore, expected to result in substantial improvements in the existing infrastructure, a key element for the successful restructuring of the Argentine economy. However, it was not obvious which enterprises should be privatized first, in what conditions and with what regulatory framework.

Furthermore, in the Argentine case, privatization was considered a powerful instrument that could be used to gain a good reputation, quickly, among the local and international establishment. The need for a good reputation was crucial to a government that belonged to a party of populist tradition and that had taken office in the middle of hyperinflationary conditions. Hence, a rapid improvement in the fiscal accounts by the sale of State enterprises that usually suffered losses and the attraction of FDI also became priority issues in the privatization program.

Subject to the requirement that the consortia participating in public auctions had to include a partner with previous experience in the same field of activity, a high share of public utility firms ended up being controlled by foreign investors. Most privatizations, however, involved joint ventures with large domestic conglomerates. Typically, the foreign partner took responsibility for the technical and operational side of the business, while the domestic partner—usually with minority shares—remained in charge of the administrative and financial side. Foreign banks often participated as providers of finance, particularly through external debt-to-equity swaps.

The evolution of the macroeconomic environment decisively shaped the details of the privatization program. Consequently, the privatization of telecommunications, completed in 1990 in the middle of a deep economic crisis, provided for modest investment commitments, a loosely defined regulatory framework, a sharp increase in telephone charges (fixed in US$ dollars since 1991 and indexed to the US$ inflation rate) and a guaranteed monopoly for a decade. Despite these benefits and the sizable potential of the telecommunications market (with considerable repressed demand for telecommunications services), only three consortia submitted offers.

By contrast, privatizations made in 1992–1993 took place in the context of a fast-growing/low-inflation economy and greatly improved expectations. This made it possible to streamline privatization procedures and regulatory bodies, as was the case with the privatization of natural gas distribution, and electricity generation and distribution.

Even then, significant incentives were offered to attract foreign and domestic investors: most companies that offered themselves for privatization were transferred without liabilities (including environmental obligations).[6] Moreover, the rate-fixing system included highly questionable clauses, such as rates fixed in US$ dollars (in consonance with the currency board in place then) and indexation mechanisms linking local rates to the US$ inflation rate. This situation, combined with the fact that many activities were natural monopolies or were granted reserved markets for extended periods of time, made high profits the norm among privatized firms.

The largest privatization was that of YPF, Argentina's largest corporation with petroleum and natural gas interests, and upstream and downstream activities in the petroleum industry. YPF was privatized in 1993 through the sale of shares in small blocks on the domestic and international markets; 58 percent of the company's stock was floated on the market and an indeterminate share was purchased by foreign portfolio investors. The national government and several provincial administrations maintained a minority stake and an employee ownership program retained control of 10 percent of the capital stock. In January 1999, at the height of the Brazilian foreign exchange crisis, the Spanish oil company, Repsol, purchased the government's 15 percent share in YPF. A few months later, in April 1999, Repsol made a public offer and acquired the remaining 85 percent of the capital that was mostly in the hands of private, domestic, and foreign investors.

State firms in manufacturing sectors, such as steel and petrochemicals, were also privatized and were mostly acquired by private firms with interests in the same sectors. Ports, airports, the postal service, the national airline company, many provincial banks, and other businesses were also privatized during this period.

In a study of the performance of privatized nonfinancial enterprises, Galiani et al. (2001) found substantial increases in their profitability and operating efficiency after privatization. Productivity indicators improved due to massive layoffs[7] and also because privatized firms increased output and introduced modern management practices, and production and organizational technologies. In fact, investment by these firms increased at least 350 percent as a result of privatization, a process that was greatly facilitated both by the easy access to the international financial market and as a result of trade liberalization in capital goods (see next section).

Privatizations often had positive impacts on the quality, availability, and, to a lesser extent, the costs of the respective services and/or products. For instance, the productivity levels of ports improved remarkably. The Buenos Aires Port, which operated with 8,000 employees before the reforms, had only 2,500 employees in 1994. In turn, several old labor regulations were abolished and this allowed substantial cost reductions.

In the electricity market, tariffs were reduced, especially for the large business sector, and the installed capacity increased from 13,267 MW to 18,100 MW five years after the privatization. In the gas sector, transport networks increased their capacity by 60 percent between 1992 and 2000 and the gas distribution network grew by 58 percent, from 66,765 to 105,614 km. In the area of telecommunications, the number of lines increased 100 percent in 1989–2000. Average productivity increased from 92 lines in service per employee in 1990 to almost 400 lines in 2000 (Gerchunoff et al., 2003). Fuel and energy exports were also boosted by privatizations (see table 4.2).

While privatizations were rather popular in the early 1990s, it is interesting to explore the reasons behind their growing unpopularity along the decade. First, sales of certain State enterprises were fraught with corruption, and there was considerable public concern about this. Second, substantial quality improvements were not attained in all cases—passenger railway services, for example, did not improve significantly after privatization. Third, while the business sector benefited most from rate reductions, households suffered rate increases in some areas such as basic telephone services. Fourth, privatizations resulted in massive layoffs and were therefore perceived as one of the main causes of the growing levels of unemployment (for more details see chapter 6).

In addition, no incentives were put in place to foster backward linkages with local suppliers (in fact, local supplies were largely replaced with imports) or to induce privatized firms to engage in innovative activities (which were even discontinued in some cases). Last but not the least, regulatory norms and agencies were very heterogeneous, and, in some cases, were not only weak or deficient but also almost inexistent. This created a situation in which the significant productivity increases in most privatized activities were not fully transferred to consumers but rather augmented the privatized firms' profits (which, to a large extent, were not reinvested in Argentina but transferred abroad) hence limiting the social benefits generated by privatizations.

Trade Liberalization

Trade liberalization measures had already begun in 1988, when Alfonsín's government limited the number of items subject to quantitative restrictions or prohibitions and the weighted average tariff rate was reduced to 48 percent. The new government carried out the second phase in foreign trade reform. From 1989 onward, successive rounds of tariff reductions were implemented. The tariff structure was extensively modified in April 1991 to include only three levels: 0 percent for raw materials, 11 percent for intermediate inputs, and 22 percent for manufactured final goods. The weighted average tariff rate was reduced to 19 percent by 1991 (see table 3.1).

As shown in table 5.1, the average effective level of tariff protection was relatively low during this period, with peaks in the areas of textiles and leather, wood and wood products, and machinery and equipment, and lows in the food and beverages sector. In turn, the government eliminated many specific duties and quantitative restrictions on imports of capital and durable goods.

In subsequent years the scheme was slightly modified: the tax on previously untaxed imports was raised to 5 percent and the tax on intermediate goods was increased by two points. During successive reforms the number of tariff levels increased again.

In 1993, a decision was made to further liberalize trade in capital goods and eliminate the import tariff for such goods.[8] Another instrument that favored the acquisition of foreign technology, during that time, was the scheme that permitted duty-free imports of "turnkey plants." There was a boost in capital goods—imports as a result of trade liberalization and the

Table 5.1 Estimates of the effective tariff protection levels, 1991 and 1997, in percentages

Sector-Description	1991	1997
31. Food, beverages and tobacco	9.2	22.5
32. Textiles and leather	23.6	22.9
33. Wood & wood products, including furniture	22.9	19.8
34. Paper & paper products, publishing & printing	12.8	14.4
35. Chemicals and petrochemicals	13.2	15.3
36. Non-metallic minerals	15.2	14.4
37. Basic metallic industries	19.1	15.7
38. Metallic minerals, machinery & equipment	26.7	17.5
39. Other manufacturing industries	22.2	26.1
Industry	**not available**	**19.1**
Weighted average	**12.7**	**17.3**

Source: Berlinski (2004).

increase in domestic investment. They rose from an annual average of US$800 million between 1982 and 1990 to over US$5.8 billion in the period from 1992 to 2000. In 1990, imports totaled US$635 million dollars, by 1994, there were in the order of US$6 billion, and in 1998 reached the maximum level of the decade, US$8.5 billion. The easy access to imported machinery and equipment favored investments and facilitated productivity gains in most sectors of the economy.

All quantitative restrictions were successively eliminated except in the automobile sector (see the section on sectoral policies below). As a result of this series of reforms, the weighted average tariff fell to 17 percent in 1993, although tariff dispersion was higher than in 1991 (see table 3.1).

In conjunction with unilateral trade liberalization, the integration process with Brazil, initiated by the previous government in the mid-1980s, was deepened with the signature of the Asunción Treaty in 1991. This treaty drew Paraguay and Uruguay into the preferential trade agreements with Argentina and Brazil, thereby creating the MERCOSUR (the Southern Common Market).

The four countries agreed upon a schedule of automatic rounds of tariff reductions for intraregional trade covering the period 1991–1994. After difficult negotiations, an agreement on a common external tariff (CET) structure—largely based on the Brazilian tariff structure—was reached in 1995. This transformed MERCOSUR into a customs union, although each country was allowed to maintain a list of up to 300 goods as exceptions to the common tariff.

Capital goods, information technology, and telecommunications goods—which were imported at a 0 tariff rate in Argentina—would converge to the CET only in 2001 and 2006, respectively.[9] A special arrangement was put in place for sugar that had never been exposed to trade liberalization within MERCOSUR due to the low competitiveness of Argentine producers. An administered trade regime was adopted for automobiles (see the section on sectoral policies below). Some other items in the chemicals, steel, paper, and footwear sectors were temporarily exempted from free intraregional trade and placed under convergence programs with gradual tariff reductions until the 0 level was achieved in 1999.

After these changes, as observed in table 3.1, the average tariff was 16 percent by 1997, slightly lower than the one in 1993. However, the effective protection increased from 12.7 in 1991 to 17.3 percent in 1997 (see table 5.1). Food, beverages, and tobacco showed the highest increase, while there was a significant reduction in the effective tariff protection in the areas of metallic minerals, machinery, and equipment.

Trade liberalization led to a significant growth in imports of manufactured goods. For the first time since 1976–1981, imported goods flowed into

Argentina forcing domestic producers to compete in the local markets by launching new products and production processes and increasing productivity. Import penetration ratios in the entire manufacturing sector rose from 5.7 percent in 1990 to 19 percent in 1999. Those ratios were much higher in the areas of unskilled labor-intensive and in technology-intensive goods. Furthermore, a significant decline in the relative prices in all manufacturing sectors was observed after 1990 and a negative and significant correlation between (relative) prices and import penetration ratios was found in some studies (e.g., Galiani and Sanguinetti, 2003).

In this scenario, and despite the government's initial commitment to liberalization, the unfavorable evolution of the trade balance (see chapter 6) and the emergence of sectoral pressures amidst growing unemployment induced the government to introduce certain ad hoc instruments to restrain imports. The "statistical tax" on imports was, for example, increased from three percent to ten percent in 1992[10] and the government made aggressive use of safeguards and defensive commercial legislation such as antidumping and compensatory duties.

The number of investigations of cases of dumping and subsidies which were subject to legal judgments increased over the decade. Cases of anti-dumping decisions increased from 24 in 1996 to 65 in 1999 and 98 in 2001—between 1996 and 2001 there were 412 of those decisions. In turn, over the decade there were 16 investigations concerning subsidies, all related to goods of European Union origin (Bouzas and Pagnotta, 2003). In fact, among MERCOSUR members, Argentina was the country with a higher number of these measures during the 1990s, and between 1992 and 1997, Argentina was among the seven World Trade Organization (WTO) countries with the highest number of antidumping investigations.

In sum, although it is clear that trade policy was more liberal than in any other period since 1930, from 1991 to 2000, there was a great number of modifications in the trade protection framework, both through changes in nominal tariffs and through the introduction or removal of special regimes, nontariff barriers and other charges (such as the "statistical tax"). While sectoral pressures, and short-term economic policy objectives—that is, those related to inflation abatement, current account imbalances, and fiscal revenues—help to explain why there were frequent changes in trade policy during the 1990s, those changes impaired the role of a tariff structure as a guideline for resource allocation by private agents (Bouzas and Pagnotta, 2003).

There was a similar evolution in the area of regional integration. Although intraregional trade expanded substantially, periodical disputes arose, especially between Argentina and Brazil, and reached their peaks during moments of economic crisis in one or more of the member countries. The disputes were aggravated by the lack of effective institutional arrangements to deal with trade or other types of conflicts, and by the absence of "deep" integration mechanisms beyond trade liberalization. Of particular importance is that MERCOSUR has never had regional competitiveness or sectoral policies aimed at taking advantage of the potential gains from integration—the automotive sector regime that is analyzed later has mostly been concerned with regulating bilateral trade between Argentina and Brazil in order to avoid a serious flight of the industry from the former to the latter. In this scenario, defensive or protective trade measures prevailed, while the underlying structural problems could not be solved.

The Brazilian devaluation in early 1999 severely hit the Argentine economy and led to huge pressures from the private sector to establish compensatory mechanisms to deal with the sudden change in the bilateral exchange rate between both countries.[11] It also fueled Argentine claims about the diversion of foreign investments from Argentina to Brazil. This situation had already been exposed during the period 1997–1998 as a result of several federal and national investments incentive packages offered in Brazil and further deteriorated during the Argentine recession in 2000 and 2001. The problems associated with the lack of any form of coordination of macroeconomic policies had their fullest impact during this period.

Although MERCOSUR as such has survived, it is evident that there has been stagnation for several years in the negotiations aimed at deepening regional integration; a fact that has not only led to the aforementioned periodic conflicts but has also prevented full exploitation of the potential advantages of the agreement.

Deregulation of FDI, Technology Transfer, and Other Areas

Deregulation measures may be classified under two headings. There are those aimed at lowering costs, generally through increased competition in the domestic market, or at opening new investment opportunities in areas where legal entry barriers existed.

Among the first group, different kinds of deregulation measures were adopted in the oil industry, agriculture, fishing, mining, foreign trade operations, electricity and gas, exchange and capital markets, professional services, wholesale and retail trade, land, water and air transport, and insurance (see Llach, 1997).

The second group of deregulation measures was related to the attraction of foreign investment and/or the technological modernization of the domestic economy. In this regard, it must be noted that, together with capital goods imports, FDI and technology transfer were viewed by the government as the potential cornerstones of competitive domestic production and productivity gains in the new trade liberalization scenario.

FDI had been already strongly deregulated in 1976 with the enactment of Law No. 21,382. Menem's administration completed this task, removing almost all the few remaining sectoral restrictions still allowed in the 1976 regime. After this round of reforms, FDI operations did not require approvals, formalities, or registration procedures or any kind. There were neither discriminatory withholding taxes toward income nor taxes applied to the remission of profits and dividends emanating from FDI.

This "investor-friendly" approach was also followed by the signing of 51 bilateral investment treaties (BITs), the endorsement of the failed Multilateral Agreement on Investment (MAI) proposed by the Organization for Economic Cooperation and Development (OECD) countries and generous concessions in the negotiations leading up to the General Agreement on Trade in Services (GATS). Following the mandate of the Agreement on Trade-Related Intellectual Property Rights (TRIPs) negotiated in the Uruguay Round of the General Agreement on Tariffs and Trade (GATT), the old Argentine patent law (Law No. 111 of 1864) was modified in 1995. Among other changes, patent protection was extended to pharmaceutical products despite the opposition of the leading domestic manufacturers. The protection period was extended from 15 to 17 years and compulsory licensing was eliminated.[12]

In the area of technology transfer, the military government had enacted a very liberal regime (Law No. 22,426) in 1981, which almost totally deregulated technology imports. Registration of contracts between independent firms was only optional,[13] while the implementation authority, the INTI[14] only had to approve legal deeds between parent firms and their local subsidiaries. This last requirement was removed when the 1993 Foreign Investment Law was enacted.

What happened with FDI inflows and technology transfer following these deregulation measures? In sharp contrast to the previous decade, when very few FDI transactions took place, Argentina was one of the main destinations for FDI inflows in the developing world during the 1990s. Between 1992 and 2001, investment of over US$76 billion flowed into the country. For several years during that decade, annual inward FDI flows accounted for over 2 percent of GDP and 10 percent of gross fixed capital formation.[15]

Most FDI inflows were related to takeovers, initially of public firms and then of private domestic enterprises. Takeovers accounted for around 60 percent of FDI inflows in the 1990s. The FDI came mainly from the United States and some European countries such as Spain, France, Italy, the Netherlands, Germany, and the United Kingdom. Neither Japan nor other East Asian countries made significant investments in Argentina. There were, however, also some major inflows from Chile and, to a lesser extent, from Brazil.

The oil industry attracted one-third of FDI inflows[16] between 1992 and 2000, while the manufacturing industry received around 22 percent of those inflows. Chemicals (especially petrochemicals), automobile, and food and beverages sectors attracted most manufacturing FDI. The rest went into services, privatizations—for example, communications, electricity, and gas supply—and also into banking, the retail trade, and others.

The main attractions for foreign investors were the abundance of natural resources and the size and growth rate of the domestic market together with privatization, price stabilization, trade liberalization, and, to a lesser extent, integration within MERCOSUR (Chudnovsky and López, 2001). Neither cheap labor costs—wages in US$ dollars were relatively high in Argentina during the 1990s—nor loose enforcement of environmental regulations were key factors in attracting FDI. The "investor-friendly" approach was perhaps a necessary precondition for the FDI boom, but, in itself, it would not have had a sizeable impact in the absence of the other aforementioned attractive conditions in Argentina.

As for payments for technology transfer, while in 1992 the contracts registered—remember that registration is only for information purposes— amounted to a total of US$74 million, the respective figure in 1996 was US$632 million and in 1999 they had climbed to US$1.45 billion, to later descend until US$765 million in 2001 (H. Rodríguez, 2004).[17] The bulk of the contracts corresponded to licenses and technical assistance (see chapter 7 for a discussion of this source of technology acquisition in the context of innovation activities in the private sector).

Complementary Policies

When the program of structural reforms was implemented, no complementary policies were initially adopted to encourage competitive restructuring in firms, such as SMEs that would face problems in adapting to the new and more competitive domestic environment. Furthermore, the program was thought to be incompatible with any kind of "old-style" industrial policy, which was blamed for many of the problems faced by the Argentine economy. The government assumed that the new rules of the game—a more deregulated and liberalized economic environment—would foster a restructuring process in which efficient firms and sectors would expand and increase productivity, while inefficient ones would disappear.

However, as early as 1991, a notable exception had to be made in the trade liberalization program: the automotive sector was placed under a special regime that protected it from the pressure of import competition. The main reasons behind the adoption of this regime were fears about the capability of the industry to face competition from imported products—it must be noted that the authorities were particularly afraid of massive layoffs in the event of a collapse of the automotive sector. The regime was presented as a way to allow a gradual restructuring of the industry, after which it would be able to compete in an open market. The extent to which this objective was attained is analyzed in the next section.

Moreover, as seen earlier, throughout the 1990s a number of trade restriction measures had to be taken in order to address the difficulties of sectors that were being damaged by import penetration. Unfortunately, at least from our point of view, those measures were never tied to serious programs aimed at encouraging productivity growth and strengthening competitiveness in protected sectors and it comes as no surprise that those sectors had been constantly calling for protectionist instruments.

Pari passu, the consequences of the reform program shed light on the existence of market failures and other types of obstacles that prevented many firms from adopting strategies aimed at adapting to the new rules of the game. These difficulties were clearly reflected in the fact that by mid-1990s many SMEs had shrunk or even collapsed,[18] while others had abandoned production for import activities. This situation led to certain horizontal public policies being adopted from 1994 onward, including those oriented toward facilitating credit access for SMEs.

The need to foster exports in the face of growing trade imbalances led to a redesign of the various incentive programs. Investments were promoted through some sectoral schemes aimed at assuring long-term fiscal stability for private firms (i.e., mining, forestry) and through the creation of the Investment and Foreign Trade Bank (BICE), which replaced the failed BANADE; as its name suggests, BICE also lends for export purposes.

Last but not the least, even though the government clearly favored foreign technology sources—FDI, capital goods imports, licenses, and others—to provide inputs for the productive restructuring process, some initiatives aimed at fostering local innovative activities have in fact been adopted since the mid-1990s. These were intended to deal with market failures that prevented domestic firms from undertaking such activities.

The aforementioned programs are analyzed briefly in the following sections. Anticipating our conclusions, it may be stated that, with the exception of the sectoral schemes, it is clear that they have not had a substantial impact on economic restructuring. In this regard, it must be noted that, by the late 1990s, only 20 percent of manufacturing SMEs had availed of at least one of the public programs in force during that decade. Most of those who had not utilized the programs argued that there was lack of information about them, while another group of firms stated that the programs were not suitable for their needs (Yoguel and Moori Koenig, 1999).

Sectoral Policies[19]

The Motor Vehicles Regime

The main elements of the special regime for this sector were put in place in 1991. The regime consisted of a combination of import quotas, investment, and balanced trade requirements for established manufacturers, minimum content rules for locally produced vehicles and preferential import tariffs for domestic producers. The program aimed at promoting specialization and fostering competitiveness among established car manufacturers in order to take advantage of the rapid increase in domestic demand that followed stabilization.

The motor vehicles regime was complemented by an agreement signed with Brazil in 1990, which significantly increased bilateral trade. The agreement established a duty-free balanced trade program for vehicles produced in both countries, subject to minimum domestic content requirements. The bilateral agreement was modified in 1994 and 1995, after the implementation in Brazil of an automotive sector regime similar to that in force in Argentina. Since 1995, trade in finished vehicles and automotive components within MERCOSUR has been free of quotas, but it has continued to be subject to compensatory rules between total exports and imports for a four-year period.

Eventually, in July 2000, a MERCOSUR common automotive sector regime was adopted. The common policy established a 35 percent CET for car imports from third countries (for parts and components the CET was set at 14, 16, and 18 percent). The regime also provided for preferential import tariff rates on extra-zone imports for established manufacturers and duty-free intraregional trade subject to balanced trade requirements (to be eventually phased out in 2005). It was envisaged that intraregional trade would be fully liberalized as of 2005, but liberalization was postponed in 2004, sine die, due to fears that Argentina would lose most of its automobile production in favor of Brazil. Negotiations on minimum local contents for bilateral trade in automobiles were particularly tough, as Argentina wanted to preserve a domestic production capacity in automotive components which the national government thought to be in danger without such regulations.

What were the impacts of these changing trade regimes on the automobile sector? Local production, which had reached a historical minimum of less than 100,000 vehicles in 1990, quadrupled between that year and 1994. The production upswing could not cater to the rapidly growing local demand and the share of imports in the market grew from 1.2 percent in 1990 to 26.3 percent in 1994. Exports, which had been historically very low, rose from 1,100 units in 1990 to 52,000 in 1995 and the export share vis-à-vis local production grew from 1.1 percent in 1990 to 18.5 percent in 1995. Both the largest shares of imports and exports were related to bilateral trade with Brazil. Production and trade of automotive components showed rather similar figures and trends.

After the Tequila crisis, production grew again until 1998, when a historical record of 457,000 units was attained. Exports reached 237,000 units (more than 50 percent of total production), and they were closely matched by imports (which accounted for over half of domestic market sales). Hence, it was quite clear that this industry had gone through a complete process of restructuring throughout the decade, not only because production was 4.5 times that of 1990, but also because from a closed market (around 1,000 units were imported and exported in 1990), foreign trade accounted for over half of both production and domestic demand in 1998.[20] However, it must be noted that this internationalization process was not the result of market dynamics, but rather the outcome of a regime of managed trade.

Investments also increased strongly in the 1990s, both from established manufacturers and from newcomers. Between 1990 and 1995, total investments in the automobile sector reached US$2 billion and, according to the automobile makers association (ADEFA), investments during the 1990s totaled US$5.6 billion. There were also substantial levels of investment in the automotive parts and components sector, in which many foreign companies acquired local firms.

While in the 1980s and even in the early 1990s many major car assemblers (Fiat, General Motors, Renault, Citroen, Peugeot, Chrysler) closed their facilities or licensed their technology and trademarks to local producers and left the country, most of them returned and newcomers also arrived (i.e., Toyota) in the 1990s. Between 1990 and 1998, the number of employees in the automotive sector increased by 32 percent, from 17,430 to 22,963. Labor productivity in the sector rose by around 250 percent in the same period.

The sectoral regime and the bilateral agreement with Brazil encouraged a division of labor between plants on both sides of the border. In contrast with the specialization that prevailed in the mid-1980s—based on intraindustry trade in parts and components—the new regime favored assembly firms and particularly those with plants in the two countries. Specialization by model type was also encouraged. In effect, while in 1990 Argentina produced 25 models, only 12 models were produced in the country in 1997 (Campos, 1998). These trends were not only facilitated by the domestic and regional policy framework, but also by changes in the global strategies of automobile TNCs that aimed at closer integration among their subsidiaries in different countries.

Considering the initial constraints and the state of the industry worldwide, the motor vehicles regime was successful in attracting market-seeking foreign investment. It also helped to promote some efficiency-seeking[21] investments by integrating the Argentine automobile industry into the broader MERCOSUR market. The regime also fostered a significant upgrading of technological capabilities and production methods. There was a remarkable increase in the productivity of local plants as a result of the exploitation of economies of scale and the introduction of modern practices, such as *just-in-time* inventory management (Bastos Tigre et al., 1999).

However, the regime has also had problems, such as a tendency to create a situation of structural overcapacity. This prevented achievement of the economies of scale necessary to compete in world markets (economies of specialization were not enough to compensate for the lack of scale).

The regime also affected the automotive parts and components sector by bringing about a significant reduction in the number of suppliers per plant in line with international trends and a relatively low domestic content in finished cars, particularly in new models. The modernization of the sector also encouraged the establishment of new parts and component manufacturers that are worldwide suppliers of terminals.

Although this improved quality, scale, costs, and delivery periods in the parts and components sector, it also forced a large number of existing domestic firms into bankruptcy, while others had to survive through specialization in the auto-parts replacement market (Kosacoff, 1999a). This frustrated the possibility of taking advantage of acquired manufacturing capacities and qualified human resources, a pattern consistent with the absence of initiatives targeted at developing local suppliers, which might have increased positive spillovers into the local economy. Furthermore, key policy issues such as environmental practices, the creation of research, development and design units, and human resource training were not included among the objectives of the regime.

The automobile industry was severely hit by the recession that began in late 1998. Production fell by 25 percent between 1998 and 2000[22] and employment was reduced by a similar percent. The fall in domestic sales was even higher. Car manufacturers could not compensate for the domestic recession with exports since Brazil's devaluation in 1999 put Argentine production at a severe cost disadvantage—exports decreased by more than 40 percent between 1998 and 2000.[23]

Furthermore, the change in the bilateral exchange rate with Brazil, together with the domestic recession and the attractive incentives in Brazil for automotive industry investments, forced several parts, and components firms to close their facilities in Argentina and move to Brazil. The same happened with some assembly lines in the finished cars segment.[24]

On balance, the automobile industry in Argentina in the late 1990s was more open and competitive than in the past, and local customers had access to vehicles technologically similar to those sold in developed countries. However, modernization came at the expense of lower linkages with local producers and a severe reduction in the local content of finished cars. Although Argentina's automotive industry did not become a *maquila* (a factory that imports materials and equipment on a duty-free and tariff-free basis for assembly or manufacturing and then re-exports the assembled product), it is clear that spillovers from car manufacturing to the rest of the economy were relatively low.

Ultimately, the automotive sector benefited substantially throughout the decade (see Llach et al., 1997 for an evaluation of those benefits),[25] even though these firms did not always meet their commitments. For instance, when the export commitments originally agreed upon had not been fully met by the automobile producers, the penalties established by the 1991 regime were deferred to May 1994 and an extra year was given to offset the huge trade imbalance. Furthermore, the conditions under which imports could be offset by exports were partially relaxed. These benefits were given in exchange for new commitments—some of them vaguely formulated— in terms of prices, competitiveness, production, investments, and exports. A few years later, those firms that were not able to offset with new exports the accumulated previous deficit, despite the more flexible regime, were obliged to cancel the debts (estimated at US$140 million) for uncompensated imports. However, in 1999, to compensate for the domestic recession, the government allowed automobile manufacturers to use the paid fines to cancel tax obligations.

The Mining Regime
Although Argentina had implemented different promotional regimes for the mining sector for years, they failed to attract significant resources to explore and exploit areas with mining potential. Following this disappointing experience, a new regime was put in place between 1993 and 1995. This regime established incentives such as the possibility to deduct expenditures for determining the projects' feasibility from the income tax and accelerated amortization procedures for investments made in equipment, construction, and infrastructure. The investors were also authorized to capitalize up to 50 percent of the value of mining reserves and to exclude it from the determination of their tax liabilities. Mining firms were also exempted from the wealth tax and from paying import levies and other charges on imported machinery, equipment, and inputs. Moreover, the regime guaranteed investors with stability in tax payments, foreign exchange availability, and import tariffs for a period of 30 years (excluding changes in the exchange rate and in export tax rebates).

The federal agreement committed provincial governments to charge investors with royalties of upto 3 percent of the value at ex-mine.

The agreement gave rise to conflictive interpretations since mining firms (endorsed by the federal government) adopted a definition of value ex-mine that deducted from royalties the amortization of fixed assets (machinery, technology, and so on). Most provincial governments did not accept this definition and their position were backed by the congress, which reformed the National Mining Law in 1999.

The new regulatory framework coincided with a remarkable increase in inward FDI, especially in 1992–1996. The bulk of new investments came from Canada, South Africa, Australia, United States, and England. In 1996, the inflow of FDI into the mining industry rose to about US$700 million. However, falling world demand after the Asian crisis and lower international prices helped to account for a sharp decline in FDI inflows after 1997.

In 1997–1998, mining production and exports increased sharply due to the entrance into production of three metal mega projects: *Bajo de la Alumbrera, Salar del Hombre Muerto*—both in the province of Catamarca— and *Cerro Vanguardia* in Santa Cruz. In effect, in 1999, mining output was 138 percent higher than in 1996. However, after six years of continuous growth, mining production started to contract at the turn of the decade, mostly due to the above mentioned fall in international prices.

Typically, the linkages of mining projects with the local economy have been very limited. Both technology and equipments were mostly imported. In turn, little progress has been made in devising a reliable framework to control the environmental impacts of mining, a fact that has generated concern in populations located nearby the new investment projects in this sector.

Enterprise Policies

As previously stated, soon after the negative effects of the reforms turned visible, the government began to launch a series of initiatives aimed at facilitating the adaptation of local firms, especially SMEs, to the new rules of the game.

In 1992, the so-called specialization regime was adopted. Industrial firms submitted programs with export objectives and tariff reductions were granted for imports of inputs and/or final goods. This regime, which was managed by the Industry Secretariat, came to an end in the mid-1990s.

Within the Industry Secretariat, a National System of Norms, Quality and Certification was created in 1994. The system was supposed to work on the coordination of the different entities involved in the issue of quality norms in the country. At the same time different programs of subsidies for obtaining ISO certifications were implemented both at national and regional levels. This brought about a significant increase in the number of ISO certifications.[26] Apart from this progress, there is no further assessment available on the impact of this system, which, in fact, never became fully operational and was abolished few years after its creation.

In 1994, the Industry Secretariat also launched a Program of Suppliers Development, with the aim of developing a reliable and efficient network of suppliers among SMEs in order to strengthen productive linkages with large firms. Due to budgetary constraints, this program had to be dismantled shortly after its launch.

A system of Productive Poles was also designed, aimed at identifying regions, zones, or sectors with the potential to undertake productive restructuring measures. The INTI provided advice on technological and organizational changes and improvements in production processes. The Industry Secretariat offered financial support in the form of different credit programs for SMEs. Although some agreements were signed under this scheme, it was also discontinued shortly after its creation.

The only partly successful public programs for SMEs in the first years of the 1990s were those that subsidized the interest rates paid by these enterprises on borrowings from the financial system. Although these programs generally assigned all the available resources, it is hard to find any evaluation of their real impact on the beneficiary firms' performance. Their rationale was based on the evidence that SME access to credit was impaired by market failures that substantially increased the interest rates paid by those firms. Later on, the problem of access to credit due to the lack of collateral was addressed through programs that assisted SMEs to obtain the necessary collateral, although there is evidence to suggest that this initiative had little impact.

In 1997, the S&T secretary designed an initiative called Program for Improving the Technological Capacity of SMEs on the basis of an analysis of the problems faced by SMEs with regard to technology and innovative activities. The program was based around a network of "technological advisers" whose function was to detect the technological problems of groups of SMEs, suggest strategies to overcome them and facilitate the development of linkages with public and private S&T institutions to solve these problems (Chudnovsky, 1999).

This is one of the few policy initiatives launched in the 1990s on which an assessment is available (Carullo et al., 2003). The firms that participated in this "technological advisers" program were largely satisfied with the results obtained, which included the implementation of quality systems, production layout modifications, reduction of idle times and improvements in the utilization of raw materials. The impact of this program on the firms' performance was, however, never evaluated.

Due to its limited budget, a very small number of firms (326 between 1997 and 2001) had access to the program. Lack of trust and an aversion to cooperation with other firms and institutions may also help to explain the limited response of targeted firms. One of the criticisms of the program concerns its lack of integration into other S&T initiatives launched at the same time (Carullo et al., 2003).

In 1997, an SME Secretariat was created. Two assistance programs were initiated during this period: the Program of Support to Enterprise Restructuring and the Program of Enterprise Restructuring for Exports (see Ventura, 2001, for an analysis of the latter). These programs offered nonreimbursable funding for the firms to avail of advisory and consultancy services in areas such as quality control, management, qualification for standards, access to external markets, and so on.

The number of programs directed at SMEs substantially increased in 2000–2001. By 2002, there were 17 programs devoted to issues such as credit access and cost, supplier development, exports, fostering SME partnerships, improvement of value chains, human resources training, and so on (see Angelelli et al., 2004). Due to budgetary constraints and institutional weaknesses there were difficulties in the implementation of these programs, although most of them are still in operation.

In 2000, an "SME Law" was approved that provided for the creation of a special fund for SMEs. The fund—which has not been implemented till date—was intended to provide long-term financing for SME investments and also to possibly serve as the cradle for the promotion of venture capital funds in Argentina.

Finally, it is worth repeating that the old BANADE was closed in 1992. Its lending capability had been impaired by nonperforming loans; the high inflation regime had frequently rendered BANADE lending rates strongly negative; loans had been granted for political reasons, and its technical capability had been damaged by the lack of institutional stability. The BICE was created after BANADE's closure. This new bank was supposed to contribute to financing investment and primarily export operations. In practice, its impact has been limited since (1) interest rates in BICE's credit lines were not very different from market rates; (2) BICE did not have contact with its potential clients and actual credit demand depended on the efforts made by commercial banks to publicize the benefits of the credit lines on offer (Bouzas and Pagnotta, 2003).

Export Promotion Policies

In the 1990s, a number of WTO-compatible export promotion policies were in force. The existing drawback and temporary admission regimes were retained with minor modifications. Exporters could also recover the value added tax (VAT) charged on domestic purchases, provided that those purchases were related to inputs used in the exported goods. This regime, however, was affected by government delays in refunding VAT, mostly due to repeated fiscal pressures.

Export reimbursements were also granted. In 1992, those reimbursements were at the same level as import tariffs, in order to compensate fully for the "anti-export" bias. However, this criterion was later modified, again mainly on account of budgetary restrictions. In addition, there were other special regimes in place that benefited certain regions and activities (see Bouzas and Pagnotta, 2003).

The Export.ar Foundation, a nonprofit organization with representatives of both the public and the private sectors, was created in the early 1990s with the aim of assisting private firms in their efforts to access, expand, and diversify export markets. The foundation's services included information and seminars about foreign markets and business opportunities, assistance in organizing business travel, and the participation of Argentine international fairs. Its performance has, however, been limited by budgetary constraints.

Science and Technology Policies

Breaking with the laissez faire approach that had traditionally predominated in this area in Argentina, some technology policy initiatives were adopted by the Science and Technology Secretariat from the mid-1990s onward (see Chudnovsky et al., 2004a for an evaluation of the respective programs). The forerunner of these initiatives was the Law for the Promotion and Support of Technological Innovation (Law No. 23,877), which was passed in 1990, and the Program of Technological Modernization launched in 1994—both programs granted credit assistance for R&D and innovative activities carried out by local firms.

In December 1997, the Government's Science and Technology Cabinet (GACTEC) approved the National Multiyear Science and Technology Plan 1998–2000. This plan, which was renewed annually, was aimed, inter alia, at setting priorities for research and innovation funding.

By the end of 1996, a National Agency for the Promotion of Science and Technology (referred to as the Agency in subsequent instances) was created within the Secretariat for Science and Technology. The aim of the Agency was to finance nonprofit research projects in the public and private sectors (through a fund called FONCYT) and promoting technological innovation in the private sector (through a fund called FONTAR). Both Argentine Technological Fund (FONTAR) and Scientific and Technological Research Fund (FONCYT) granted subsidies and credits for S&T projects.

A recent survey shows that only 25 percent of SMEs know about FONTAR's existence, while around four percent have used funds from that organization (INDEC-SECYT-CEPAL, 2003). Lack of information, bureaucracy, difficulties in getting the required collateral, and the inability to document projects were the reasons mentioned by the firms as to why they were unaware of FONTAR and/or have not used its funds.

Some studies help to shed light on the impact of FONTAR's programs. Sanguinetti (2005) finds that FONTAR funding has had a positive effect on

R&D expenditures and none on total innovation expenditures. In turn, Chudnovsky et al. (2006a), focusing on a program of nonreimbursable grants, find that FONTAR funds have had a positive impact on total innovation expenditures (i.e., no total crowding out effect has existed), but have failed to foster an increase in the amount of resources devoted by benefited firms to innovation activities (i.e., no additionality has been observed). Although these studies reveal some positive impacts of FONTAR's funding, it is worth recalling that, given budget restrictions and other limitations of the program (and of the local environment), its effects have been rather limited.

A fiscal credit for R&D expenditures by private firms was established and became operative in 1998 (see Chudnovsky, 1999, for details). From 1998 to 2000, 243 firms benefited from fiscal credits for R&D projects (76 percent of those firms were SMEs). In 2001, the program was discontinued due to budgetary restrictions, but in 2002 it was again in operation (34 of 100 project submissions were approved). The program is still operating on the basis of annual requests, and its original budget was raised from $20 to $25 million.

A survey of 55 firms that benefited from the program between 1998 and 2001 showed a positive impact on the magnitude and quality of their innovative activities and that the program had facilitated the implementation of projects that would otherwise not have been carried out (Chudnovsky et al., 2004a). R&D expenditures rose from 0.3 to 0.8 percent of the sales of firms surveyed, comparing the periods 1995–1997 and 1998–2002. However, no rigorous cost-benefit evaluation has been carried out to date and, by financing specific projects, the program fails to give firms an incentive to adopt R&D as part of their core activities.

In the 1990s, the government also tried to foster public S&T institutions in order to establish closer linkages with the private sector. In the case of the CONICET, this objective was pursued with little enthusiasm or success.[27] The same can be said to a large extent for the university system.[28] Regarding INTI, too much emphasis was placed on self-financing, which reinforced the historical bias of the organization in favor of metrology and routine tests. Naturally, the not very relevant innovative and research activities were further displaced within INTI (see Chudnovsky et al., 2004a).

In this scenario, it comes as no surprise to find that universities and public S&T institutions ranked among the least important sources of information for innovative activities in manufacturing firms and that technological linkages of private firms with those organizations were weak (INDEC-SECYT-CEPAL, 2003; INDEC-SECYT, 1998).

To complete this section, it is relevant to take a look at the evolution of expenditures in S&T during the 1990s, although, from what has been discussed earlier, it is difficult to establish a link between that evolution and the aforementioned programs. The share of S&T expenditures[29] in GDP

Table 5.2   Average S&T and R&D expenditures as a percentage of GDP

	S&T expenditures/GDP	R&D expenditures/GDP
1985–1990	0.32	not available
1991–1995	0.41	not available
1996–2000	0.50	0.41

Source: SECyT (Secretariat of Science and Technology).

increased from 0.3 percent between 1985 and 1990 to 0.5 percent between 1996 and 2000. The R&D expenditures reached 0.45 percent of the GDP in 1999, with an average of 0.41 percent from 1996 to 2000 (see table 5.2).

Despite these slight increases in the 1990s, the figures are low by international standards, both in relation to developed countries and the "Asian tigers" and also vis-à-vis neighboring nations such as Brazil and Chile.

If the composition of the expenditure by sector is analyzed, the most important change is the increase in the share of the business sector, which grew from almost 16 percent of the total S&T expenditures in the second half of the 1980s to 31 percent in 1998—pari passu, the relative share of public institutions declined.

However, the share of the private sector in the financing and performance of R&D expenditures is low vis-à-vis both developed nations and developing Asian countries. In part, this is explained by the small size in Argentina of the productive sectors that in developed countries have the highest R&D expenditures relative to their sales: informatics, aviation, fine chemicals, and so on. However, certain sectors in developed countries (e.g., the pharmaceutical, automotive, and industrial chemicals sectors) spend considerable shares of their sales in R&D, but do not show the same performance in Argentina. As a consequence, the low expenditure on R&D is only partly a result of differences in the productive specialization pattern in Argentina compared to that of developed countries. The innovative patterns in the Argentine private sector are analyzed in greater depth in chapter 7.

Concluding Remarks

The adoption of a currency board jointly with a massive privatization program, trade and capital account liberalization, and deep market deregulation were the key policies adopted in the early 1990s.

While these "first generation" reforms had a favorable impact on certain economic indicators (as those examined in the next chapter) and became very popular in the first half of the 1990s, the public mood toward them gradually began to change and, by the end of the decade, they were often associated with the most negative consequences of the economic regime adopted during that period.

The deficiencies in the design, sequencing, and implementation of the structural reforms—which were mainly a consequence of a poor institutional setting—explain to a large extent the growing disappointment with the reforms' outcomes. However, the lack of effective complementary policies aimed at dealing with the difficulties experienced by many domestic enterprises in adapting to the new rules of the game is also responsible for the failures of the 1990s.

Not only were most complementary policies put in motion some years after the reforms were launched, but they never received adequate attention in terms of government priorities and human and financial resources.

Moreover, as said before, there was a low response of SMEs to these programs. By the late 1990s, only 20 percent of manufacturing SMEs had availed of at least one of the public programs in force during that decade (Yoguel and Moori Koenig, 1999). Angelelli et al. (2004) mention some factors that could explain this low response of SMEs, including weak management capability, excessive bureaucracy, the lack of private sector involvement in their design, and operation and institutional instability with resulting high staff rotation levels and frequent budget cuts. In addition, there was a lack of coordination among the different programs and no strategic or global vision underlying their design. Furthermore, they have rarely been subject to serious evaluations, which give rise to uncertainty as to their actual results. Last but not the least, it has often been the case that the firms who used the programs were those with greater dynamism and competitive skills. Then, it is probable that, at least to some extent, the policies under analysis have contributed to growing heterogeneity among domestic SMEs (Yoguel et al., 1998).

In this scenario, it is no surprise to find that complementary policies had no substantial impact on the economic restructuring process of the 1990s. In contrast, the few sectoral schemes in force were rather effective in attracting foreign investment inflows and expand production capacity and exports, but their ability to generate positive spillovers for the rest of the economy remained very limited.

In the next two chapters an analysis of the main results of the economic policy regime of the 1990s is made. Chapter 6 deals with the macroeconomic, productive, and social evolution. Chapter 7 studies the nature, determinants, and impacts of firms' behavior.

CHAPTER 6

ECONOMIC AND SOCIAL PERFORMANCE DURING CONVERTIBILITY "HIGH GROWTH" YEARS

Macroeconomic Performance

With the program of structural reforms launched by Menem's administration and the application of a currency board scheme in 1991 (the Convertibility Law), the Argentine economy entered into a stabilization-cum-growth path that lasted until 1998 (only interrupted with the recession in 1995 due to the Tequila effect)—see table 2.2 and graph 2.3.

Between 1991 and 1998, GDP grew at an annual average rate of 5.9 percent. From the hyperinflation levels reached in 1989 and 1990, the consumer price index dropped to 84 percent in 1991 and 17 percent in 1992. Single-digit rates had already been registered in 1993 and 1994, and since then there was practically no inflation during the rest of the 1990s.

The success of the Convertibility Plan in first reducing the wholesale and then the retail prices, and hence the inflationary tax (see graph 2.7), led to growing public support for the government policies. This support was enhanced by the increasing availability of consumer credit and the reduction in the real interest rate that in turn resulted in a consumption-led growth in 1992–1994. At the same time, these macroeconomic conditions and significant receipts from the sale of state enterprises led to an improvement in fiscal accounts.

However, in a context of a fixed nominal exchange rate, the rise in domestic prices (especially in nontradable goods and services) at rates higher than that of international inflation led to a real appreciation of the peso during the first years of the Convertibility Plan. This, together with trade liberalization and the recovery of domestic demand, favored a rapid growth in imports—in 1998 total imports were 280 percent higher than in 1991.

Exports also grew (see table 4.2), especially since 1994, favored by the regional integration process in MERCOSUR, the improved international prices for commodities (at least until 1998), the growth in agricultural output (see section on the agricultural production boom) and the maturation of some large industrial and energy projects. As a result of these factors, in 2000, exports doubled from the 1993 levels.

However, as imports grew far more than exports, significant trade deficits appeared in most of the Convertibility years (see graph 6.1). The only exceptions were 1995–1996, when the effects of the Tequila crisis had a contractive impact on imports, and 2000–2001, due to the recession that would finally end with the Convertibility era. Trade deficits were financed by growing inflows of foreign capital, both through portfolio capital as well as through FDI[1]—see graph 6.2.

Foreign investment also helped to close the gap between domestic savings and investment (on an average, savings were 15.5 percent of the GDP between 1991 and 2001, while fixed investment reached 18.5 percent).

As previously stated, the external shock from the "Tequila effect" resulted in a financial crisis and recession in 1995. However, the recovery was rapid and the economy resumed growth in 1996–1998, with higher investment and export coefficients than in 1991–1994.[2] In turn, productivity growth and the effect of the 1995 recession on consumer prices reduced the real appreciation of the peso in the mid-1990s.

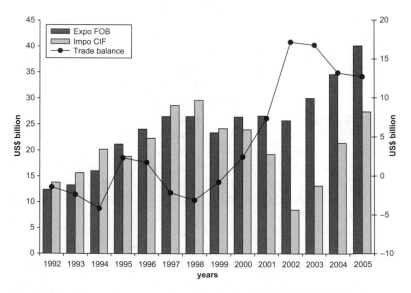

Graph 6.1   Exports, imports and trade balance, 1992–2005 (US$ billion)

Source: Authors' elaboration on the basis of INDEC's data.

or regulations over M&A operations in Argentina. The government did not use any special instrument to encourage or discourage cross-border M&A versus greenfield investments, and the 1980 Antitrust Law (Law No. 22,262) contained no special provisions for mergers, acquisitions, or joint ventures. In addition, this law was generally deemed outdated and ineffective in the 1990s. Arguments had been put forward that competition from imports might compensate for the lack of efficient antitrust legislation, but the experience of the 1990s showed that, in spite of trade liberalization, market-distorting practices and abuse of dominant positions persisted, and that an improved enforcement of domestic competition legislation[10] was necessary. In any case, the apparent trend toward growing concentration was also a source of discontent among SMEs.

As stated in chapter 2, growth during 1991–1998 was mainly lead by TFP increases (see table 2.4). However, heterogeneity is also observed when analyzing TFP evolution. On the basis of information from both large firms and SMEs, a study by FIEL (2002) shows that, while TFP grew in firms that belonged to nontradable sectors, the opposite occurred with firms in tradable activities. The study argues that this finding may be due to a fall in relative prices of tradable goods—as a consequence of trade liberalization—to decreases in the international price of certain export commodities (oil and meat) and to the peso overvaluation.

However, the finding suggests that trade liberalization in the context of the Convertibility Plan had a negative impact on many firms in the manufacturing industry, and that, far from forcing them to increase productivity, the contrary effect was observed. On the other hand, positive TFP evolution in nontradables may reflect, to some extent, productivity gains in privatized sectors and other services where extensive microeconomic inefficiencies were present before the 1990s. In this context, it is not surprising to find that the industrial sector lost share in terms of employment and GDP, while the share of services increased (see table 2.1).

In the described scenario, it is no wonder to find that, whereas large and foreign-owned enterprises (especially those participating in the privatization process and generally in the provision of services) largely supported the Menem government's policies, while local manufacturing firms (and SMEs in particular) were less enthusiastic about them.

It was then in a not too solid macroeconomic situation, with important business interests that had had serious difficulties to adapt to the new rules of the game in the 1990s, and in the context of growing social discontent with the result of the reforms, that the Argentine economy suffered the external shocks resulting from the Russian and Brazilian crisis in 1998 and 1999. The two main consequences of these crisis were, first, a "sudden stop" in capital inflows, and second, a new round of peso overvaluation—after

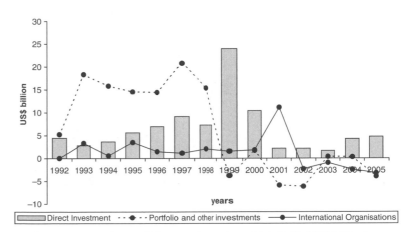

Graph 6.2   External capital flows to Argentina, 1992–2005 (US$ billion)
Source: Authors' elaboration on the basis of the Ministry of Economy data.

Table 6.1   Evolution of the public sector fiscal surplus (% GDP)

	1993	1994	1995	1996	1997	1998	1999	2000	2001
Income	21.4	19.8	19.5	17.5	18.9	19.0	20.6	19.9	19.1
Expenditures	20.3	20.0	20.0	19.5	20.4	20.3	22.3	22.3	22.3
Total surplus	1.2	−0.1	−0.5	−1.9	−1.5	−1.4	−1.7	−2.4	−3.2
Primary surplus	2.4	1.1	1.1	−0.2	−0.5	0.9	1.2	1.0	0.5
Primary surplus excluding social security	2.0	1.6	1.8	1.7	2.2	2.7	3.5	3.4	3.2

Source: Authors' elaboration on the basis of Ministry of Economy' data.

At the same time, however, the fiscal accounts started to worsen[3] (see table 6.1). The increasing fiscal deficit since 1994 was due, among other things, to the growth in the interest paid on the external debt, the growing public expenditures (exacerbated by the electoral cycle before the reelection of Menem in 1995 and then in anticipation of the presidential elections in 1998–1999) and the fall in fiscal revenues. The latter was related to the social security reform that was approved after tough negotiations with the congress in 1993 and became operative in 1994.[4] The result of the accumulation of fiscal imbalances was growing indebtedness (see graph 6.3).

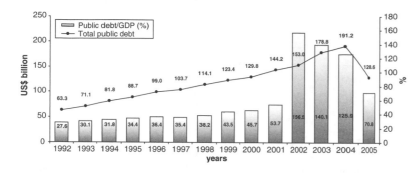

Graph 6.3   Evolution of the national public sector debt, 1992–2005 (US$ billion and percentages)

Source: Authors' elaboration on the basis of Ministry of Economy and ECLAC's data.

On the other hand, unemployment—in particular after 1995—gradually became a serious problem. While in May 1992 the unemployment rate in urban concentrations reached 7 percent of the working population, it climbed to 18.4 percent in May 1995. Although there was a subsequent decline, unemployment rates never fell below 12 percent again and in May 2000 reached a level of 15.4 percent (see graph 2.10).

Faced with rising unemployment, the government tried to deepen labor market reforms. In 1991, an employment law (Law No. 24,013) was passed. This law introduced fixed-term and special training contracts for young workers and created an unemployment benefit system. Employer wage taxes were reduced in 1994. In 1995, a new law (Law No. 24,465) formalized the fixed-term contracts regulated by the previous law and introduced a trial period of up to six months. This was supposedly an important step since the business sector had always been seeking more flexible contracts, given the burden of severance payments imposed by legislation (Galiani and Gerchunoff, 2003). Later on, in 1998, short-term contracts were eliminated as a result of criticism of their implications. Some segments of the labor movement and members of the opposition stated that they did not have an impact on unemployment but rather made labor relations more precarious.

During this period, union membership was largely maintained and labor negotiations remained within the scope of the collective working agreement, although some individual company-level agreements were settled. In fact, although some unions opposed the reforms, most of them supported the government (Etchemendy, 2001). This was reflected in the decline in union activities. The number of general strikes decreased from 13 in the Alfonsín

administration to 2 in the first Menem government and 5 in the second. In return for the unions' support, the government maintained their power through collective bargaining[5] and by leaving untouched the union–administered welfare organizations (*obras sociales*) that were a key source of financing the unions' activities. These organizations were very important in the health market in which no significant reform had taken place.

Stabilization-cum-growth, together with the adoption of tough Basel regulations by the Central Bank, was not enough to overcome the old deficiencies of the financial system. The capital market went through booms and busts during the decade, but failed to become a relevant source of finance for domestic firms.[6] The banking system, in turn, discriminated against SMEs and generally had a bias toward financing private consumption and government needs rather than productive investments.

Even in the context of increasing financial bolstering in the first years of the Convertibility Plan, Argentina still lagged behind by international standards, even vis-à-vis other developing countries. This led to high interest rates and high intermediation costs in the domestic market. As previously stated, social security reform was supposedly to channel funds for private investment, but in practice failed to fulfill that role.

Large firms had much easier access than SMEs[7] to both domestic and international credit markets that were opened again to Argentine firms. The SMEs were restricted in the international credit markets and had limited access to financing from large domestic banks. Hence, they mostly resorted to small banks with higher interest rates on loans to fulfill their borrowing needs (Fanelli and Machinea, 1995). The situation deteriorated further when many of those small banks were sold to foreign banks with more conservative credit policies than their domestic counterparts.[8] Stricter financial regulations from the adoption of Basel norms also reduced the access of SMEs to credit.

Another key outcome of the reform process was the boom of mergers and acquisitions (M&A) that not only reflected worldwide trends, but also was fostered by changes in the domestic business environment. Data from Argentina's Secretariat of Industry, Commerce and Mining show that M&A exceeded US$70 billion between 1990 and 1999—of which US$22 billion concerned privatizations. Cross-border M&As totaled over US$58 billion during the same period (nearly 83 percent of all M&A activity). The same source estimates that total investments amounted to US$32 billion between 1990 and 1999.

Although no precise data exists on the subject, these trends led to increasing concern about the effects of the growing market concentration process that was taking place in most sectors of the Argentine economy.[9] In this regard, it must be noted that, until 1999, there was no effective control

the Brazilian devaluation, but also due to the US$ dollar appreciation (in relation to the euro). In these conditions, external debt indicators (in relation to GDP and to exports) reached dangerous levels, increasing the country's risk premium and resulting in growing capital flight. Recession was the outcome of these trends, jointly with deflation. The final outcome of this process, the worst crisis in Argentina's history, is analyzed in chapter 8.

The Evolution of Productive Sectors

Industrial Restructuring

Value added in the manufacturing industry showed almost a 19 percent increase between 1991 and 2000. However, the share of industry in Argentina's GDP fell steadily during that decade, from 18.5 percent in the early 1990s to 17 percent in 1998, and to less than 16 percent in 2001. In other words, industry grew at a slower pace than the rest of the economy both during the growth as well as during the recession periods. The services sector, including privatized public utilities, gained the share lost by the manufacturing industry.

During 1991–1998, the physical volume of production grew by 4.0 percent and the number of workers fell by 2.7 percent per year. This impressive difference in the evolution of both variables explains the remarkable growth observed in labor productivity (see table 3.3 and graphs 3.1. and 3.2).

Although available data does not allow us to make a precise analysis of the sources of productivity increases, there are some factors that have surely made a contribution to that phenomenon. First, the fall in industrial employment was to a large extent due to outsourcing and subcontracting practices. Hence, workers who were previously considered as belonging to the manufacturing industry are now counted as services workers, although they probably performed the same task in the same manufacturing plant as before.

Second, informal employment has grown over the past two decades. The statistics presented include to some extent informal workers, but do not capture the whole magnitude of the phenomenon. If the gap between total effective employment and formal employment has been widening, official statistics may be overestimating the magnitude of the fall in the industrial workforce.

Hence, although there is a consensus to the fact that employment in the manufacturing industry substantially fell during the 1990s,[11] the real magnitude of the fall is perhaps lower than that reported.

In any case, beyond the uncertainty surrounding its real magnitude, there was a reduction in industrial employment during the 1990s, both in relative as well as absolute terms. The first part of this phenomenon—known as deindustrialization—is the reduction of the capacity of industry to generate employment vis-à-vis other sectors of the economy and, in particular services. It is a process that takes place in most industrialized countries in the world. Instead, absolute decreases in industrial employment are less frequent, especially with the magnitude observed in Argentina.[12] The following paragraphs discuss the reasons behind this phenomenon.

The industry response to trade liberalization was a quantitative adjustment, reducing the number of jobs and increasing the length and intensity of the working day. The growing share of imported goods in the local market and the difficulties of adapting through higher prices on account of the intense competition in a context of price stabilization led the industry to seek higher levels of labor productivity to enable enterprises to survive over the decade (CEP, 1999).

There were five main factors behind the reduction of employment in the manufacturing industry during this decade: (1) the implementation of *soft technologies*—improvements in the organization, productive processes and procedures with more efficient use of personnel and longer working days; (2) the substitution of foreign parts and inputs for those of domestic origin; (3) the use of new labor-saving equipment and technology as a result of the extreme change in relative prices between capital and labor at the beginning of the decade (on account of trade liberalization in capital goods); (4) the bankruptcy of firms with old productive processes and their replacement by new enterprises operating in line with international state-of-the-art practices and lower labor requirements; (5) subcontracting or outsourcing of activities previously undertaken inside the firm (see Bisang et al., 1996).

But labor productivity increases are also explained by industrial restructuring in the post-ISI stage. As observed in table 6.2, resource-processing

Table 6.2 Changes in the relative share of different industrial sectors, 1970–1996

Industrial sectors	1970	1996
Metal-working industry (excluding automobiles)*	15.6	13.1
Automobiles**	9.9	12.1
Natural resource-intensive industries. Foodstuffs, beverages and tobacco*** and resource-processing industries****	36.2	45.7
Labor-intensive industries*****	38.2	29

*: ISIC groups 381, 382, 383, 385.
**: ISIC group 384.
***: ISIC groups 311, 313, 314.
****: ISIC groups 341, 351, 354, 355, 356, 371, 372.
*****: ISIC groups: 321, 322, 323, 324, 331, 332, 342, 352, 361, 362, 369, 390.

Source: Katz (2001).

industries increased their share in manufacturing production by 9.5 percent between 1970 and 1996. These industries are highly capital-intensive and often have low domestic value added. In turn, labor-intensive industries reduced their share by more than 9 percent. Hence, sizeable shares of the increase in labor productivity and the reduction in industrial employment may be explained by changes in the composition of manufacturing production.

When comparing the years 1993 and 2000, the "winning" sectors—that is, those with the highest growth rates—were food and beverages, petroleum refinement, chemicals, rubber and plastics, and, to a lesser degree, metals, pulp and paper. These activities mainly depend on the stock of natural resources and/or produce industrial commodities with scale-intensive processes. In general, they are able to easily enter external markets in times of falling local demand.

The sectors that declined in importance in terms of industrial production included textiles and clothing, metallurgy and machinery, electrotechnology, and transportation equipment. These are sectors with either high levels of unskilled (textiles) and skilled (machinery) labor or that are engaged in areas in which there are rapid technological advances (electronics) take place. They were also severely affected by the trade liberalization of the 1990s.

What happened to the evolution of labor productivity in manufacturing industry vis-à-vis that of the United States? While at the beginning of the 1970s labor productivity in manufacturing in Argentina was 52 percent of that recorded in the United States, the gap was reduced initially in that decade and then expanded again in the 1980s. In 1990, the gap was around the same level as in 1970 but since then, domestic labor productivity in Argentina rapidly approached that of the United States (see table 4.1).

It must, however, be noted that these trends may be the outcome of different factors. In particular, being an aggregate, industrial labor productivity movements comprise both changes in productivity levels in each industrial sector and in the composition of the manufacturing output. Hence, the closing of the gap may be the result of productivity levels in Argentina's different manufacturing sectors approaching those of the United States, as well as of changes in the relative share of each sector in the aggregate manufacturing output in both countries (this is of importance in the light of the commented contraction of labor-intensive industries in Argentina).

Furthermore, the real gap between the Argentine and the U.S. productivity levels is probably higher than that documented in table 4.1. Since the 1990s, manufacturing value added figures in Argentina include an estimate of the "black market" contribution, although as previously stated, informal employment is not recorded in official industrial statistics. Hence, real productivity levels in Argentina are undoubtedly lower than those on which the comparisons presented in table 4.1 are based.

Industrial exports grew substantially throughout the decade (the annual average for the period 1995–1999 was over 80 percent higher than that of 1990–1994) and their share on total exports grew from 27 to 31 percent along the decade (see table 4.2). However, heterogeneity was also observed in export performance. Chemicals and petrochemicals, together with motor vehicles (where a sectoral promotion regime was in place, as discussed in chapter 5), accounted for around 60 percent of the increase in manufacturing exports between 1990 and 2000. Paper and pulp, steel, and machinery and equipment contributed to another 25 percent. In contrast, exports of shoe and leather goods declined and the share of textiles in total nonresource industrial exports fell from 6.3 to 3.7 percent during the same period.

MERCOSUR (the Southern Common Market)—the regional integration agreement that joined Argentina, Brazil, Paraguay, and Uruguay—was the main destination for the growing industrial exports, accounting for almost 70 percent of the increase in nonresource based manufacturing exports between 1990 and 2000. MERCOSUR's share on those exports jumped from 23 to 49 percent over that period.

These figures indicate the positive role played by MERCOSUR for a large part of Argentine industry. Nonetheless, the low share of developed markets as destinations for manufacturing exports reflects both the weak competitive capabilities in many sectors and the influence of TNC affiliates' strategies. The latter factor is very important considering the growing affiliates' share on the country's foreign trade;[13] these issues are discussed in detail in chapter 7.

The Agricultural Production Boom

In the 1990s, the elimination of taxes and withholdings on agricultural exports, the substantial reduction of import tariffs on inputs and capital goods, and the deregulation of several markets, all created favorable conditions for a large expansion of production volumes of cereals and oilseeds—from 26 million tones in 1988–1989 to over 67 million in 2000–2001 (see graph 3.3). Production increases were particularly remarkable in the case of soybean, which soon became Argentina's leading export item (see the following paragraphs).[14]

Growing production led to a substantial increase in exports against a background of erratic international prices and in the face of though competition from other countries, which, unlike Argentina, benefited from government subsidies for agricultural production and exports.

The extraordinary growth in agricultural production was mainly a result of a substantial expansion of the planted area[15] and higher yields (see graph 3.4) following extensive adoption of new technologies.[16] In addition, with the increase in the planted area, the Pampa's agricultural sector succeeded in reversing job loss trends that had been experienced over the previous decades and went on to generate almost 200,000 jobs between 1993 and 1999.

It is, however, important to take into account that there was an increasing concentration of production in the agriculture sector, mainly due to the fact that new technologies increased the minimum efficient production scale. At the same time, the incorporation of new technologies led to massive indebtedness and in this scenario, it comes as no surprise to find that many small farmers were unable to continue with their production activities (Sonnet, 1999; Bisang, 2003).

Technological modernization was achieved in different ways. Sales of capital goods increased sharply. Trade liberalization permitted not only imports of cheap and more efficient agricultural machinery, but also induced domestic machinery producers to replace parts produced domestically with imported inputs, lowering costs and improving quality, but at the cost of lower linkages with local suppliers.

The use of fertilizers, herbicides, and pesticides also boomed, favored by trade liberalization, but also associated with the expansion of domestic capacity in those product categories. With regard to the environmental impact of increased use of chemical inputs, it must be noted that they are still used much less intensively than in developed countries, and that old polluting pesticides and herbicides have been replaced by new more "environmental-friendly" products (Chudnovsky et al., 1999).

Another key change was the introduction of transgenic crops in agriculture. The first transgenic crop commercially released into the Argentine market in 1996 was soybean tolerant to glyphosate herbicide. Later on, the local authorities approved transgenic varieties of corn and cotton tolerant to herbicides and resistant to insects.

The area planted with herbicide-tolerant roundup ready RR soybean shot up from less than 1 percent of the total area in the 1996–1997 season, to more than 90 percent (around nine million hectares) in the 2000–2001 season. The adoption of lepidoptera-resistant corn has also been rapid, accounting for 20 percent of the total cultivated area during the 2000–2001 farming season (the third year after its introduction). The diffusion of BT (Bacillus thuringiensis) cotton has, however, been very limited, amounting to only 7–8 percent of the total planted area.

At present, Argentina ranks second only to the United States in terms of agricultural area cultivated with transgenic crops and is therefore a major player in the international genetically modified organisms (GMOs) arena (Trigo et al., 2002).

Argentina enjoyed favorable conditions for a rapid adoption of GMOs. The seed industry profited from the active involvement of national companies, subsidiaries of multinational corporations, and public institutions.[17] To top it off, the country also cherished a long-standing tradition in the field of germplasm improvement. The aforementioned elements, along with the fact that Argentina constitutes the major area (up to 26 million hectares of cultivable land) for the potential use of new technologies outside their country of origin, provided the appropriate incentives and a most favorable environment for the rapid adoption of these biotechnological inputs.

However, in the case of the most successful GMO crop, RR soybean, other factors were also in place to foster its rapid diffusion,[18] including, first, the manner in which the RR gene was first transferred to Argentina. Following a series of business deals in the United States and Argentina, when Monsanto, the company that bred the RR soybean, tried to patent the gene in Argentina, it was unable to do so because it had already been "released." Therefore, Monsanto could not meet the conditions, that entitled it to charge a technology fee or restrict the use of the seed by farmers, as it is the case in the United States.[19]

Second, according to the Argentine legislation and under the International Union for the Protection of New Varieties of Plants (UPOV) Convention of 1978, farmers can legitimately keep seeds for their own use. There are, however, clandestine operations (the so-called "white bag") through which seed multipliers offer seeds without the authorization of the companies holding the legal production rights. Both factors have driven down the price of RR soybean, thus promoting the rapid adoption of that technology.

Third, the glyphosate price substantially decreased during the 1990s due to fierce competition in local markets following the introduction of new firms in the manufacturing and commercialization of the herbicide.

In this scenario, and bearing in mind that Argentina has encountered no difficulties till date in accessing target markets for its RR soybean exports and that, in spite of the perceptions of foreign consumers, price differentials between conventional and RR soybeans in the world market do not penalize the latter, it is hardly surprising that almost all Argentine soybean crop is RR. Nonetheless, the INTA (2003) has expressed serious concerns about the consequences of the soybean boom, since the crop has often been introduced at the expense of crop rotation. Furthermore, the "agriculturization" process triggered off by the soybean expansion in the ecologically fragile northeastern and western areas of the country is unsustainable. This development could affect both the quantity and quality of the country's natural resource endowment and lead, in the future, to a fall in agricultural production.

The outstanding increase of no-tillage practices[20] was another major technological innovation introduced during the past decade. The range of application of this planting system rose from approximately 300,000 hectares in the 1990–1991 season to over 9 million hectares in the 2000–2001 season. This technology constituted an important factor in the expansion of production, as it increased the area cultivated with late soybean, planted after the wheat harvest. During the 1999–2000 season, for example, this generated a further 3 million hectares of arable land.

The combination of no-tillage planting techniques and herbicide-tolerant soybean joins two technological concepts: new mechanical technologies that modify crop interaction with the soil and the utilization of general use, full range herbicides—with glyphosate in first place—which are environmentally neutral, due to their high effectiveness in controlling any kind of weed as well as their lack of residual effect. While a more intense use of inputs is now necessary, this was nonetheless deemed positive because it simultaneously lowered the consumption of herbicides with the highest toxicity levels.

Other innovations introduced over the past decade included modern agronomic practices (related to soils and nutrients management, efficiency improvements in the use of chemical and mechanical technologies and crop rotation) and the diffusion of irrigation techniques (Chudnovsky et al., 1999; Sonnet, 1999).

Finally, although it is clear that a remarkable technology modernization process took place in Argentine agriculture during the 1990s, and this allowed a substantial increase in production and exports, it is also true that the spillovers of this process to the rest of the economy were limited by two factors: (1) the local agricultural machinery industry went through a restructuring process that involved both plants closures and a strong reduction in the domestic content of locally produced machines; (2) the new chemical and genetic technological packages that are increasingly crucial for agricultural production are provided by a handful of affiliates of TNCs affiliates that seldom engage in biotechnology R&D activities in Argentina. This means that the focal point of technological innovation, which in previous decades was mainly the Argentine Pampas, has now been transferred abroad (Bisang, 2001).

Education, Growth, and Inequality

Argentina is in a relatively good position among developing countries with regard to educational indicators. Illiteracy rates are very low and the Argentine population over 25 years has, on average, 8.5 years of education, compared to 5.9 in Latin America, 8.4 in Central and Eastern Europe, and 7.6 in East Asia (Holm-Nielsen and Hansen, 2003).

Table 6.3   Net schooling rates, 1980–1997

Year	Primary	Secondary	Third-level
1980	90.7	42.4	9.8
1991	98.4	61.3	20.5
1997	95.2	69.0	27.6

Source: Etchart (1999).

The education system in Argentina has always performed well when measured against other developing countries and over the last decades, the trend toward steadily improving access to education was maintained (see table 6.3). However, data suggest that progress in this area for the past 30 or 40 years has been slower than in other developing countries—and, in some cases, Argentina has lagged behind some nations that previously had worse educational records (such as Spain, Korea, or Taiwan).

Moreover, if we consider the population over 25 years, Argentina's performance is in line with international trends in terms of its GDP per capita. However, the country falls well short of these trends when only the population with a full secondary or higher education is considered.

Beyond quantitative data, when it comes to quality assessments the trends observed are not very positive. A number of studies have shown that the quality of education has been declining over the past decades. A 1993 survey revealed that 40 percent of secondary school graduates could not read and write in accordance with acceptable standards (World Bank, 1998). An annual test undertaken by public authorities—to investigate the language and mathematics skills in primary and secondary schools reveals mediocre results and no clearly improving trend and—in some cases, it indicates that standards in fact worsened during the 1990s (in spite of the initiatives launched since the mid-1990s to improve the quality of education).

There are few international comparisons of educational quality available that include Argentina. The 1997 United Nations Educational, Scientific and Cultural Organization (UNESCO) comparative study of language and mathematics skills in primary schools throughout the Latin American region found that Argentina was one of the better performing countries, along with Brazil and Chile (UNESCO, 1998). However, a recent study of reading literacy in grade 4 reveals a bad performance of Argentine students, whose skills rank well below European students, and also lag behind those of students from Turkey or Colombia (NCES, 2003).

Another study shows that Argentina ranks below Thailand and Mexico in reading literacy of 15-year-old students, and only slightly above Chile, and found that it had the highest within country variation among the countries surveyed. Results are similar when mathematical and scientific literacy is considered—in fact, Argentina's relative performance in scientific literacy is clearly worse than in the other two areas—(OECD/UNESCO, 2003). Students' performance is strongly associated—even more strongly than in most of the other surveyed countries—with family background, that is, educational attainments, income, wealth, and so on.

The low expenditure per student in primary and secondary schooling is one of the most important factors behind the declining quality of education (Llach et al., 1999). The public sector is responsible for the bulk of educational expenditure in Argentina. Hence, fiscal crises have direct and far-reaching consequences for the educational budget. Among those consequences, budget restrictions limit the possibilities of improving the teachers' or professors' professional skills and lead to insufficient spending on goods and services, such as classroom equipment.

Teachers' salaries are below par than those paid in other Latin American countries such as Chile and Mexico, and remain relatively stable throughout their professional life cycle. This means that, while in other countries, for instance, Brazil, teachers at the top levels of salary scales are substantially better paid that teachers entering the profession, progression is less significant in Argentina. Hence, the teaching career is, in the long run, economically less attractive in Argentina. This makes it difficult to attract and retain the most qualified candidates and the rigid wage structures fail to motivate a better performance on the part of teachers (Holm-Nielsen and Hansen, 2003).

As previously indicated, there is a wide disparity in educational quality and students performance, not only compared with the situation 30 or 40 years ago, but also vis-à-vis other developed and developing countries. Predictably, students from poor families and regions tend to receive a lower quality of education[21] and are also affected by the fact that they often need to work in order to help their families. This helps explain why the attendance rates and the numbers of students completing their studies are low both at primary and secondary school levels (Llach et al., 1999; Decibe and Canela, 2003).[22]

Some institutional reforms undertaken since the late 1980s may have contributed to increasing disparity in the quality of education. In 1978, primary schools and some secondary schools were transferred to the provinces. In 1992, this transfer process was completed and the provinces took full responsibility for secondary education with the result that they now control 90 percent of total education expenditure (Holm-Nielsen and Hansen, 2003).

Although a study by Galiani and Schargrodsky (2002) suggests that, on balance, decentralization resulted in better performance of students in public schools, it has been stated that the transfer process has had two main weaknesses that may explain why wide performance disparities still exist: (1) most provinces lacked the budget and the administrative capabilities needed to guarantee the efficiency and quality of the educational system; (2) decentralization, at least in 1992, was not specifically aimed at enhancing the quality of education, but was motivated by fiscal considerations (Decibe and Canela, 2003). In fact, Galiani and Schargrodsky (2002) find that the effects of decentralization were negligible in provinces with significant fiscal deficits, while positive in provinces with balanced budgets.

A particular source of concern from the point of view of industrial development is the low quality of technical education. The equipment in technical schools is often obsolete, programs are outdated, and professors underpaid. Linkages between technical schools and the business sectors are very weak with the result that the schools cannot adequately cater to the technical needs of enterprises (Winkler, 1990; Fuchs, 1994). Private and public training programs exist, but are heterogeneous in their quality and limited in their coverage.

Moreover, it has been stated that the educational system does not promote the creation of "higher-order" skills related to adaptability, flexibility, and the capability to identify and access relevant information and make independent analysis based on the data (Del Bello, 2002, quoted in Holm-Nielsen and Hansen, 2003). This is the outcome, among other things, of outdated teaching strategies and curricula.

What is the situation regarding the university system? Since the return of democracy in 1983, when quotas and entrance tests for public universities were removed, there was a notable increase in enrolment rates. The number of students who completed their studies also increased, albeit at a much lower rate. In fact, in Argentina, only 5 percent of total students graduate annually, while this rate is almost 15 percent in Brazil and Chile. As suggested by Holm-Nielsen and Hansen (2003), high dropout rates may be the result of the poor quality of teaching and the low level of students' motivation.

Budget constraints also affected the quality of public university education,[23] in a context in which, since the 1980s, the monetary resources increased at a much slower rate than the numbers of students. Professors' salaries, which account for the bulk of the university budget, have fallen substantially in real terms, while there has been a marked increase in the students/professor ratio. The low wages fail to attract and retain the best qualified young professors (who often prefer to teach at private universities or go abroad), and the resulting ageing population of professors show little willingness to update curricula or address other issues in need of improvement. Furthermore, only 12 percent of Argentine faculty had a doctoral degree in 1997 (Holm-Nielsen and Hansen, 2003).

Lack of competition among universities has been mentioned as another weakness of the system. The Fondo para el Mejoramiento de la Calidad

Universitaria (FOMEC) program launched in the 1990s aimed at alleviating that problem by offering competitive funding for projects presented by the universities—related to curricular reform and updating of equipment and faculty skills. Till date, the program appears to have been successful, but doubts remain as to its long-term impact on the institutional flaws that have plagued the public university system (Holm-Nielsen and Hansen, 2003).

Entry to public universities has traditionally been difficult for people with low resources, and, in the 1990s, the differences in access possibilities between rich and poor candidates widened, although public universities are still free (Echart M., 1999). Of each 100 pesos expended by the national government on university education, only 6 pesos benefited the poorer segment of the population (Decibe and Canela, 2003). Some grant programs exist, but they have a low coverage—3,000 grants for 40,000 potential candidates (Del Bello, 2002).

As for the relevance of education for the needs of industrial restructuring, Argentine students, as stated earlier, have traditionally been more likely to choose "liberal" professions, while science and engineering enrolment rates were relatively low. This bias was reinforced even in the 1990s, when a significantly higher proportion of university students opted for social science careers (see table 6.4). The number of engineering students in terms of the total population of Argentina is low compared to countries such as Korea, Chile, Spain, Portugal, or Greece. In contrast, the country has more physicians per inhabitant than Canada, the United States, Japan, or the United Kingdom (UNDP, 1999).

The university system has historically had very weak linkages with the business sector and this situation has not improved in recent decades, despite some negligible government initiatives (it must be noted that public universities have the autonomy to determine their curricula and policies; see Decibe and Canela, 2003). Universities—and the educational system as a whole—do not cultivate entrepreneurial thinking or capabilities

Table 6.4   First-level university graduates, 1990 and 1999, percentages

	1990	1999
Total	100	100
Natural and Pure Sciences	12	8
Engineering and Technology	13	16
Medical Sciences	21	16
Agricultural Sciences	4	4
Social Sciences	36	45
Humanities	13	12

Source: Authors' calculations based on RICYT.

(Kantis et al., 2000) and given this situation, it is hardly surprising to find that Argentine executives in general see the university system as being of little relevance to the needs of the economy (Holm-Nielsen and Hansen, 2003).

With regard to postgraduate university education, the available data shows that the number of doctorate students is low. In 1996, around 400 students completed their doctoral studies and 1,000 their master's degree. Brazil produced almost 2,500 doctoral graduates that year. The quality of postgraduate studies in Argentina is, to say the least, heterogeneous, and there is a lack of good educational facilities for many careers (Barsky, 1994).

A problem that has further strongly diminished the stock of human capital is the so-called brain drain phenomenon—the emigration flow of qualified individuals since the late 1970s—a consequence of ideological persecution and the economic crises (see Albornoz et al., 2002a, 2002b).

On balance, although the availability of human capital has been traditionally seen as a strong competitive advantage for Argentina, the declining quality and low relevance of educational skills for the needs of the economy have seriously constrained the contribution of education to productivity growth in Argentina.

In contrast, educational trends have had an impact on growing unemployment and income inequality. Educational attainments are negatively correlated with unemployment rates (Llach and Kritz, 1997). Higher education levels lead to a wage premium (Echart M., 1999), although this apparently does not apply to the same extent to the poorer income groups (Holm-Nielsen and Hansen, 2003). Moreover, wage gaps among groups with different educational qualifications increased during the 1990s (Gasparini, 1999).

Gasparini, Marchionni, and Sosa Escudero (2004), on the basis of evidence for 1986–1998, and considering not only returns to education but also returns to experience and unobservable factors and transformation in the occupation, age, and educational structure find that changes in the returns to education explain a very significant part of the increase in income inequality in 1992–1998. Changes in the returns to unobservable factors—such as talent, responsibility, and disposition to hard work, among others—and in the hours of work had also a significant role. Despite the significant increase in the unemployment rate in this period its effect on inequality was low.

According to the authors mentioned this is explained by the fact that the increase in unemployment was to a large extent accompanied by a decrease in the inactivity rate of roughly the same magnitude, implying that the sum of unemployed and inactive individuals did not vary much in the period.[24]

Regarding wage inequality, reference is made in the following considerations to a study undertaken by Bebczuk and Gasparini (2001). As in other countries, women and skilled workers have increased their share in the labor pool in Argentina. Furthermore, as shown in table 6.5, college and

Table 6.5 Share of employment by educational group, 1980–1998

	Share				Change in share			
	1980	*1986*	*1992*	*1998*	*80–86*	*86–92*	*92–98*	*80–98*
Without a high school degree	63.0	55.2	45.8	38.2	−7.8	−9.4	−7.6	−24.8
High school graduates	25.2	29.9	32.6	34.1	4.7	2.7	1.5	8.8
College graduates	11.8	14.9	21.6	27.8	3.1	6.7	6.2	16.0

Source: Bebczuk and Gasparini (2001).

Table 6.6 Hourly wages by educational group, Greater Buenos Aires, 1980–1998, in dollars

	1980	*1986*	*1992*	*1998*
Without a high school degree	12.03	7.79	6.39	6.57
High school graduates	20.25	11.93	9.55	10.12
College graduates	35.97	20.97	14.77	20.26
Total	15.16	9.80	8.25	9.75

Source: Bebczuk and Gasparini (2001).

high school graduates increased their share in employment, especially in the period from 1992 to 1998. This contrasted with the decreasing share of unskilled workers in the labor supply and employment.

Assuming stable labor demand, these shifts in supply would imply a fall in the relative wage of skilled workers. This is the case until 1992, but not in the more recent period. As shown in table 6.6, wages of college graduates increased by almost 50 percent between 1992 and 1998, whereas they remained roughly the same for less skilled employees in the same period.

As relative wages of skilled employees increased despite the large rise in the number of college graduates, the explanation must be found on the demand side. During the 1990s, the growing demand for skilled labor was the result of shifts within and between sectors. Within most sectors, a growing share of skilled personnel (and especially college graduates) has been apparent since 1980 and in the 1990s in particular. Regarding shifts between sectors, the increase in skilled labor demand was led by public sector employment in the period 1986–1992 and by the professional and business sector during 1992–1998.

However, sectoral reallocation, in great part due to trade liberalization, explains a significant, though smaller part of the wage premium (see also Galiani and Sanguinetti, 2003). The increase in the intensity of use of skilled labor seems to be a more important factor. Growing demand for skilled labor was probably induced by a fall in the relative price of machinery and equipment and the introduction of new skilled labor-intensive technologies.

Summing up, it is apparent that disparities in access to and the quality of education as experienced by different socioeconomic groups further reinforced income inequalities. This vicious circle, in spite of some initiatives mentioned, could not be broken by educational policies put into force during the past decade.

Concluding Remarks

As a result of the implementation of the currency board and some key structural reforms, Argentina was able to put an end to the various mechanisms that had contributed to the high inflation regime that was in place since 1975 and that had finally led to the hyperinflation episodes registered at the end of the 1980s. Price stabilization was an important achievement of the 1990s. It became a valuable public good as in any other country. However, price stabilization would not come without costs—that is, exchange rate overvaluation, the loss of adjustment mechanisms in front of external shocks—which would become evident since 1998. The vulnerability of the Argentine economy was reinforced by the progressive worsening of the fiscal accounts, which led to growing indebtedness (for a detailed discussion see chapter 8).

In 1991–1998, the country experienced relatively high growth rates, at the beginning based on consumption and then on increasing investments and exports. As imports grew more than exports, trade deficits emerged but they were financed by foreign capital inflows in an international context where ample liquidity existed. Foreign investment also contributed to finance the gap between domestic savings and investment.

Although the relative prices setting favored nontradable goods and services, many tradable activities also had a very good performance, including agriculture, oil, mining, and several manufacturing branches. Significant productivity increases were attained in many sectors, which were largely based on the incorporation of imported machinery and equipment, technology transfer from abroad and heavy reliance on FDI. Technological modernization implied changes in production functions leading to a growing demand for skilled personnel, a trend that contributes to explain growing inequality during the 1990s.

In the case of the manufacturing industry restructuring came along with a very heterogeneous performance among the different industrial branches.

Resource-processing and capital-intensive sectors gained share at the expense of labor and knowledge intensive ones. This, along with the widespread adoption of organizational and process innovations, led to a severe fall in manufacturing employment during the period under analysis.

Labor destruction in the manufacturing sector—and in privatized firms—was not compensated by the growth in employment in services. The early rise in unemployment rates along with growing income inequality quickly reversed the initial success of the Convertibility Plan in reducing poverty rates.

Hence, even before the external shocks that affected the Argentine economy since 1998, high unemployment, growing poverty, and income inequality heavily reduced the developmental impact of the growth process we have just referred to. Furthermore, the lack of progress in dealing with the serious educational problems faced by the Argentine society eroded the quality of human capital, limiting its contribution to productivity growth and aggravating the vicious circle between the (lack of) educational skills and income inequality.

Substantial heterogeneity at enterprise level was also a key feature of the modernization process. Whereas large and especially foreign-owned firms often had easy access to the assets required to run business in the new and more demanding local and international environment, this was not generally the case with small and medium size firms. As mentioned in chapter 5, the complementary policies launched by the government once the structural reforms were in force were not very effective in facilitating the restructuring process in this key segment of the enterprise population. Hence, it comes as no surprise to find that the attitude of business toward Convertibility was split, with larger firms often supporting it and SMEs being generally more critical.

Nonetheless, not only did the large and foreign-owned firms perform well in the new business environment but a number of SMEs were able to survive and grow in the 1990s as well. The nature and determinants of the restructuring process at firm level in the manufacturing sector is precisely the topic to be discussed in the next chapter.

CHAPTER 7

THE MICROECONOMICS OF INDUSTRIAL RESTRUCTURING DURING THE CONVERTIBILITY ERA

The Changing Entrepreneurial Strategies

The structural changes analyzed in the two previous chapters had a strong impact on entrepreneurial strategies and performance. It is important to bear in mind that most manufacturing firms had been established during the ISI period and engaged in the learning processes in a highly protected domestic market, where growth was interrupted by recurrent crises and where institutional and political instability was the norm (see López, 2006, for an analysis of the changing interaction between institutions and firms behavior in the different historical phases of the Argentine economy).

Since the mid-1970s, this scenario had been changing, initially with trade liberalization and then with a "forced" closing of the economy, albeit in a situation of stagnation and increasing macroeconomic instability. The best-adapted strategies to this peculiar environment were those with short-term horizons, a bias for high liquidity preference—to take advantage of speculative financial transactions—and avoidance of long-term commitments (i.e., investments in fixed assets and in innovative activities).

Naturally, reforms–cum–price stabilization constituted a sudden change in the rules of the game that forced private firms to redefine their strategies to adapt to the new economic regime. However, and contrary to what is often supposed in the neoclassical tradition, firms do not instantaneously adapt to changes in the environment in which they operate. On one hand, firms' strategies have a strong path–dependent component—that is, inertia may delay the adaptation to the new environment. On the other hand, even if firms perceive the need to restructure their activities, market failures (related to finance, innovation, and so on) may prevent them from doing so.

As seen earlier, even if some public policies had been adopted in the 1990s to deal with these problems, they did not have a substantial impact on the general course of the economic restructuring process.

In the initial years of the reforms "defensive" measures, aimed primarily at cost reduction, were mostly adopted. Then, as the firms perceived that reforms seemed irreversible, and growth and price stabilization appeared to have been consolidated, several significant transformations occurred in the manufacturing sector. These transformations included: (1) a bias toward less labor-intensive "production functions"[1]; (2) a substantial reduction in the degree of vertical integration of local production due to the substitution of local inputs for imported inputs; (3) a higher level of specialization of local firms as a result of product mix reduction—taking advantage of trade liberalization made it possible to complement domestic supplies with imported goods; (4) a trend toward outsourcing of auxiliary services; (5) introduction of managerial and organizational innovations; (6) an increasing importance toward marketing and advertising activities and (7) increasing attention toward quality and environmental issues (Kosacoff, 1998).

The need for adaptive technological initiatives was far less important than in the past. On one hand, changes in global TNC strategies have often led to worldwide production systems, in which products and process technologies used by affiliates in different parts of the world are more standardized than they have been in the past. On the other hand, trade liberalization has made imported capital goods and inputs cheaper and more easily available. Moreover, modern equipment usually embodies computer-based process technologies that are far more efficient than outmoded electromechanical production techniques. This renders unnecessary a number of engineering activities carried out either to extend the life cycle of old machines or to perform technical operations; these are now incorporated in the new equipment. Similarly, R&D and project engineering departments may be reduced or directly eliminated when affiliates become part of worldwide integrated production systems, and R&D and engineering efforts are centralized at headquarters.[2] In this scenario, foreign technology sources acquire even more preeminence over domestic sources than in the past (see Katz, 1999b; Cimoli and Katz, 2003).

Notwithstanding the existence of these general trends, when examining the magnitude and impact of R&D and other innovative activities in the Argentine manufacturing industry during the 1990s, a less somber and more nuanced picture emerges, as discussed later.

Predictably, beyond the above mentioned general features of the manufacturing restructuring process, the available evidence suggests that heterogeneity was the norm in terms of firms' performance and strategies in the 1990s.

Affiliates of TNCs[3] were the main "winners" in the restructuring process (Chudnovsky and López, 2001). Mainly through takeover of public or private domestic firms, the number of TNC affiliates among the 500 Argentine leading firms increased from 219 in 1993, to 318 in 2000, and to 340 in 2003. Their share in total production value augmented from 60 percent to 79 percent and to 82 percent in the respective years (data from INDEC).

Similar trends and figures are observed when only the manufacturing industry is considered. In fact, the share of TNCs in manufacturing during the 1990s was notably higher than that observed in the ISI stage. Considering, for example, the group of leading industrial firms in each year, while in 1963 affiliates of TNCs accounted for 46 percent of valued added and 36 percent of employment, in 1997 the same figures were 79 and 61 percent respectively. Moreover, the TNC share in the sales of the leading 100 manufacturing firms moved from 43 percent in 1974 up to 61 percent in 1998 (Chudnovsky and López, 2000). In the next section we show that manufacturing TNCs affiliates also performed better than domestic firms in terms of labor productivity during the 1990s.

The available evidence suggests that as in the ISI stage, market-seeking strategies were predominant among TNCs affiliates.[4] However, most foreign firms also took advantage of the opportunities created by MERCOSUR and in some cases, for example, the automotive industry, had efficiency-seeking objectives. As discussed later, they were also more prone to be engaged in foreign trade than domestic firms.

In contrast to the TNCs growing presence in the Argentine economy, local conglomerates showed heterogeneous strategies and performances, although, as a whole, they lost the central role they had played since late 1970s. Although some of these conglomerates disappeared or shrank drastically,[5] others—such as Techint and Arcor—strengthened their positions in the domestic market, often concentrating their activities on their "core business." At the same time, these successful conglomerates increased their presence in external markets, combining exports and FDI (Kosacoff, 1999b).

Considered as a whole, the domestic conglomerates undoubtedly showed a series of weaknesses both in terms of their impact on the local economy and the evolution of their own business activities: (1) their development had been mainly based on activities that generate limited linkages with the rest of the economy; (2) they usually operated in resource-intensive sectors, having a low presence in R&D based activities[6]; (3) in their respective markets, their size was frequently small vis-à-vis the international leaders—the above mentioned cases of Techint and Arcor are an exception to this rule (Bisang, 1998). Hence, it comes as no surprise to find that these conglomerates failed to become, as a group, "national champions."

Regarding SMEs, before the reforms most of them had obsolete machinery, inefficient production layouts, lack of skilled human resources, an excessively diversified product mix, little or no export experience, few cooperation linkages with other firms and organizations—including those offering technological or entrepreneurial services—weak quality control systems and marketing capabilities, and a management style strongly based on the technological and other expertise of the owner. Naturally, these deficiencies seriously affected their competitive potential and in any event, SMEs were generally more exposed to market failures in fields such as finance, technology, information, and others. As already mentioned, these aspects were hardly addressed successfully by the set of public policies in force in Argentina in the past decade (see Cepeda and Yoguel, 1993; Gatto and Yoguel, 1993; Yoguel, 1998 and 1999).

The SMEs process of adaptation to the new market conditions was especially difficult. Many of them went bankrupt, while others lost market share, had to retreat to the lower end of their respective markets, sold their businesses and totally or partly became importers. However, there was a group of dynamic SMEs, estimated to be around 20 percent of the SME manufacturing sector, who managed to survive and expand in the domestic market, and, in many cases, could even export,[7] on the basis of their accumulated and/or enhanced technological capabilities, management skills and human capital stock (Yoguel and Rabetino, 2002).

In the following sections we further analyze the "microeconomics" of the restructuring process by focusing on three key issues: innovation, FDI, and environmental management. The aim is to learn more about the impact of the Convertibility and the reforms not only on variables related to firms' economic performance—such as productivity and trade—but also on their environmental behavior.

This analysis is mainly derived from a series of studies elaborated by us on the basis of data from two large manufacturing surveys carried out by INDEC (Argentina's National Statistical Institute) and made available to us through a special agreement with that organization. The next section presents some basic statistical data that describes the performance of surveyed firms, while the rest of this chapter presents the key findings that emerge from the analysis undertaken to address the above mentioned issues. The econometric strategy and analysis is not reproduced here but can be examined in the respective papers.

The Statistical Data

With the purpose of analyzing the magnitude and diffusion of innovation activities in the Argentine manufacturing industry, two innovation surveys (designed in accordance with the methodology suggested by the Oslo and Bogotá Manuals[8]), were carried out in the past years (1998 and 2003, see next paragraph).

While the first survey covered the period 1992–1996 and included 1,639 firms (INDEC-SECYT, 1998), the second survey collected information for 1,688 firms during 1998–2001 (INDEC-SECYT-CEPAL, 2003).[9] Both samples were randomly drawn from the National Economic Census of 1993 and from the Input-Output Matrix survey of 1997, respectively. This way, they were intended to be representative samples of the manufacturing industry at the beginning of the periods they covered,[10]

On the basis of these surveys it is possible to learn about the performance of industrial firms in Argentina from 1992 to 2001. With this purpose, we have elaborated a series of statistical tables that shed light on the evolution of different groups of firms in terms of key performance variables. These tables are based on information for a matched panel of 718 firms interviewed in both the 1992–1996 and 1998–2001 innovation surveys. In other words, our analysis is restricted only to the subset of firms that were sampled in both surveys, a balanced panel data set.

While most of the firms that compose our data set (69 percent) were created before 1975—hence, they were born during the ISI phase—only 7 percent were created during the 1990s. However, more than 50 percent of the firms created before 1975 have changed ownership. These changes occurred mostly in the 1990s and often involved the acquisition of indigenous firms by TNCs.

SMEs and domestic firms accounted for the majority of the 718 firms. In both 1996 and 2001, 582 firms (81 percent of the sample) employed less than 300 employees. On the other hand, the share of foreign firms (i.e., firms with a share of foreign capital greater than 10 percent) increased from 11 percent in 1996 to 19 percent in 2001.

From table 7.1, it can be appreciated that food and beverages, chemicals, textiles, and machinery and equipment sectors accounted for almost one-half of the firms. While natural resources-intensive sectors accounted for almost one-third of the firms, R&D intensive was the least numerous group.[11]

The performance of manufacturing firms was irregular throughout the 1990s. Considering the evolution of labor productivity (measured by sales per employee),[12] table 7.2 shows that between 1992 and 1998, firms surveyed experienced a period of high growth (37 percent), while the opposite occurred during 1998–2001 (−12 percent). In turn, total employment showed a steadily decreasing trend throughout these years. In 2001, the average number of employees in manufacturing firms was 20 percent smaller than in 1992. However, there was a significant composition effect, since the weight of skilled labor (the share of professionals in total employment)

Table 7.1 Distribution of firms according to sectors

Sector (CLANAE* classification)		All firms		Innovators (1992–1996)		Innovators (1998–2001)	
		Firms	%	Firms	%	Firms	%
Scale intensive	Rubber and plastics	46	6.4	38	6.6	32	7.5
	Common metals	24	3.3	20	3.5	18	4.2
	Metal products	39	5.4	30	5.2	19	4.5
	Machinery and equipment	59	8.2	53	9.2	42	9.9
	Radio and TV equipment	9	1.3	8	1.4	8	1.9
	Vehicles	31	4.3	30	5.2	22	5.2
	Other transport equipment	10	1.4	6	1	2	0.5
Scale (total)		**218**	**30.4**	**185**	**32.1**	**143**	**33.6**
Labor intensive	Textiles	67	9.3	47	8.2	25	5.9
	Wearing	15	2.1	10	1.7	7	1.6
	Leather and footwear	13	1.8	11	1.9	10	2.4
	Edition and printing	38	5.3	32	5.6	18	4.2
	Furniture	27	3.8	19	3.3	12	2.8
Labor (total)		**160**	**22.3**	**119**	**20.7**	**72**	**16.9**
R&D intensive	Chemicals	75	10.4	65	11.3	55	12.9
	Electrical machinery	24	3.3	22	3.8	17	4
	Medical instruments	10	1.4	7	1.2	6	1.4
R&D (total)		**109**	**15.2**	**94**	**16.3**	**78**	**18.4**
Natural resources intensive	Food and beverages	144	20.1	114	19.8	83	19.5
	Tobacco	1	0.1	1	0.2	1	0.2
	Wood	21	2.9	9	1.6	5	1.2
	Paper	21	2.9	18	3.1	13	3.1
	Petroleum	6	0.8	6	1	5	1.2
	Fabricated and non ferrous minerals	38	5.3	30	5.2	25	5.9
Natural resources (total)		**231**	**32.2**	**178**	**30.9**	**132**	**31.1**
Total		**718**	**100**	**576**	**100**	**425**	**100**

* National Classification of Economic Activities.

Source: Chudnovsky et al. (2006).

Table 7.2   Performance and innovation activities

	1992 Average*	%**	1996 Average*	%**	1998 Average*	%**	2001 Average*	%**
Performance								
Sales/ Employment 1992 = 100	100		127		137		122	
Growth (%)			27		8		−12	
Employment 1992 = 100	100		93		91		80	
Skilled labor/ Employment (%)	6.8	75	7.4	75	7.7	76	8.7	77
Exports/ Sales (%)	14	44	15	60	17	51	19	54
Imports/ Sales (%)	14	64	15	73	18	62	15	60
Innovation activities*								
R&D	0.89	22	0.83	29	0.86	25	0.94	28
Technology acquisition	4.99	28	4.22	45	4.26	33	2.82	31
Total expenditures	3.93	46	4.08	59	3.91	45	3.04	45

* Calculated for firms that report a positive value of the respective variable.
** Percentage of firms that report a positive value of the respective variable.
*** Expenditure as a percentage of total sales.

Source: Chudnovsky et al. (2006).

increased without interruption throughout the 1990s, from 6.8 percent in 1992 up to 8.7 percent in 2001.

In addition, throughout the decade, there were more firms importing than exporting (e.g., 73 percent and 60 percent, respectively, in 1996). However, as a share of sales, the intensity of these activities was similar between importers and exporters (see table 7.2). This trend changed in 2001 when, affected by the domestic recession that began in 1998, the intensity of imports decreased significantly, as opposed to exports.

Technological Innovation, Productivity, and Trade

In spite of the heterogeneity in their behavior and performance in the postreform scenario, it could be expected that, overall, manufacturing firms would increase their investments in technology modernization and make efforts to improve their productivity levels in order to face the challenges of trade liberalization.

This was in fact the case as revealed by the first national survey on innovative activities in manufacturing firms carried out in 1997 (INDEC-SECYT, 1998). In an environment of booming sales and productivity, innovation expenditures (including R&D activities, acquisition of related capital goods and expenditures on training, consultancy engineering and design services) increased from 3.0 percent in 1992 to 3.7 percent of total sales in 1996. In addition to increasing their innovation expenditures during this period, manufacturing firms were also very active in introducing new product and process technologies.

What happened once the growth cycle was over? In the adverse conditions that prevailed since 1998, a drastic reduction in innovative activities could have been expected in a situation in which firms were trying to cut expenditures and postpone investment decisions in order to face the recession. This presumption was confirmed by the second national survey on innovation in the manufacturing sector (INDEC-SECYT-CEPAL, 2003), which showed that, as sales (as well as productivity and investment) fell sharply, innovation expenditures were drastically reduced between 1998 and 2001 (-28.5 percent). Understandably, there were also fewer firms that introduced new technologies during this period.

However, and unexpectedly, in-house R&D expenditures increased substantially (21.5 percent), although they remained at modest levels. The ratio of R&D expenditures to total sales of firms surveyed increased from 0.15 percent in 1992 to 0.17 percent in 1998 and to 0.26 percent in 2001. However, it must be noted that one firm alone—a TNC affiliate—contributed to 32 percent of R&D expenditures in 2000. Since the firm did not have R&D expenditures in 1998, it accounted for the entire increase in the aggregate between that year and 2001 (INDEC-SECYT-CEPAL, 2003).

An interesting finding relates to the number of workers assigned to R&D activities. In the context of a drastic reduction in employment in the surveyed firms (6 percent between 1992 and 1996 and 8 percent between 1998 and 2001), the number of workers in R&D activities grew by 14 percent between 1992 and 1996 and 19 percent in the following period. As a consequence, the share of R&D personnel in total employment increased from 1.2 to 1.7 percent between 1992 and 2001. Based on this data, in INDEC-SECYT-CEPAL (2003) it is estimated that there were around 14,000 people working in R&D activities in the manufacturing industry in 2001.

What was the position with regard to sources of foreign technology during this period? Payments from foreign technology transfer remained at around 0.4 percent of total sales of the firms surveyed. Considering only large firms, the ratio is only somewhat higher (0.5 percent).

Capital goods acquisition was, during the whole period under analysis, the main source of technology on innovative activities. At the same time, this area of expenditure was more sensitive to the changes in the macro-economic cycle. Between 1992 and 1996, over half of the capital goods associated with the introduction of new technologies came from abroad. The growth rate of capital goods imports almost tripled from that of purchases of domestic capital goods.

What happens when one considers only our sample of 718 matched firms? Turning to innovation activities, total expenditures figures (reported in table 7.2) include not only R&D and technology acquisition, but also management, engineering, and industrial design investments related to innovation activities. This broad definition is desirable for analyzing innovation activities in developing countries such as Argentina.[13]

Table 7.2 shows that, after increasing in 1992–1996, the number of firms engaged in innovation activities (i.e., firms with positive innovation expenditures) decreased markedly—from 59 percent to 45 percent—between 1996 and 2001. Furthermore, among these firms, the intensity of total expenditures on innovation activities decreased to almost 3 percent of total sales in 2001, from a maximum higher than 4 percent, reached in 1996.

This trend is explained largely by the main component of innovation expenditures during the decade, which was the acquisition of technology external to the firms. The latter includes capital goods (related to innovation activities within the firm) and technology transfer (patent rights, licenses, trademarks, designs) acquired domestically or abroad. After a substantial growth during 1992–1996, the share of firms that invested in technology acquisition decreased markedly (from 45 percent in 1996 to 31 percent in 2001). At the same time, the intensity of these expenditures decreased from 5 percent in 1992 to 2.8 percent in 2001.

However, table 7.2 shows that the share of firms that undertook R&D activities increased from 22 percent to 28 percent in 1992–2001. Moreover, the intensity of R&D expenditures among these firms also increased, reaching 0.94 percent of total sales in 2001.

Graph 7.1 shows that while most firms (80 percent) were innovators[14] in 1992–1996, their number decreased notably during 1998–2001, though still accounting for 59 percent of the sample. Even though these figures may appear surprisingly high at a first glance, it is important to take into account that the European Community Innovation Surveys reported that 50 percent of European manufacturing firms had introduced a product or process innovation during 1990–1992 (Archibugi and Sirilli, 2000), a shorter period than those covered by the Argentine surveys. Furthermore it cannot be ignored that since the implementation of a program of structural reforms in the early 1990s, the Argentine industry was radically transformed, inducing firms to adopt new strategies (to innovate, among them) to be able to survive.

When innovators are classified according to the type of innovations reported (only products, only processes, or both products and processes),

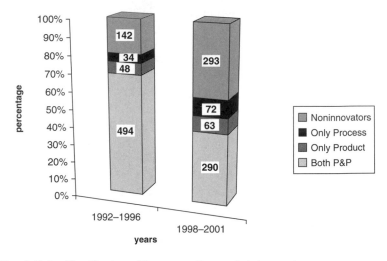

Graph 7.1   Classification of firms according to their innovative output
Source: Chudnovsky et al. (2006).

we can observe a significant change in the composition of this group. In particular, graph 7.1 shows that the share of firms that introduced both products and processes fell between the two periods analyzed (from 86 percent to 68 percent of innovators).

In general, the group of innovators has a higher presence of large and foreign firms than in the whole sample. In 2001, for example, SMEs represented 75 percent of innovators, while foreign firms accounted for 24 percent. Furthermore, table 7.3 shows that innovators reached labor productivity levels that were, at least, 1.3 times higher than in noninnovators. Nevertheless, productivity growth rates were similar in both groups.

This was not the case for employment, with noninnovators reducing labor considerably faster than innovators.[15] The share of skilled labor has also been higher in the latter. For example, in 2001, while skilled labor accounted for almost seven percent of total employment in noninnovators, this figure was 10 percent in innovators (the gap in the use of skilled labor between both groups increased during the period under analysis). Table 7.3 also shows that innovators were more involved in international trade during the 1990s. In 2001, while 67 percent of these firms exported, only 35 percent of noninnovators did so (although export intensities have been lower in innovators). In the case of imports, these percentages were 74 percent and 40 percent in 2001, respectively.

Table 7.3 Performance in innovators and noninovators

	1992 Average*	%**	1996 Average*	%**	1998 Average*	%**	2001 Average*	%**
Innovators								
Sales/ Employment 1992 = 100	100		130		146		130	
Growth (%)			30		12		−11	
Noninnovators***	1.36		1.62		1.34		1.36	
Employment 1992 = 100	100		94		109		96	
Skilled labor/ Employment (%)	6.9	81	7.5	82	8.5	85	9.6	87
Exports/ Sales (%)	13	49	15	67	16	64	18	67
Imports/ Sales (%)	14	71	15	80	16	76	15	74
Noninnovators								
Sales/ Employment 1992 = 100	100		110		145		126	
Growth (%)			10		31		−13	
Innovators***	0.74		0.62		0.75		0.73	
Employment 1992 = 100	100		83		89		76	
Skilled labor/ Employment (%)	6.2	53	6.6	51	6.3	64	6.9	63
Exports/ Sales (%)	18	20	16	34	18	32	23	35
Imports/ Sales (%)	11	33	11	42	20	41	15	40

* Calculated for firms that report a positive value of the respective variable.
** Percentage of firms that report a positive value of the respective variable.
***Quotient of average sales per employee between innovators and noninnovators.

Source: Chudnovsky et al. (2006).

Table 7.4 shows that the majority of innovators engaged in innovation activities. Moreover, this share increased considerably during the period analyzed (from 55 percent in 1992 to 70 percent in 2001). Correspondingly, these figures indicate that a minor (though significant) number of firms introduced innovations without making innovation expenditures.[16] In contrast, expectedly, the share of noninnovators who engaged in innovation activities was small, except in 1996 (see table 7.4).[17] In other words, relatively few manufacturing firms allocated resources to R&D and/or technology acquisition without introducing innovations during the 1990s.

In turn, the data in table 7.4 shows that the intensity of innovation expenditures was similar between innovators and noninnovators during the 1990s. In other words, innovative firms that engaged in innovation activities did not allocate higher investment efforts than noninnovators that also

Table 7.4   Innovation expenditures in innovators and noninnovators

	1992 Average*	%**	1996 Average	%**	1998 Average	%**	2001 Average	%**
Innovators								
R&D	0.89	27	0.84	35	0.87	40	0.93	45
Technology acquisition	5.03	33	4.10	53	4.29	50	2.79	50
Total expenditures	3.93	55	4.00	69	4.00	68	3.06	70
Noninnovators								
R&D	0.70	1	0.40	3	0.70	3	1.20	4
Technology acquisition	4.20	7	5.90	16	3.90	7	3.30	4
Total expenditures	3.80	9	5.40	19	3.00	10	2.80	8

* Calculated for firms that report a positive value of the respective variable.
** Percentage of firms that report a positive value of the respective variable.
Source: Chudnovsky et al. (2006).

undertook these activities. Tentatively, the data suggest that, in order to explain the type of firms that became innovators during the past decade, it might be more relevant to consider whether firms engaged in innovation activities, rather than emphasizing the intensity with which these activities were undertaken.

Following the methodology employed in studies for industrialized countries and using matched panel data from both Argentine innovation surveys, in Chudnovsky et al. (2006b) an econometric study was undertaken in order to learn about the determinants and impacts of innovative activities by manufacturing firms during 1992–2001. The main questions addressed in that paper are as follows:

1. Which types of attributes and assets (i.e., size, ownership, market orientation, labor skills availability, and so on) make firms more prone to engage in innovation activities and to launch new products and new processes to the market?
2. Do firms that engage in innovation activities have a higher probability of introducing a new product and/or process in the market? Furthermore, do in-house innovation activities have a different impact on the probability of becoming an innovator vis-à-vis technology acquisition expenditure?
3. Do firms that introduce product and/or process innovations perform better than those that do not?

According to the findings of the mentioned paper, large firms are more prone to engage in innovation activities[18] and to launch innovations in the market. In contrast, foreign ownership does not have any effect on those variables. While labor skills have a positive and significant impact on the probability of undertaking innovation activities, the same does not happen with export activity. On the other hand, labor skills and exports have a statistically significant impact only on the relative likelihood of obtaining both product and process innovations.[19]

Performing innovation activities (in-house R&D and technology acquisition) enhances the probability of becoming an innovator, but in heterogeneous ways. While technology acquisition does not affect the relative likelihood of the innovation output outcomes, R&D increases the odds of both product and process and only product innovations vis-à-vis only process innovations. Finally, innovators performed better than noninnovators in terms of labor productivity, during 1992–2001.[20]

While in the paper we have just referred to exports was considered only as control variable on the impact of innovation activities on innovation outputs and productivity, in another study (Chudnovsky et al., 2006c) the relation between innovation and export activity was analyzed with data from the second innovation survey.

In this case, the analysis shows that along with other factors—such as size, labor productivity, share of skilled labor, and foreign ownership—being an innovator had a positive impact on export activity by manufacturing firms in Argentina during 1998–2001. While launching product innovations new to the market improves the probability of being an exporter, adopting a process innovation new for the firm increases exports levels and propensities. These findings may suggest that in order to be able to compete in foreign markets firms need to have state-of-the-art products, while the amount and relative magnitude of their export activity is more related to process innovations that are presumably related to costs reduction and/or productivity and quality enhancements.

The Impact of Foreign Direct Investment

As it was the case during the ISI period, a key source of foreign technology during the 1990s was FDI. As we have already seen, the presence of TNCs affiliates in the Argentine economy increased substantially during the 1990s.

Foreign firms were expected to introduce new products, process, and organizational technologies that would be reflected in their performance (i.e., exports, productivity, and so on). These are the direct effects of FDI. Furthermore, indirect effects from FDI may occur through different kinds of spillovers for domestic firms that may arise from the presence of foreign firms:

1. There may be an increase in the human capital stock in host countries through the growing availability of workers, technicians, and engineers trained by the TNCs affiliates.

2. TNCs affiliates are usually more productive than the local firms with whom they compete. Thus, horizontal or intra-industry spillovers may appear when domestic firms are induced to increase their productivity or improve the quality of their products by reorganizing their businesses, increasing their innovative efforts and/or acquiring machinery, equipment and disembodied technologies. Sometimes, knowledge leakages (in areas such as work process organization, product design, marketing, and so on) that can help domestic firms enhance their productivity levels may arise from the presence of TNCs, although the latter have an incentive to prevent these spillovers (Kugler, 2000).

3. Contrary to the above case, TNCs affiliates may have an incentive to promote vertical or inter-industry spillovers. The diffusion of knowledge across sectors could benefit them to the extent that it helps their clients and/or suppliers to increase their productivity and become more competitive and efficient. For instance, TNCs may provide technical and marketing assistance, information, training, and so on. to their suppliers contributing to generate positive spillovers. Furthermore, it has been argued that affiliates established through acquisitions are likely to source more locally than those taking the form of greenfield projects. While the latter have to put time and effort in developing local linkages, the former can take advantage of the supplier relationships of the acquired firm (Javorcik, 2004).

However, it was just not positive spillovers that occurred from TNCs presence. Foreign affiliates could also lead to negative horizontal spillovers when domestic firms are forced to reduce their production—causing lower productivity in their establishments if they are operating with high fixed costs—or even to exit the market, as a result of the increasing presence of TNCs (Aitken and Harrison, 1999). Negative vertical spillovers may also appear when, for instance, domestic suppliers are displaced from the market as a consequence of the affiliates' bias in favor of foreign suppliers.

An important conceptual consideration must be made at this point. If FDI spillovers are associated with knowledge leakages, then discussing negative spillovers makes no sense (since we would be forced to assume that domestic firms reduce their productivity because of those leakages). However, if FDI spillovers include the effects derived not only from technological and geographical proximity but also from TNCs competition with domestic firms it is possible to consider the possibility of negative spillovers.

Most recent studies on spillovers in other countries, which are mostly based on panel data, either failed to find a significant effect or find negative horizontal spillovers[21]; in some cases, positive spillovers are found only for certain groups of local firms. In turn, some recent studies have found evidence of positive vertical spillovers (a finding that makes sense in the light of above arguments).

TNCs affiliates could also generate *market access (export) spillovers*, to the extent that their export activity may reduce the cost of access to information about foreign markets and/or facilitate an export learning process for domestic firms.

Data from innovation surveys made possible to undertake research in order to establish how foreign firms performed in Argentina and what kind of spillovers they had generated. Before turning into the results of the econometric analysis, it is worth presenting some descriptive statistics.

As expected, table 7.5, shows that foreign firms, during the period under analysis, had labor productivity levels between 1.5 and two times higher than domestic firms. In turn, whereas between 1992 and 1998 productivity grew 49 percent in the former, this rate was 25 percent in the latter. The reduction in productivity that affected both groups of firms in the recessive period was lower in foreign firms (10 versus 14 percent).

Table 7.5   Domestic and foreign firms' performance

	1992 Average*	%**	1996 Average *	%**	1998 Average *	%**	2001 Average *	%**
Foreign firms								
Sales/Employment 1992 = 100	100		121		149		135	
Growth (%)			21		23		−10	
Domestic firms***	1.61		1.55		1.88		1.98	
Employment 1992 = 100	100		88		85		72	
Skilled labor/ Employment (percent)	13.7	94	12.7	96	14.1	95	14.8	96
Domestic firms								
Sales/Employment 1992 = 100	100		124		125		108	
Growth (%)			24		0.9		−14	
Foreign firms***	0.62		0.65		0.53		0.50	
Employment 1992 = 100	100		86		80		70	
Skilled labor/ Employment (percent)	5.8	73	6.1	72	5.9	72	6.6	72

* Average per firm. Calculated for firms that report a positive value of the respective variable.
** Percentage of firms that report a positive value of the respective variable.
*** Quotient of average sales per employee between domestic and foreign firms.

Source: Authors' calculations based on data from Argentine Innovation Surveys.

Table 7.6 Innovative expenditures in domestic firms and in TNCs affiliates (percentage on sales)

Innovative expenditures		1992		1996		1998		2001	
		TNCs	Domestic	TNCs	Domestic	TNCs	Domestic	TNCs	Domestic
R&D	Average	0.46	0.97	0.59	0.89	0.63	0.95	0.56	1.10
	%*	36.2	20.8	39.5	26.8	36.9	23.2	41.3	25.2
Technology	Average	2.81	5.67	5.06	3.97	4.65	4.11	2.51	2.94
acquisition	%*	69.6	24.1	71.1	41.2	46.2	30.5	49.0	27.6
Total	Average	2.87	4.12	5.14	3.81	4.15	3.80	2.69	3.15
	%*	81.2	42.7	78.9	56.7	62.3	42.1	65.0	40.5

* percentage of firms (on each group) that reported a positive value for the respective variable.

Source: Own elaboration based on data from the National Innovation Surveys 1992–1996 and 1998–2001.

The contrasting trends in labor productivity were recorded against a background of falling employment in both groups of firms, though to a lesser extent among foreign firms.

R&D and technology acquisition activities are more common in affiliates of TNCs than in domestic firms. However, R&D intensity (R&D expenditures/sales) in domestic firms is higher than in foreign firms—the average ratio in the former was between 50 and 100 percent higher than in the latter during the period under analysis. While foreign firms invested relatively more in technology acquisition in 1996 and 1998, the opposite occurred in 1992 and 2001 (see table 7.6).

This suggests that in-house technology development is of less importance in affiliates of TNCs than in domestic firms, as the former naturally tend to rely on foreign sources—mainly, though not exclusively internal to the corporation to which they belong.

On the basis of the aforementioned database and employing econometric techniques, Chudnovsky et al. (2004c) show that, expectedly, TNCs affiliates have higher productivity levels than domestic firms. Nevertheless, evidence is found neither of positive nor of negative horizontal spillovers for domestic firms from FDI presence.

In another ongoing study, in this case, based on comparing the performance of domestic firms that were taken over by foreign investors during the period under analysis with that of those firms that were retained by local owners, a number of issues related to the direct and indirect impact of FDI on trade, productivity, and innovation were analyzed through the use of econometric techniques (Chudnovsky et al., 2006d). The main findings of this study are as follows:

1. Labor productivity increased after the firm was acquired by foreign investors. As expected, the growth in productivity has been

taking place gradually since the year in which the firm changed ownership.

2. The probability of introducing a new (or improved) product and/or process innovations may have increased after the firm was acquired. This probability did not augment since the year in which the firm was taken over suggesting that this effect takes place at the beginning. In contrast, takeover by foreign investors has no effect on the intensity and composition of innovation expenditures in the acquired firms.

3. Exports and the intensity of exports (i.e., exports/sales ratio) increased after the firm changed ownership. The findings are similar in the case of imports and the intensity of imports.[22] As expected, the increase in exports and in export intensity took place gradually since the takeover. The same trend is similar in the case of imports.

4. There have been neither positive nor negative spillovers from TNCs' presence. This result is valid both for horizontal and vertical spillovers.

5. In the case of innovation and trade no evidence is found of horizontal and backward spillovers, except for the case of positive backward spillovers on the innovation output (meaning that firms that supply to sectors where takeovers have taken place may have been induced to launch new products and processes to the market).

These results provide robust econometric evidence that FDI through takeovers of domestic firms increased labor productivity, exports, and imports in a gradual way since the year in which the firm changed ownership, and had an immediate effect on the probability of introducing new products or processes in the market.

The new owners of the domestic firms seem to have transferred inputs (such as organizational and production technologies) to the acquired firms that allowed them to launch new products and to increase labor productivity and trade more than in the control group of always domestic firms. However, neither technology acquisition nor research and development activities seem to have been affected by the takeover.

While the direct effects of FDI through takeovers seems to be positive on the variables analyzed so far, the results on the indirect effects of the higher foreign presence in Argentine manufacturing industry are less encouraging. The finding of positive backward innovation spillovers suggests that the new owners have taken advantage of the network of local suppliers of the acquired firms and may have provided inputs to launch new products and processes of production. This is clearly beneficial for both the supplier and the foreign firm that took over. However, we did not find any evidence that this type of spillovers were significant in the case of innovation activities, productivity, or exports.

Environmental Management in the
Manufacturing Industry

In the context of increasing concerns worldwide on the relation between economic growth and the protection of the environment (as seen in chapter 1), it is relevant to discuss the available evidence on the environmental dimension of industrial restructuring through the analysis of environmental management activities (EMA) undertaken by manufacturing firms in Argentina during the 1990s.[23]

Argentine environmental policy comprises both federal laws (which can be adhered to voluntarily by provinces) and provincial and municipal norms. These legal provisions establish command-and-control style environmental regulations. Performance standards are fixed and firms are fined if they fail to meet them. Market-based norms—for example, pollution taxes, tradable permits, and so on are almost nonexistent (see OECD, 1994 for a discussion of both kinds of instruments).

As far as the division of responsibilities between the federal government and the provinces is concerned, the 1994 constitutional reform established that natural resources belonged to each province, but that the provinces delegate to the nation the capacity to determine "minimum environmental standards." This process is embodied in pieces of legislation establishing uniform environmental parameters throughout the nation to secure adequate protection of the environment. Nevertheless these norms are applied according to complementary laws passed by each provincial government.

It must be mentioned that the Argentine legal environmental protection parameters are often very strict, as they were established in line with prevailing standards in developed countries. Nevertheless, the legislation is often implemented by technically and financially weak local and provincial authorities.

These often assume—correctly or not—that if they strictly apply the environmental legislation, many firms in their area, especially SMEs, will have to close down or face higher costs that will affect their competitiveness. In other words, the enforcement of environmental norms is often weak, but notwithstanding this, environmental regulations have played a major role in the adoption of environmental protection practices in the local manufacturing industry (see below).

Another relevant aspect to take into account is that environmental policy is formulated exclusively in terms of setting performance standards, while the connection between the environmental and the productive and technological dimensions of industrial restructuring is simply overlooked. Hence, enterprise and technology initiatives are totally disconnected from environmental policies, although EMA in private firms is closely linked to their innovative and productive capabilities (see below).

As for the evidence on EMA, questions related to the type of EMA and to the main motivation for engaging in those activities were raised in the Second Innovation Survey. In Chudnovsky and Pupato (2005) the information for the same panel of firms analyzed in this chapter was processed, referring only to 1998–2001 because similar questions were not raised in the first survey. Table 7.7 shows that there were sharp differences among firms that had and had not undertaken EMA. The former were larger and better performing firms, as measured by the number of employees and total sales, respectively. In addition, they employed more skilled labor and engaged in innovation expenditures more intensively (as shares of sales) both in 1998 and in 2001. Therefore, it is unsurprising to find that while 84 percent of the firms that undertook EMA were innovators (i.e., introduced new products or processes) during that period, less than a third of the firms without EMA managed to do so.

Table 7.7 Descriptive statistics for firms with and without EMA

		Firms that undertook EMA	Firms that did not undertake EMA
Average total sales (millions of dollars)	1998	61.6	10.7
	2001	54.2	7.5
	% change	−12.0	−29.9
Average total employment	1998	343	125
	2001	317	107
	% change	−7.6	−14.4
Skilled employees on total employment (%)	1998	40	27
	2001	43	29
	% change	7.5	7.4
Foreign firms (%)	1998	27	9
	2001	29	9
R&D / sales (%)	1998	0.33	0.08
	2001	0.37	0.14
	% change	12.1	75.0
Technology acquisition/sales (%)*	1998	1.92	0.75
	2001	1.38	0.32
	% change	−28.1	−57.3
Innovators (%)**		84	31

* Technology acquisition includes expenditures in capital goods (related to innovation activities within the firm) and technology transfer (patent rights, licenses, trademarks, and designs) acquired domestically or abroad in 1998.
** Firms that introduced new products or processes during 1998–2001.

Source: Chudnovsky and Pupato (2005).

Table 7.8   Type of EMA in surveyed firms

EMA type	Percentage of firms undertaking each activity
1. Incorporated treatment and waste disposal systems	31
2. Implemented environment remediation actions	18
3. Improved water, input and energy use efficiency	36
4. Established in-site or off-site recycling	26
5. Replaced or modified pollutants processes	21
6. Substituted pollutant inputs or raw materials	18
7. Developed more environment-friendly products	11
8. Achieved environmental management certification*	8
9. Other EMA	5

* ISO 14001, IRAM 3800, OHSAS

Source: Chudnovsky and Pupato (2005).

The types of environmental activities covered by the innovation survey are shown in table 7.8. Efficiency improvements in the use of water, energy and other resources were the most widespread environmental activity (36 percent of the firms), followed by effluent treatment (31 percent), and recycling (26 percent).

The analysis of the different types of EMA is important in the light of the changes observed in recent years in the way environmental management is treated both by firms and by public authorities, in developed as well as in middle-income developing countries. Until some years ago, environmental management had been mainly focused on treatment of pollution once it has been created, the so-called "end-of-pipe" (EOP)[24] approach. However, the situation has recently been changing as "industry is moving from an 'end-of pipe' reactive strategy that focused on capturing and disposing of pollutants generated during manufacturing, to a more holistic approach that integrates environmental considerations more effectively over a broader range of firm functions—including product design and procurement practices, as well as production processes" (OECD, 2001, p. 9).

This new approach toward environmental management is usually referred to as "pollution prevention," clean production (CP), or "eco-efficiency." The key idea is to shift from a "corrective" approach to a "preventive" one, as well as to try to transform what has traditionally been seen as a source of additional private costs—to meet environmental regulations—into a source of potential benefits—through environmentally friendly products or production processes.

CP actions can be distinguished according to their level of complexity. There are some "simple" ones—with small investment requirements, low technological complexity, and short implementation periods—as water, energy, and input savings. At the other end, there are more "complex" measures— generally involving greater investments, longer lead times, and higher technological complexity and uncertainty—for example, the development of new cleaner technologies.

The distribution of the firms in our dataset according to the quality of their environmental management[25] and nationality is summarized in table 7.9. Although 47 percent of the firms were not engaged in EMA, there is a concentration of firms around higher quality environmental management among those facilities that were engaged in EMA. For example, considering the whole sample, the number of firms that undertook complex CP (30 percent) was five times larger than those that undertook EOP management (6 percent). At the same time, foreign firms have introduced complex CP far more often than domestic firms.

There is a significant dispersion across sectors in terms of the proportion of firms engaged in EMA and the quality of EMA undertaken (Chudnovsky and Pupato, 2005). This might reflect, among other factors, sectoral differences as a function of the magnitude of individual environmental problems, the strength of regulation enforcement, the existence of technological opportunities to improve environmental performance and the type of firms prevailing in each activity.

With regard to the motivations for undertaking the EMA described in table 7.8, the main motivation is the need to comply with local environmental regulations (or, "regulatory pressure"), which was identified by 33 percent of the firms in the sample. In turn, as a benchmark for comparison, improving the firms' environmental image (which is a source of "market pressure") was a motivation for undertaking EMA in 29 percent of the firms in the dataset. Export market requirements have also promoted the adoption of EMAs in some sectors. Moreover, an improved environmental performance was often achieved as a by-product of the efforts made to reduce costs and

Table 7.9 Quality of EMA and firm nationality

EMA	Firms (percent)		
	All	Domestic	Foreign
No environmental management	47	52	22
End-of-pipe	6	6	5
"Simple" clean production	18	18	18
"Complex" clean production	30	24	55

Source: Chudnovsky and Pupato (2005).

increase production efficiency to face the growing competition in domestic and export markets (Chudnovsky et al., 2000).

As to the obstacles for improving the level of environmental management in SMEs, technology seems to be the most important one. This includes: (1) the high cost of some technologies; (2) the lack of information about feasible technical alternatives; (3) the inadequate availability of technology suited to the specific needs of SMEs (INDEC-SECYT-CEPAL, 2003). Lack of information is also an obstacle for SMEs to engage in EMA, coupled with the perception on their part that complying with the environmental legislation would have a negative impact on their costs (although this is not necessarily the case, as discussed in the received literature—see OTA, 1994; Porter and Van der Linde, 1995).

In Chudnovsky and Pupato (2005) we aim at answering the following questions:

1. What are the determinants of the probability of undertaking EMA and of their quality? In particular, is the adoption of EMA and their quality influenced by the innovative activities performed by manufacturing firms?
2. What types of EMA are encouraged by environmental regulatory pressure on manufacturing firms? Are innovation activities stimulated in firms that are under environmental regulatory pressures?
3. Are foreign firms more prone to undertake EMA than domestic firms? Do foreign firms' EMA spillover to domestic firms? Do spillovers depend on the absorptive capabilities[26] of domestic firms?

Briefly, we found that firm size and technology acquisition expenditures increase both the probability of undertaking EMA and the quality of environmental management.[27] In addition, we find a positive impact of environmental regulatory pressure on innovative behavior, though such regulatory pressure induces "end-of-pipe" at the expense of simple CP management. Finally, despite the fact that foreign ownership is associated to a relative decrease in the quality of environmental management, foreign firms are more prone to undertake EMA and generate positive environmental spillovers, by inducing simple CP management in domestic firms with high absorption capabilities.

In any case, it is important to handle the results with due caution. Although we have measured the explanatory variables at the beginning of the period covered by our dataset and included sector fixed effects in our regressions in order to obtain more robust estimations, endogeneity problems still remain. The latter may stem from the impossibility, given data availability, of controlling for firm fixed effects and other unobservables that may be correlated with both the regressors and the dependent variables. For these reasons, the results should be interpreted with caution. We prefer to view our findings as indicating conditional correlations between variables, rather than proper causal relationships.

Concluding Remarks

During the 1990s, the economic policy setting supposedly aimed at efficiency and modernization. Trade liberalization jointly with access to state-of-the-art technology (through FDI, capital goods imports, technology payments, and so on) would give both the incentives as well as the means to improve productivity and gain competitiveness. These processes effectively took place in the industrial sector, but favoring mostly large and/or foreign owned firms.

In turn, the SMEs process of adaptation to the new market conditions was especially difficult. Many of them went bankrupt, while others lost market share, had to retreat to the lower end of their respective markets, sold their businesses, and totally or partly became importers. However, there was a group of dynamic SMEs that managed to survive and expand in the domestic market, and in many cases even export, on the basis of their accumulated and/or enhanced technological capabilities, management skills, and human capital stock.

However, heterogeneity in firms' performance went beyond the determinants associated with size or ownership. Though most manufacturing firms were born during the ISI and survived in the same volatile Argentina's economic and institutional scenario, they had accumulated different kinds of productive, organizational, and technological capabilities. Hence, not all firms were equally equipped to meet the challenge of the reforms in the 1990s.

In this regard, it is worth noting that before the 1990s manufacturing firms had developed routines and strategies adapted to an inward-oriented economy, with relatively low levels of competition and a permanent macroeconomic and institutional instability. Reforms forced firms to rapidly adapt to very different rules of the game, something that proved very difficult for most SMEs, not only because their low capabilities levels but also because of the lack of public policies aimed at helping their adaptation to the new environment.

The findings of the studies surveyed in this chapter help us understand better the determinants of firms' performance and to derive policy lessons. As for innovation, an important conclusion is that in spite of low R&D expenditures in Argentina's manufacturing industry, a number of firms have begun to consider R&D activities part of their routines and a valuable asset to be preserved even during bad times. The results show that firms do so for good microeconomic reasons, since R&D contributes to becoming an innovator and, hence, to higher productivity levels than competitors who do not innovate.

It is very relevant to take into account that continuous R&D efforts have a considerably larger impact on the probability of having an innovative output when compared to discontinuous expenditures. Hence, discontinuing in-house R&D activities would have a negative impact on the results of those activities. This finding reminds us of the importance of the fact that firms also learn to innovate and that this learning must be a continuous process to be effective.

Since knowledge and innovation processes have a strong cumulative nature, it comes as no surprise to find that better results are obtained when firms internalize R&D activities as part of their routines than when they undertake isolated innovation projects. While this finding may not be unexpected when developed countries are analyzed, it is interesting to find that it is also valid for developing countries. Hence, technological policies should aim at fostering firms to maintain permanent innovation departments instead of only subsidizing specific projects—as it is still the case in Argentina.

Although R&D activities as such had no impact on EMA, technology acquisition expenditures were an important variable in enhancing EMA and their quality at firm level. At the same time, the finding that there is a strong and positive conditional correlation between regulatory pressure and the launching of new products and processes by firms suggests the importance of combining environmental and technology policies.

This is very relevant taking into account that in Argentina environmental policy is formulated exclusively in terms of setting performance standards, while the connection between the environmental and the productive and technological dimensions of industrial restructuring is simply overlooked. Hence, enterprise and technology initiatives are totally disconnected from environmental policies, although environmental management in private firms is closely linked to their innovative and productive capabilities.

Regarding FDI, although its direct effects in terms of productivity, trade, and innovation were mainly positive, the scenario is less encouraging when analyzing its indirect effects. Innovation output spillovers to domestic firms were found to be positive in case of backward linkages, but the same did not happen when analyzing trade and R&D activities. As for trade and productivity spillovers the results are not statistically significant. Taken as a whole, these findings suggest that positive FDI spillovers may arise when they also benefit TNCs—because TNCs may be interested in helping their suppliers to enhance their technological capabilities.

While some vertical positive spillovers may arise without policy intervention this effect was hampered in the Argentina's case due to the fact that many TNCs replaced domestic suppliers with foreign ones. Hence, policies aimed at helping domestic firms to enhance their competitive assets might have had a positive impact since they could have helped many of those firms to be able to remain as TNCs suppliers and to enhance their possibilities of reaping positive FDI horizontal spillovers.

Finally, it is relevant to discuss the implications of the findings related to SMEs performance. Surveyed studies have found that the smaller the firm the lower the probability of engaging in innovative activities, of becoming an innovator, of exporting and of having EMA. As involvement in innovative activities enhances the probability of a firm to become an innovator, and as innovators perform better than noninnovators, the aforementioned finding implies that smaller firms are at a disadvantage in terms of productivity performance (in fact, large firms have, per se, higher labor productivity levels).

Although no comprehensive study has been undertaken on the reasons why SMEs have a lower probability of engaging in innovation activities and of becoming innovators, the innovation surveys—and other scattered evidence available on the subject—suggest that lack of access to credit is the main obstacle to innovative activities in SMEs.[28] Furthermore, Chudnovsky et al. (2004b) found that, during recession periods, small firms may become even more restricted in their ability to undertake innovative activities. A key challenge for policy-makers is to remove the obstacles, which may be preventing SMEs from engaging in innovative activities.

These obstacles include not only access to credit but also others mentioned by SMEs such as lack of skilled personnel, information failures and weak cooperation links with others firms and institutions. As seen earlier, although some policies aimed at dealing with these issues were put in place during the past decade, their impact to date has been negligible. This is a key area on which far more and better focused public efforts should be concentrated.

CHAPTER 8

FROM CRISIS TO RECOVERY, 1998–2006

Introduction

During 1998–199, the Argentine economy suffered a series of external shocks as a result of the Asian, Russian, and Brazilian crises. These shocks, combined with the weaknesses of the Argentine economy, led to a long recessive period that ended in the biggest crisis in the country's history in 2001–2002. Not only did the GDP record a drastic fall (see graph 8.1), but there was also a banking crash. The economic crisis turned into a deep political crisis, and finally led to the default of the external debt and to a huge peso devaluation in the middle of a sharp increase in the unemployment rate and in the number of families under the poverty line (see graphs 2.9 and 2.10).

The management of the crisis was shouldered by a provisional government that took office in January 2002 in the middle of deep economic instability and high levels of social protest. However, the crisis was eventually overcome, a quick economic recovery ensued during the second quarter of 2002, and a new government was elected in May 2003.

As the Argentine crisis has certain similarities in its origin to the Mexican, Asian, Russian, and Brazilian crises, we begin this chapter with a stylized account of the key causes accounting for those episodes. Then we analyze the specific factors explaining the roots of the Argentine crash; we review the management of the crisis and finally we comment about the external debt restructuring that took place in early 2005.

The main factors that lie behind the strong economic recovery since 2003 are briefly discussed at the end of this chapter. Although the emphasis in our analysis is on the economic issues, attention is also paid to the political and institutional aspects that we consider equally important for having triggered the crisis and defined its evolution.

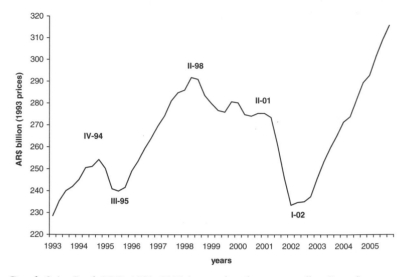

Graph 8.1   Real GDP, 1993–2005 (quarterly values, seasonally adjusted)
Source: Authors' elaboration on the basis of INDEC's data.

From the Mexican Financial Crisis to the Brazilian Currency Crisis

By mid-1990s, the "fundamentals" of the Mexican economy were relatively stable and there had been progress in the implementation of orthodox reforms such as privatizations and trade liberalization (including the launching of the North American Free Trade Agreement), which were perceived as necessary by the international financial community. However, the over-valuation of the RER (the nominal exchange rate was fixed since November 1991) and the growing current account deficit forced the government to implement a currency devaluation in March 1994.

Within a difficult political context, there were continuous runs against the Central Bank reserves leading ultimately to the collapse of the currency regime at the end of 1994. The currency crisis in turn led to a banking crisis and to a sharp GDP fall in 1995.

The financial assistance of the IMF and the strong support of the U.S. government avoided the default on the external debt and facilitated the quick recovery of the economy. However, this opened a debate among many analysts who argued that the expectation of a financial bail out by the IMF was considered a source of moral hazard since it encouraged foreign investors to lend with little regard to the risk profile and the viability of the projects they finance in emerging markets.

While Calvo and Mendoza (1996) interpret the Mexican event as a "death foretold" in view of the inconsistency between the currency regime and the structural imbalances of the economy, Sachs et al. (1996) consider that it was a "sudden death" provoked by a shift in investors' expectations after the first peso devaluation, which finally led to a self-fulfilling prophecy (the so called second generationcrisis models in the received literature). Ros (2001) provides a more comprehensive explanation of the various factors accounting for first the currency and then the debt crisis.

The contagion effect of the Mexican crisis was relatively limited— Argentina was the country that received the more significant impact of the "Tequila" effect. On the contrary, the next crisis that began in Thailand in mid-1997 quickly spread over the region, mainly affecting Philippines, Indonesia, Malaysia, and Korea—by the end of November all of these countries had devalued their currencies.

These countries (and specially) Korea had experienced high growth rates during many decades, with large savings and investment rates and strong export performances. While they had been more cautious than the Latin American countries with regard to import liberalization and privatization, in the 1990s, they started to liberalize the capital account and to deregulate their financial systems.

The Asian crisis was very surprising as most of those economies exhibited stable fundamentals and high growth rates. Although there were both current account deficits and currency appreciations, these two key indicators were generally lower than in Mexico—the same happened with the external debt/exports ratio, as shown in table 8.1.

Despite these good initial conditions, speculative attacks sharply reduced reserves and the changes in market expectations and the herd behavior by foreign investors led to a self-fulfilling prophecy, generating a currency and a banking crisis. Instead of restoring confidence among investors, the fiscal and monetary policies recommended initially by the IMF contributed to the panic and aggravated the crisis (see Sachs and Radelet, 1998; Stiglitz, 2002 for sharp critiques). It was only in 1998 that the IMF modified its original strategy. This change, together with the policy initiatives taken by the countries themselves (Malaysia did not require the IMF assistance), facilitated a quick recovery in most cases.

When the East Asian economies had started on their recovery, the next crisis episode took place in mid-1998 in Russia. Although the contagion from the East Asian crisis and the fall in oil prices were influential causes of this crisis, internal problems were at the root of the Russian episode. After a huge cumulative fall in GDP in 1990–1995 and a controversial privatization program, Russia began a growth process in 1997, attracting foreign portfolio investment.

Table 8.1   Currency overvaluation, current account deficit and external debt ratios before the crisis (percentage)

Country	Currency overvaluation*	Current account deficit/GDP	External debt/ GDP	External debt/ Exports
Mexico (94)	18	−7	33	197
Thailand (96)	11	−8	59	151
Malaysia(97)	12	−6	47	51
Indonesia (97)	8	−2	63	215
Korea (97)	4	−2	29	83
Russia (97)	69	0	30	124
Brazil (98)	20	−4.3	31	410
Argentina (01)	30	−1.7	52	456

* Currency overvaluation measures the change in the relation between the domestic consumer price index and the U.S. index in the period prior to the crisis. The years considered in each case are 1990–1994 (Mexico), 1990–1996 (Thailand, Malaysia, Indonesia, and Korea), 1993–1997 (Brazil), 1993–1996 (Russia) and 1990–2001 (Argentina).

Source: Authors' elaboration on the basis of World Bank's data (World Development Finance) and International Financial Statistics.

However, there was a strong currency appreciation (see table 8.1) and high levels of fiscal deficit and external public debt. In this scenario, and despite the significant financial assistance received from the IMF, the successive speculative attacks on the ruble sharply reduced the reserves and finally led to a large currency devaluation and a debt default in 1998 (see Kharas et al., 2001). The IMF attempted to prevent the crisis by providing liquidity and policy advice. However, they were not enough to change investors' expectations and mostly contributed to increase the capital flight (see Stiglitz, 2002). The effects of the Asian and Russian crises were universal and a sudden stop in net capital flows to emerging markets took place since 1998.

The next crisis took place in late 1998 in Brazil. The currency overvaluation in an economy with serious fiscal problems, current account deficit, and high external debt made it vulnerable to attacks on the domestic currency by foreign investors.

After spending huge amounts of reserves in defending the currency, in early 1999, a devaluation of the real finally took place. Nevertheless, a banking crisis and a default on the external debt were avoided and some of the fiscal measures that could not be taken before the crisis—due to political constraints—were agreed upon. Although the economy did not enter a recession and the assistance from the IMF was not an issue, it is noteworthy that there was very poor growth performance and huge debt levels in the Brazilian economy after the crisis (see Roubini and Setser, 2004).

The Main Causes of the Argentine Crisis

The Argentine crisis was a result of multiple economic causes, which cannot be fully understood unless we refer to the main features of the political system and the poor quality of the institutional context in which key economic decisions were made before and during the crisis.

With the benefit of hindsight, though not much time has passed, there are a number of academic studies that try to shed light on the several factors that gave rise to the crisis. The fiscal imbalances that contributed to the steep rise in the external debt, the RER appreciation, and the impact of external shocks are pointed out in all studies. However, authors differ in the relative value they assign to each factor, as well as in the interpretation of the process that finally brought about the crisis (for an initial survey see Nofal, 2002).

For some authors (especially Mussa, 2002 but also Teijeiro, 2001 and Krueger, 2002) the main factor accounting for the crisis was the continuous public sector imbalance throughout the Convertibility years. The dynamics of the resulting external indebtedness from fiscal indiscipline became unsustainable in a context of RER appreciation, and strong and adverse external shocks.

In contrast, other authors focus their attention on the "sudden stop" in capital flows to emerging markets since the Russian crisis in August 1998 (e.g., Calvo et al., 2002). They particularly highlight some features of the Argentine economy that magnified the effects of the sudden stop, including: (1) the small share of tradable goods output relative to domestic absorption of tradable goods led to a big swing in the RER; (2) the liability dollarization in nontradable sectors (including the government) made them highly susceptible to big balance sheet effects following a peso devaluation; (3) there was a high level of public debt denominated in foreign currency.

A third group of studies emphasizes the role played by expectations. Hausmann and Velasco (2002) state that in the Argentine case two negative factors were combined since 1998. First, expectations of a future increase in the value of exports diminished given the external shocks and the RER appreciation. Second, the financial constrain became more important. In a context of deteriorated export prospects, international investors were not willing to finance the current account deficit necessary to sustain growth.

Within the same group of studies, Galiani et al. (2003) point out that the dynamics of both fiscal accounts and the RER have to be understood in the light of economic agents' expectations about the future path of the economy. The agents define their spending (and their indebtedness levels) in accordance with the future prospects of the GDP as well as of the production of tradable goods (that will define the capacity of the country to generate income in foreign currency).

In the Argentine case the fulfillment of growth expectations under the Convertibility regime were contingent on the realization of a good set of productivity effects, international conditions for exports, consistent fiscal policies and a willingness of foreign lenders to supply credit. Adverse external shocks had a large negative impact on those expectations in a context in which it was not possible to make a significant adjustment in the dollar value of spending and incomes without putting into question the whole contractual framework.

An important contribution made by Galiani et al. (2003) is that, in contrast to other studies that regard as faulty some of the economic policies Argentina implemented during the Convertibility years, they explain certain economy policy decisions (such as the dollarization of the financial system) as endogenous to the prospects of growth and to the need of obtaining external funds. In this regard, they argue that the adoption of the currency board provided a framework that helped to recover the value of contracts by restricting the degree of freedom of monetary policies and their potential impact upon inflation.

In relation to this, it is important to consider that Convertibility became a sort of core economic institution in a country where many institutions are not reliable and rules are not widely respected. In addition, the initial success that Convertibility had in reducing inflation and subsequently in resisting the negative impact of the Tequila crisis made it harder and costly to exit this regime in an orderly manner. The exit costs were further aggravated because of the growing amount of financial contracts in dollars, both from the government and the private sector.

Likewise, another study (de la Torre et al., 2002) states that the Convertibility was the core or main contract that gave origin to every other economic contract in Argentina during the 1990s. In the same vein as Galiani et al. (2003) in this study some key economic policy measures (i.e., the dollarization of the financial system, the issue of public bonds denominated in dollars) are seen as dependent on government's objectives (to increase financial intermediation to facilitate the growth process). Nevertheless, in contrast with the two studies mentioned above that emphasize aspects related to the expectations on future production of tradable goods, more emphasis is placed on the real and financial shocks that since 2000 gave rise to the so-called exchange trap (overvaluation)—growth (recession)—debt (high indebtedness) circle.

Finally, the work of Perry and Serven (2002) does not focus on any shock or vulnerability in particular but considers the combination of these crucial factors for causing the Argentine crisis. These authors argue that the shocks did not affect the Argentine economy more than any other Latin American economy. Convertibility and the nominal inflexibility of prices imposed an extended deflationary adjustment in response to the different shocks (see next section) that provoked a RER appreciation. On the other hand, the deflationary adjustment reduced the nontradable sector's (including government's) payment capacity. Given the banks exposure to "government risk," the financial tension aggravated. Meanwhile, the weak fiscal policy implemented throughout the decade aggravated the imbalances that emerged in the aftermath of the external shocks.

External Shocks and the Vulnerability of the Argentine Economy

The extent to which the series of external shocks from the Asian to the Brazilian crisis affected the Argentine economy is illustrated in table 8.2.

It is important to note that these shocks were different in their features and repercussions from those that resulted from the 1995 crisis. While the capital outflow was a financial disturbance on both occasions, only in the latest crisis were the real shocks negative. In this connection, the devaluation of the Brazilian real, the appreciation of the U.S. dollar, and the fall in export prices and the terms of trade, resulted in a dramatic fall in the export sector's profitability and, therefore, affected its capacity to obtain foreign currency.

This is clearly reflected in graph 6.1 which shows that exports stagnated since 1998. As argued earlier, the poor behavior of the export sector meant a fundamental restriction for a country that, at the same time, faced increasing difficulties in accessing the international capital market after the Russian crisis.[1]

Table 8.2   The impact of external shocks on Argentina's economy (1998–1999)

Fall in the terms of trade (% variation)	11.1
Fall in export prices (% variation)	20.0
Fall in exports to Brazil (% variation)	30.0
Devaluation of the Brazilian real vis-à-vis the Argentine peso (wholesale price index)	18.4
Appreciation of the U.S. dollar vis-à-vis the euro (%)	10.0
Net capital outflows (% of GDP—excluding FDI—)	1.4
Increase in public sector interest payments (% of GDP)	1.0

Source: Fanelli (2002), based on ECLAC data.

However, many other Latin American countries were also affected by these external shocks, though on a different scale in each case. Therefore these shocks cannot explain by themselves such a profound crisis as the one Argentina went through.[2] The evolution of Argentina's economy since 1999 must then be explained paying special attention to largely domestic factors.

The structural reforms that Argentina underwent in the first half of the 1990s, the quick exit of the crisis of 1995 and the strong recovery that started in 1996—in which growing investment and exports had a key role—were, to the eye of investors and analysts, positive signals regarding the evolution and prospects of the Argentine economy.

Moreover, the high requirements of net worth and liquidity in the banking system that were adopted after the "Tequila crisis" (though, as shown, these prudential rules had also some negative effects) and the significant presence of foreign banks seemed to give an unusual strength to the Argentine financial system as compared to those in other emerging countries.

However, despite these assets, the Argentine economy showed important weaknesses that made the absorption of the external shocks difficult. First, in the context of Convertibility, there were few available adjustment mechanisms to deal with the increasing appreciation of the RER. Second, the public sector had a poor fiscal discipline (see the following paragraphs). Third, there were restrictions on economic policy decisions that mainly came from the disenchantment of wide sectors of the civil society as a consequence of the evolution of unemployment, income distribution, and poverty during the 1990s.

The RER's overvaluation was favored by the nominal rigidity imposed by the Convertibility regime. During the first years of the 1990s, the real appreciation of the peso—explained in great part by the nominal fixation of the exchange parity in 1991 in a still inflationary context (especially at the consumer prices level)—could yet be considered an equilibrium phenomenon. This argument was mainly based on the fact that reforms implemented since the beginning of the Convertibility regime had led to significant productivity improvements that might have justified the appreciation of the peso.

In contrast, by the end of the decade and in view of the external shocks mentioned above, different estimates supported the idea that the RER was overvalued in relation to both its historical value and its "equilibrium value." Perry and Serven (2002) estimated the real effective exchange rate (REER)[3] with respect to its "equilibrium value" in 35 percent in 1999 and 55 percent in 2001. They explain two-thirds of this figure by the combined effect of the dollar appreciation and the devaluation of the Brazilian real.

During the Convertibility regime, the adjustment of the REER could not come from the variation of the nominal exchange rate; it could exclusively come from the changes in the relative levels of domestic prices vis-à-vis the prices prevailing in the main Argentina's commercial partners. In this manner, the devaluation of the Brazilian real and the appreciation of the U.S. dollar made Argentina adjust the REER through a reduction of the domestic prices. Therefore, since 1999, there was a deflation of consumer prices of around 1 percent per year that would last until the devaluation of the peso.

Last, but not the least, it is important to note that during the Convertibility years considerable changes were introduced in the relative prices structure that tended to favor the nontradable vis-à-vis the tradable sectors. In this sense, those changes, which were introduced as part of the privatization process, resulted in a more rigid set of relative prices. Most of the contracts following the privatization of public services established indexation clauses that were incompatible with the type of adjustment the economy needed so as to absorb the external shocks. In a deflationary context, the prices of privatized public services showed a growing nominal trend, opposed to what it would have been expected after an external shock, when it is necessary to increase the competitiveness of the tradable sector (Fanelli, 2002).

As it has already been noted, another vulnerability of the Argentine economy was the performance of the public accounts throughout the decade, in contrast to the requirements of fiscal discipline inherent to the Convertibility regime. The fiscal imbalances—mainly derived from the social security reform that created the Private Pension Funds in 1994—together with the poor capacity of the Argentine tax collection system to effectively tax partly explains the public sector's increase of both domestic and foreign debt. On the other hand, the recognition of former liabilities (with State suppliers and retired people) also had significant incidence in the mounting State debts.

Between the end of 1994 and 2000, the debt rose around US$47.7 billion while the deficits accumulated in the 1996–2000 period added around US$25.9 billion (Hausmann and Velasco, 2002). The difference was the result of the debt recognition and the accumulation of financial assets (such as the Central Bank reserves). In this context, the public sector debt increased from around a third to more than half the GDP between 1994 and 2001 (see graph 6.3).

The federal government public spending in the 1993–2001 period registered a 29.7 percent growth. This was mostly explained by the increase in foreign debt interests (55 percent). The increase in the expenditures of the public social security system accounted for another 30 percent (a transitional cost derived from the pension system reform) and the remaining 15 percent was due to the increment of current transfers to the provincial governments. The latter was due, in part, to structural changes in budget allocation between the nation and the provinces during the analyzed period.[4]

It is important to note that the evolution of (public) spending takes us back to the political cycle influence. As Fanelli (2002) highlights, 1998 and 1999 were years of mounting political activity and President Menem was seeking another reelection. These events coincided with a strong debt increase and primary public spending, both at the national and provincial level.

Naturally, these factors explain a great part of the evolution of the national government's fiscal balance (see table 6.1), with a permanent growing deficit from 1994 (0.1 percent of the GDP) to 2001 (3.2 percent). It is worth emphasizing that the primary fiscal balance of the national government (which excludes the public debt interest payment) registered a continual surplus of around 1 percent of the GDP during the same period, though surprisingly, such a performance was particularly weak in the growth phase (1996–1998). Table 6.1 also illustrates the crucial role the social security system reform had on the fiscal performance, since it implied the loss of fiscal incomes while the expenditures in that connection remained constant (or even increased).

On the other hand, table 8.1 shows that the Argentine external debt in relation to the GDP was one of the highest among the countries that suffered crises. It was also remarkably high in relation to the exports. In this context, the large public sector's funding requirements together with the decline of the economy's capacity to obtain international currency through exports led, at the beginning of 2000, to the implementation of policies that not only had to deal with the problem of liquidity in the short term but that also had to guarantee the public sector's solvency in the medium and long run.

Finally, and following Fanelli (2002), the combination of fiscal imbalances with the adoption of stricter banking regulation after the Tequila crisis had undesired effects. The changes in banking regulations contributed to constrain the available credit to the private sector and introduced a bias in favor of the allocation of resources to the public sector, starting a crowding out process of the private sector regarding the access to credit—which particularly affected SMEs.

An important point to emphasize is that, in this scenario, only a few voices within the country (i.e., Eduardo Conesa) and abroad (i.e., Paul Krugman) raised the issue of modifying the exchange regime. Those comments were discredited for underestimating the effects that such a policy could have had in an economy with a highly dollarized contractual structure and financial system. Hence, it is not surprising that the continuity of the Convertibility regime was a common proposal among the presidential candidates on the eve of the national election that took place in October 1999. In particular, the continuity of the Convertibility was of great importance to the opposition movement that won the elections.

The End of Convertibility

Having opted for the continuity of the Convertibility system, the *Alianza* administration, headed by Fernando de la Rúa (who came to power at the end of 1999) faced the challenge of reactivating the economy. In that sense, it was compelled to satisfy two different kinds of requirements: those of the "markets"—which were uncertain about the new government's strength to reduce the fiscal deficit so as to fulfill the external commitments—and those of the citizenry, which experienced growing discontent with the legacy of the 1990s.

The new authorities considered the recovery of the economic activity a precondition for improving the solvency of the economy and for keeping the confidence of domestic and foreign investors. It was also the only way to reduce the high rates of unemployment and poverty that were of great popular concern in a context in which the suspicions of corruption had brought about the loss of legitimacy of the political system as well as of many other institutions.

In this scenario, the strategy selected by the *Alianza* administration was to induce the recovery of the economy through the improvement in the fiscal accounts. This was expected to lead to a reduction in the country's risk premium and hence in interest rates that would, in turn, foster an increase in the aggregate demand.

Under those circumstances the government decided to increase some taxes (the so-called *impuestazo*) to put in motion the so-called federal commitment to deal with the fiscal problems of the provinces and to sign a new agreement with the IMF. In this sense, it is worth mentioning that from the very beginning, the new administration counted on substantial support from the IMF, which played a decisive role in the country's access to external funds[5] from 1998 to 2001. As shown in graph 6.2, the scarcity of private external capital flows was severe in 2000 and particularly through 2001 (in 1999, the external funds mostly came from the FDI of the Spanish firm Repsol in the acquisition of YPF), a year in which the IMF funds helped to postpone the crisis for a while.

In this fashion, the new administration tried to solve what seemed to be a problem of liquidity in the short term. In fact, at that time, despite the adverse external situation, there were no significant perceptions of the public sector insolvency for two reasons.

The first and main reason had to do with the possibility that the implemented policies would result in an economic recovery or that, for exogenous reasons, the adverse external situation would revert (e.g., an improvement of the international prices for Argentine exports, a U.S. dollar devaluation vis-à-vis the euro or a reevaluation of the Brazilian real).

The second reason was that, even without improvements in the external situation, the authorities could still avoid the insolvency by implementing the necessary fiscal adjustments that were required to allow the payment of the contracted debts. At that point, the administration's degree of freedom to make these decisions was not clear, but its chance would depend on the extent of the required adjustment (the lesser if there was no deepening of the recession) and also of the image of cohesion and leadership conveyed to the citizenry.

Time would prove that reasons for optimism were not well founded. Recession was not overcome and the international scenario did not improve for Argentina. In turn, the government's scope to reduce fiscal imbalances was small in a context where the Senate and the provinces were controlled by the opposition and the citizens were reluctant to support the typical policies of public spending adjustment.[6] It is important to highlight that this balance of forces made it very difficult for the government not only to put in practice an effective solution to the fiscal imbalances but also to implement the structural reforms that were required by the "markets" and the international institutions.[7]

In May 2000, amid unfulfilled expectations of an economic recovery, the government reduced the salaries of public employees and promoted reforms in the labor legislation. Though these reforms were approved in the Parliament, the nontransparent negotiation process in which the law was passed resulted in the discredit of the *Alianza* administration among its supporters. These events had a negative impact on the government coalition and resulted in the vice president's resignation in October 2000.

The rise in the country's risk premium that followed this last event (see graph 8.2) reflected the market's distrust toward the capacity and coherence of the *Alianza* administration to fulfill the agreements made with the IMF. The loans the government received from international institutions and the government of Spain (the so-called *blindaje* or the financial shield) were the only relief Argentina received from the financial markets[8] at that time. Nevertheless, the fact that the economy was not recovering, along with the unfulfilled fiscal targets that had been agreed upon with the IMF, increased the uncertainty and provoked the resignation of the Minister of Economy José Luis Machinea, in March 2001.

The president decided to replace him with Ricardo López Murphy. The policies announced by the new minister focused on the need to reduce the fiscal deficit. His attempt to do that through a cut in public expenditures in items such as the university budget or the oil subsidies in Patagonia found opposition from the public and several members of the cabinet, who resigned soon afterward. This situation forced López Murphy out of office only two weeks after being appointed. López Murphy's failed attempt to

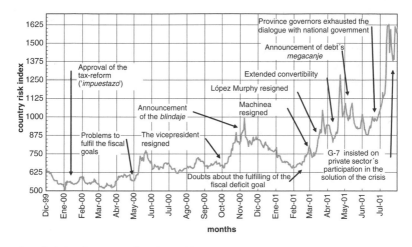

Graph 8.2   Country risk index, 1999–2001

Source: Authors' elaboration on the basis of Ministry of Economy' data.

eliminate fiscal imbalances through a reduction in public spending was a clear sign that the orthodox recipe could not be applied by a weak government, full of internal contradictions, in a highly sensible civil society. After these events, it became clear that the government had scarce possibilities of achieving an adjustment that would ensure the fiscal solvency and avoid a default.

The fact that there was neither economic recovery nor a significant fiscal adjustment transformed the initial liquidity problem into an insolvency problem during the first months of 2001. This had important consequences for the future unfolding of the crisis. In the new context, there was a general loss of confidence among domestic and foreign investors.

The economic policy followed by the new minister of economy, Domingo Cavallo, can be understood as a succession of attempts aimed at generating resources that would avoid the debt default. This occurred in a context in which there was a limited set of viable mechanisms of adjustment, particularly after López Murphy's experience. In a first phase, Cavallo aimed to promote (through the so-called competitiveness plans) production and exports in tradable sectors through tax incentives and commercial policy instruments, which were hardly effective to alleviate the lack of competitiveness in those sectors.

Later on, the public disagreement with the Central Bank's president with respect to the monetary policy[9]—Cavallo advocated for a softer monetary policy while the Central Bank defended the rules in force in the belief that a change in this area would weaken the Convertibility regime—also discredited Cavallo vis-à-vis the international investor's eyes,[10] though he was supported by the IMF.

Cavallo also attempted to reduce the burden of the public debt through a so-called *mega-canje* (a plan for a voluntary debt swap) that took place in June 2001. The results of this operation showed that investors considered the public sector solvency extremely fragile: they required high returns in order to accept the long-term debt (in compensation for the risk inherent in the operation) in exchange of a modest reduction of the debt burden in the short term.[11]

Given the impossibility of obtaining external financing, in July 2001, the government reduced by 13 percent public employees' salaries and retired people's pensions and announced a "zero-deficit" policy, which consisted in maintaining current expenditures (consumption, interests, social security, and transferences) at the level determined by current income. Later measures applied by Cavallo regarding debt restructuring[12] and the IMF reluctant support[13] did not change the financial market appreciation, well reflected in the country-risk indicators, which reached record values (see graph 8.2).

In this frame, the financial-system prudential regulations and the strong presence of foreign banks could not prevent either a deposit decrease (during 2001 it reached 22 percent of the total available at the beginning of the year, see graph 8.3) nor a capital flight (see graph 6.2).

At the same time, the adverse results of the parliamentary elections in October 2001 gave evidence of the steep popular dissatisfaction with a government that failed systematically in taking effective measures to deal with the crisis.

From the beginning of December 2001 on, the notable disequilibria in the financial and currency markets and in the public sector accounts, together with the impossibility of obtaining new credit from the IMF (domestic sources had almost been exhausted) derived in the imposition of restrictions on cash retirements from banks (the so-called *corralito*) and on capital movements.

Some days later, after a popular revolt, the president resigned and, at the end of 2001, Adolfo Rodríguez Saá's new provisional government, appointed by congress, declared the public debt default with private creditors. This president resigned after almost one week, blaming the rest of the Peronist provincial governors for their lack of political support.

The Management of the Crisis

On January 1, 2002, Eduardo Duhalde assumed a transitional administration. The initial economic measures of the new government comprised the

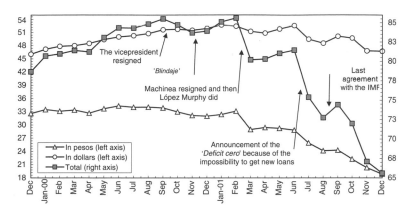

Graph 8.3   Bank deposits ($ and US$ billion)

Source: Authors' elaboration on the basis of Ministry of Economy' data.

Convertibility regime abandonment, the peso devaluation and the pesification of internal contracts, obligations, and public services rates.

In order to get a better understanding of the economic policy strategy followed by the new government, it is worth bearing in mind that, at this first moment, priorities were not so much related to reactivating the economy (an important GDP fall was expected) but rather oriented to prevent new—and, possibly, more virulent—social revolts, restrain the unavoidable inflationary pressures that would emerge from the peso devaluation (an hyperinflationary outbreak was feared and this contributed to resist a floating-exchange rate regime as requested by the IMF) and avoid the definitive financial system collapse.

In addition, there were some strong sociopolitical restrictions and determinants that conditioned the political economy decision-making process throughout 2002: (1) the population—and many politicians—had mostly hostile attitudes toward banks and privatized enterprises; this generated support for some policies (such as the freezing of public utilities rates) and rejection for others (such as compulsive deposit exchange—see the following paragraphs); (2) even though the plundering that had been characteristic of the end of De la Rúa administration vanished quickly, the level of social protest was still high, in a context of strong poverty increase—starting from already high levels (see graph 2.9). This forced the government to implement massive assistance measures (the so-called *Plan Jefas y Jefes de Hogar*, which implied a significant fiscal cost); (3) the Executive Branch entered into conflict with the Supreme Court of Justice (which the former intended to displace given its identification with President Menem government, with whom Duhalde had a severe dispute). This created a permanent uncertainty regarding the judicial validation of governmental measures, especially, as we see in the following paragraphs, in relation to the constitutionality of the norms linked to the financial system restructuring; (4) although the new government had a majority in the Senate, it was the first minority in the Deputies Chamber and most provincial governors belonged to the same political party, as 2002 went by (and the time to make decisions regarding the next national elections—programmed for April 2003—arrived) disputes within the progovernment party also started to affect the decision-making process, especially in parliament, where the Executive Power encountered increasing difficulties in getting their projects of interest approved.

In this complex scenario, it was initially intended to settle a "controlled" devaluation, with an official market—where the exchange rate was fixed at 1.40 pesos to 1 dollar—and a free one. At the same time, foreign currency control measures were implemented with the aim of preserving existent currency stocks and converting trade surpluses into a higher currency supply, helping this way to restrain the rise in the free dollar price.

At the beginning of February, due to IMF pressures, the foreign exchange market was liberalized. At that moment, the free dollar value reached near 2 pesos. At the end of April, after liberalization, it already exceeded 3 pesos— at that moment, the first economy minister appointed by Duhalde, Jorge Remes Lenicov, resigned. The exchange rate went on increasing until June, when it approached 4 pesos, in spite of Central Bank's US$7.500 million cumulative intervention aimed at defending the local currency.

From that moment on, the dollar stabilized around 3.5 pesos during the second half of 2002, and then it adopted a decidedly decreasing tendency to stabilize it between 2.8 and 3 pesos from March 2003 onward. In this second stage, the Central Bank began to absorb dollars and, in fact, it made active interventions in order to prevent further decreases in its price, retrieving its previously lost reserves through high levels of monetary emission.

Which were the factors behind the initial exchange rate overshooting and its subsequent appreciation? In the first half of the year, economical and political uncertainty reigned, which favored the overshooting. Once these conditions disappeared or, at least, attenuated, in a context of a strong commercial surplus (see graph 6.1), the exchange rate first found a plateau and later began descending.

One of the main factors of pressure on the exchange rate during the first half of 2002 was the continuous financial system money flight that converged to dollar buying. At the beginning of 2002, it was decided to deepen the restrictions imposed in 2001 to deposit withdrawals. Therefore, all fixed-term deposits and some foreign currency demand deposits were transitorily immobilized (the so-called *corralón*) allowing demand deposits denominated in pesos and the remaining foreign currency accounts to be used for transactions (the abovementioned *corralito*).

In spite of these restrictions, a continuous deposit flight took place as a result of the legal protection granted by judges to those trapped in the *corralón* the money extractions within the allowed limits, the exceptions to the *corralito*/*corralón* and other factors.

An important issue for understanding these movements is related to dollar deposit pesification at 1–1.4 parity at the beginning of February 2002 (it is worth keeping in mind that the free dollar was highly above that level at that moment). Deposit reprogramming and pesification generated strong conflicts among the government, the banks and the depositors, who claimed for their property rights. Judicial decisions tended to favor depositors, not only through legal actions but also with regard to the validity of norms related to reprogramming and pesification (which were declared unconstitutional).

In this scenario, the government first tried to initiate a voluntary policy based on exchanging reprogrammed deposits for bonds (which was unsuccessful); later, a compulsory exchange (which failed due to the opposition of the congress to support this norm—this led to the resignation of minister of economy Remes Lenicov) and, finally, already with the new minister of economy Lavagna in charge, a return to the voluntary exchange, this time with better results. In any case, a good proportion of depositors could retrieve, through the previously described means, their savings, feeding this way the demand for dollars.

The situation began to change in the middle of the year due to a conjunction of various factors: (1) after a violent popular revolt in which two people died, the governmental mandate was shortened in June 2002 (from December 2003 to May 2003); this helped appease the social and political conflicts; (2) the Central Bank, through bill emissions, began to regenerate the necessary conditions for the emergence of a market interest rate with the aim of allowing banks to offer attractive returns and therefore rebuild their deposit portfolio (which began increasing from July 2002 onward); (3) controls and regulations aimed at increasing exporters' foreign currency supply were reinforced; (4) inflation began to decelerate, after a strong initial increase and, in general, the economic situation recovered a minimum level of stability. In this more stable context, restrictions regarding deposit withdrawal could even be gradually relaxed.

Another key economic policy issue during 2002 was the financial system restructuring management. In this regard, a relevant issue was that the private sector's foreign currency debts with the financial system were pesified at the Convertibility exchange rate (the so-called asymmetric pesification, given that deposits were pesified at 1.4 pesos per dollar while credits were at 1–1 exchange rate). In addition, the banks asset portfolios had deteriorated, among other reasons, due to the fact that they were made up by a defaulted government's bonds and by credits granted to nontradable sectors. To make matters worse, a few months later it was determined that an actualization rule based on past inflation would be applied to pesified deposits, while an important proportion of credits was covered by a different actualization index and a smaller expected rate of increase (the so-called asymmetric indexation). Evidently, this set of decisions had a detrimental effect on a number of banks net worth.

The State made itself responsible for compensating banks and depositors for their decisions, with the consequent fiscal cost.[14] These measures also had a probably negative redistributive problem. Even though those depositors who remained trapped in the *corralón* had, in average, lower incomes than those who could early withdraw their deposits (see Halac and Schmukler, 2003), it is important to bear in mind that people with bank accounts in Argentina belong, also on average, to a higher income segment than those who have no relationship at all with the banking system (therefore, it is presumable that transfers toward depositors were, in the end, also regressive).

In addition, pesification implied a transfer from the whole society to those firms and people indebted in dollars (who, we may suppose, belonged to a higher average income class than those nonindebted), although it must be pointed out that if debts had not been pesified, it would have been impossible to repay them, and the outcome would have been a massive firm bankrupt and particular assets liquidation.

What happened, in the mean time, with regard to the relationship with the IMF? Initially, the authorities expected a fast and substantial assistance from the institution. At the beginning of January, the government intended to obtain US$15–20 billion of external loans, which would be allocated, among other objectives, to strengthen reserves, reprogram maturities, finance exports, and settle social programs. Nevertheless, IMF negotiations turned up to be much longer and traumatic than expected, being this another factor that led to the resignation of Minister Remes Lenicov.

Even though the IMF agreed (since there were no viable alternatives) with the debt default and devaluation, they advised from the beginning—something that would become a constant motto during 2002—that they would only support an economic and political "sustainable" program (the U.S. authorities, as well as other G-7 members, went in the same direction).

In fact, from the first moment, the IMF showed its dissatisfaction with some of the measures adopted by the new administration. Besides expressing its disagreement with the exchange market unfolding (a measure that, as we have seen earlier, was rapidly corrected), the institution criticized other initiatives that, in its view, raised doubts on the validity of property rights and implied unpredictable risks over private investors.

The IMF also insisted on the fact that, in order to make progress in the negotiations, internal political consensus was needed, including an agreement among legislators, governors and presidential precandidates, aimed at guaranteeing the fulfillment of the agreement under discussion (replicating what had happened in Brazil).[15] The latter was not achieved and, although some political compromises were obtained—in April 2002 and November 2002—which favored negotiations continuity, they took long to unbind.[16]

In any case, beyond the specific claims, it became apparent that the IMF was limiting its help to Argentina as a way of "punishing" the country for the behavior it had shown in the recent past. Obviously, it is a hard-to-test hypothesis, and it is not clear which was the essential cause that led the institution to adopt that hostile attitude (the default declaration—it does not seem to be a good candidate given that the IMF implicitly encouraged it—the way Rodríguez Saá declared the default, the "populist" inclinations of Duhalde government, a self-criticism for having helped Argentina with significant funds when it was clear that the crisis was unavoidable, and so on). Anyway, we should not disregard a priori the argument that the IMF severity was due to an intention to apply an "exemplary" treatment as an example to other indebted countries (as well as their creditors) that intended to follow Argentina's steps not to expect rescue operations in the future.

In this scenario, the negotiations aimed at achieving an agreement with the IMF extended more than expected at the beginning of the year and the assistance obtained was also much less than expected.[17] In fact, during 2002 almost US$3.5 billion (in net terms) were paid to international financial institutions (this was an unusual case of a country in crisis that, instead of receiving external help, is obliged to repay debts with institutions whose mission, in theory, is helping to prevent and solve these type of crisis). When the delayed agreement was finally achieved in January 2003 (and with validity only until August 2003), Argentina did not receive further payments; it was only possible to reprogram maturity dates.

In September 2003, a three-year agreement to refinance the debt with the institution was signed with the IMF. A conditionality clause of a fiscal primary surplus equivalent to 3 percent of the GDP was established only for the first year and it was stated that the government had to negotiate in good faith with external creditors.

The debt restructuring process was initiated in September 2003 in Dubai at the annual meeting of the IMF and the World Bank (this process was undertaken under a new government led by President Kirchner, who won the May 2003 elections). The Dubai proposal was a 75 percent cut on a defaulted debt stock of about US$87 billion. The new bonds would reach a maximum amount of about US$21.8 billion and the proposal was consistent with the budget surplus that was agreed with the IMF.

Given the negative reaction of the financial markets to the Dubai proposal and the pressures of the IMF and of the G-7 finance ministers, in June 2004, a new proposal was made by the Argentine government in Buenos Aires. In exchange for a defaulted debt stock of US$81.8 billion new bonds would be issued for a total of US$38.5 billion, in case the level of acceptance of the swap was lower than 70 percent and US$41.8 billion in case it was higher than that benchmark (for more details see Damill et al., 2005).

The bondholder's organizations rejected the new proposal, considering that the country should pay more than what was offered. The reduction in the emerging market risk premium in view of the greater liquidity at world level played in favor of the Argentine offer. At the same time, the government mentioned that with a 50 percent level acceptance it would be satisfied.

On May 3, 2005, six weeks after the start of the restructuring process, the government announced that 76.2 percent of the defaulted debt was accepted. With the achieved cut the new debt stock was reduced from US$191.2 billion in 2004 to US$128.6 billion in 2005. As a proportion of the GDP, the fall was from 126 to 70 percent (see graph 6.3).

Finally, and after months of unsuccessful negotiations and disagreements about the course of the economic policy, on December 15, 2005 the Argentine government decided to cancel the outstanding debt with the IMF (US$9.5 billion) with the accumulated reserves.

The Economic Recovery

As shown in graph 8.1 the economic recovery started in the second quarter of 2002 and since then the GDP has been steadily growing. While in 2002 the GDP growth was negative, in the following three years the economy grew at 9 percent per year—while GDP per capita has been growing at more than 7.5 percent annually since 2003 (see table 2.2). As a result, in a "V-shaped" trajectory the economy reached the GDP level of 1998 in the first quarter of 2005. In the last quarter of 2005, the GDP was 8.2 percent higher than in the second quarter of 1998 (the highest point in the 1990s) and 35.2 percent higher than in the first quarter of 2002.

Inflation control, which as mentioned earlier was the main objective of the government in 2002, was progressively achieved on the basis of fiscal surpluses, frozen public services rates, and scarcely augmented salaries (far below inflation in a context of high unemployment rates). Hence, after two-quarters of high increases in price indexes (particularly, in wholesale prices), inflation began to decelerate in late 2002—the wholesale prices index even showed a decrease in the last quarter of 2002, also helped by the dollar stabilization. The monetary policy also contributed in this sense. Even though after the Convertibility exit the country recovered its capacity to emit money without foreign currency support, an inflationary outburst was feared, and this led to a moderate monetary expansion which was validated by the higher demand for funds.

However, inflation has become a problem once more since 2005 (in that year the rise in the consumer price index was 12.3 percent). Some analysts attributed inflation resurgence to monetary expansion resulting from the government's goal of maintaining, a stable and high RER and accumulating large amounts of international currency reserves. Others saw it as a natural result of high growth and the consequent changes in relative prices. Distributive conflicts, which have given place to high levels of wage increases in 2005 and 2006, were also blamed by some as causing inflation pressures. Finally, suspicions of market distortions due to oligopolistic practices have also been expressed, and the government seems to have taken note of this diagnostics as it has placed much emphasis on price agreements with different productive sectors to reduce inflation.

However, reasons for optimism regarding macroeconomic stability exist and are mainly based on the existence of twin surpluses since 2002. As shown in graph 6.1, the external trade adjustment started before the devaluation mainly due to the sharp reduction in imports that started first with the recession and was accentuated by the crisis. At the same time, the increasing trend in the value of exports since 2003 in a context of very high international prices for commodities made it possible to maintain a relatively large trade surplus even when imports started to grow again with the economy recovery and increasing investment. Trade surplus, in turn, caused a change of sign in the current account balance that has been positive since 2002.

Although exports values have augmented 56 percent between 2002 and 2005 it is important to take into account that most of that growth has been associated with price increases, that between those years world trade has grown at a higher rate (60 percent) and that export increases in Argentina's neighbors such as Brazil and Chile have been significantly higher (96 percent and 118 percent respectively).

In the case of fiscal accounts, the Consolidated Public Sector global result progressed from a deficit of 5.6 percent of GDP in 2001 to a 3.5 percent surplus in 2004. The rise in the national government's primary surplus is mostly explained by the tax on exports,[18] although revenues of other key taxes such as those on value added, incomes and financial operations had also large increases with the economic recovery. The other factor explaining the fiscal bonanza is the contraction of interest payments resulting from the debt default (see Damill et al., 2005, for details).

GDP growth was fueled both by consumption as well as by investment growth. According to data from the Economic Commission for ECLAC gross capital formation as percent of GDP (in constant 1993 prices) increased from a low of 11.3 percent in 2002 to 20 percent in 2005 (still lower than the level achieved in 1998 that was 21 percent). The growth in gross investment has been taking place both in construction and in machinery and equipment, although the former had in 2005 a slightly higher share on total investment vis-à-vis its share in 1998 (62 against 58 percent). Although no official data exist on the subject, information from different sources lead to think that investment in machinery and equipment has been to a large extent carried out by SMEs, while it is apparent that new significant investments by large enterprises is still mostly absent.

In a context of external and internal credit rationing (and in addition to retained profits in enterprises) a key source of financing for growing investment and consumption has been the wealth effect resulting from the huge external assets holdings of the private resident sector (estimated in more than US$100 billion) that sharply increased their value in pesos since 2002.

In turn, while FDI flows were very low in 2001–2003, a recovery was visible in 2004 and 2005 (see graph 6.2). While in absolute terms FDI inflows in the beginning of the twenty-first century have been much lower than in the 1990s, in relation to the GDP and to the gross capital formation they are similar to those registered in the second half of the 1990s.

It is important to take into account that Convertibility exit brought about conflicts between the government and foreign investors in two areas: in banking, due to the problems generated by the "asymmetric pesification" and in privatized services, because of rates freezing. In the former case, many firms brought suits against Argentina in the International Centre for Settlement of Investment Disputes (ICSID) (see Bouzas and Chudnovsky, 2004).[19] Hence, it is no surprise to find that some investors in banks and privatized companies have sold their equity mainly to domestic investors and other Latin American firms (especially from Brazil). Anyway, those disinvestment cases were more than compensated with new investments in different areas, including takeovers of large private Argentine firms by Brazilian firms.

The deep change in relative prices after devaluation has favored sectors producing tradable goods. According to ECLAC data, the share of goods producing sectors increased from 29.3 to 31.7 percent between 2001 and 2005, with the subsequent decrease in services' share. The same happened when analyzing the sectors of destination of FDI (the services sector fell from 43 percent in 1992–2000 to 27 percent in 2001–2004).

Import substitution has taken place in many industrial sectors. For instance, some labor-intensive sectors such as textiles and shoes, which had been badly affected by trade liberalization and exchange rate appreciation, recorded large increases in production levels between 2002 and 2005. But production also grew at high rates in skill-intensive sectors such as industrial and agricultural machinery. At the same time and in spite of the presence of export taxes, new records were achieved in agricultural production (see graph 3.3).

Due to economic growth the unemployment rate decreased from the extremely high levels reached in 2002 (see graph 2.10). In 2005, the unemployment rate was lower than that registered in 1998 and similar to that recorded in 1994. However, it is important to bear in mind that people receiving government subsidies are counted as employed in the official statistics. Without taking them into account, the unemployment rate in 2005 was still higher than in 1998.

The progress made in poverty reduction has been less significant than in the unemployment area. As shown in graph 2.9, the percentage of people living below the poverty and indigence lines in 2005 were still similar to that of 2001 but much higher than in 1998. In turn, the Gini coefficient was only slightly better in 2005 than in 1998 (see graph 2.8). Then, although as compared with 2001–2002 social indicators show a better picture, they are still as bad in the current recovery than in the late 1990s.

Unfortunately, corruption is another key area in which the country did not make any progress in recent years as is clearly visible in table 2.5 on trends in perceived corruption. After some initial positive changes in the Supreme Court where some judges appointed by the Menem government resigned or were separated by congress, and new judges were appointed following a new and more transparent procedure, little progress has been made in reforming the Judiciary and generally on dealing with the serious institutional feebleness of the Argentine society (human rights is probably the area where most advances have been made, specially since President Kirchner took office).

Concluding Remarks

The last Argentine crisis inscribes itself within a series of similar episodes that have been, in fact, frequent during the past decade. In this frame, even though the Argentine case tends to stand out given the unusual magnitude of the collapse, it can be considered as another milestone in the series of crisis that have been affecting the emerging markets in the globalization scenario.

Nevertheless, there are some key factors that are worth pointing out in order to understand the specificities of the Argentine case. First, a crucial element to be considered is that the Convertibility scheme was much more than a fixed exchange rate system. In practice, Convertibility was the basis over which the whole contract system of the country was established. Therefore, currency devaluation implied not only a relative price change but also a general modification of the domestic contractual order.

Second, the degree of dollarization of the Argentine economy—and, in particular, of the banking system—was unusually high. In this scenario, and in spite of the existent prudential regulations, it was clear that currency devaluation would massively impact on the whole financial system, beyond the higher or lower level of soundness of each particular institution. Given these two factors, it is understandable why the collapse of the currency board in Argentina had more severe repercussions on the economy (and on the institutions' functioning) than those observed in other crisis episodes.

In addition, these elements also explain the great delay in exiting Convertibility—given the fear to the predictable consequences of such exit—when it was more evident, each time, that the socioeconomic context made impracticable the solutions by means of the fiscal adjustment (without being in sight other viable economic or political alternatives). Perhaps the most surprising element in this context was the government's opposition to proposing a deep debt-restructuring program with substantial capital cuts and/or important interest rate reductions that could have eventually prevented the debt default and, maybe, avoided the banking crisis and saved the Convertibility.

On the other hand, an important aspect that distinguishes the Argentine crisis is that it was more a progressive landslide—characterized by a combination of recession and deflationary adjustment—that ended in a collapse instead of a typical boom-and-crash episode. Probably, the long duration was related to the above-mentioned key role that Convertibility played in the Argentine economy and the relative (and apparent) soundness of the financial system.

With regard to the role of IMF, it is worth pointing out the contrast between the treatment Argentina received before and after the end of 2001. Throughout 2000, and in particular in 2001, the IMF led or supported different salvage trials and granted substantial loans to the country. The fact that Argentina was an apparent example of reform success during the 1990s might contribute to explain, among other factors, the abundant aid that was granted.

Given the evidence that the sociopolitic context of that time made it impossible to fulfill the conditions that, according to the IMF, were necessary for overcoming the crisis within the Convertibility program, in practice the institution precipitated the outcome of the crisis by denying some previously compromised funds at the end of 2001. At that moment, it was evident that the IMF accepted, was resigned (or even fostered?) not only a currency devaluation but also a debt restructuring.

Nevertheless, after the devaluation and the default declaration with private creditors the IMF applied an "exemplary punishment" strategy to Argentina, each time requiring new compromises that were mostly being accomplished by the Argentine government, were not enough to satisfy the institution's demands. Hence, during 2002, Argentina implemented some policies that were to a large extent influenced by the IMF recommendations but, curiously, did not receive any funds and in fact the country repaid previously contracted debts with the IMF and others multilateral institutions—see graph 6.2.

Therefore, unlike what happened in previous episodes in other countries, the management of the crisis was undertaken without any financial assistance from the institution (on the contrary, during 2002–2004 Argentina made net capital payments to the IMF of more than US$2.1 billion and to US$1.9 billion in interests, see Damill et al., 2005).

Finally, there is no doubt that the current recovery of the Argentine economy has been very important. The high rates of growth, the recovery of investment and consumption, the reduction in unemployment and in poverty rates, the debt restructuring process and a better management of the fiscal accounts are certainly good news. But to transform the recovery into a more sustainable growth and development process will require significant endeavors in many areas of the economic and social agenda and specially a systematic institutional building effort for improving the quality of the policymaking process and to reduce corruption, which remains at very high levels. Some observations on the policy agenda faced by Argentina in order to get long term sustainable growth are discussed in the next chapter.

CHAPTER 9

CONCLUSIONS AND POLICY IMPLICATIONS

The Elusive Quest for Growth in Argentina:
From the Postwar Development Consensus to the
Washington Consensus

In a country that has exhibited high political instability, deep economic volatility, and persistent institutional fragility (and in spite of the rich base of natural and human resources) it is hardly surprising to find a poor long-run economic and social performance. In fact, this was the outcome of the long period analyzed in this book.

However, two growth spurts took place during this epoch, the first in 1964–1974 and the second in 1991–1998. What were the determinants of growth in both spurts and what went wrong—what made it impossible to attain a sustainable growth process—are the key questions that this book has tried to answer.

The first growth spurt was mainly the result of an ambitious industrialization plan undertaken by a *desarrollista* (developmentalist) government that relied on the ideas of the Postwar Development Consensus. Although economic growth was substantial during this period, it took place in the middle of persistent inflation, severe distributional conflicts and recurrent balance of payment, and political crisis. Within this unfavorable framework, the manufacturing industry led the economic growth favored by protectionism and investment promotion policies. While the economy was virtually closed to imports of domestically produced final and intermediate goods, it was open to foreign direct investment and technology inflows, and duty-free capital goods imports were allowed under industrial promotion mechanisms. In turn, domestic innovative efforts were relatively low and mostly adaptive.

The entrepreneurial response to this incentives scheme was a substantial growth in investments—mainly undertaken by TNCs—which naturally led to a remarkable increase in industrial production capacity and employment. Pari passu, a technological learning process took place at the firm level and a local technological capability gradually accumulated in the manufacturing sector, which first allowed productivity gains—with growing industrial employment—and then increasing manufacturing exports—also favored by the reduction in the trade policy anti-export bias.

At the same time, the export-oriented agricultural sector left behind almost two decades of stagnation and resumed growth at a fast pace. In this scenario, by the end of the ISI period, it seemed possible that the "stop and go" cycles that had periodically affected the Argentine economy and exacerbated distributional conflicts could be finally overdue to an expanded export capacity.

However, some of the main structural problems of the ISI model were far from being resolved, including excessive levels of vertical integration, diseconomies of scale, and deficient quality of most manufacturing production. In this scenario, it is no surprise to find that GDP growth in 1962–1974 was mainly extensive, being based on factor accumulation, while TFP growth was only moderate.

Public policies in force during this period did little to attend these issues. Protectionism cum technology imports was the base of the "developmentalist" project, which aimed at "completing" the Argentine industrial structure by promoting investments in heavy- and capital-intensive sectors. Efficiency, quality, exports, or domestic technological development were, at best, secondary objectives, and it would be only in the late 1960s when some of those issues began to be addressed by public policies, although in an increasingly unstable political context. Institutional fragility also impaired public policies ability to deal with problems such as access to finance, given the frequent changes not only of public authorities but also of policy orientations.

Notwithstanding policy failures, as mentioned earlier, industrial productivity gradually improved and some ambitious technological projects were undertaken in sectors such as pharmaceuticals and electronics. Unfortunately, we are not able to guess whether this process—probably under a better designed industrial policy setting—would have finally led Argentina beget a more competitive manufacturing sector. Increasing political violence and growing macroeconomic turbulences paved the way for a military coup in 1976. The new economic policy after the coup meant a departure from the old regime and the beginning of a long recessionary period that lasted 15 years.

Between 1976 and 1981, in a context of ample international liquidity, an early "neoliberal" experiment in trade and financial liberalization was made by the military government. Trade liberalization took place in a context of growing appreciation of the domestic currency—the latter was used as an anti-inflationary tool. The outcome of this process was first irregular growth and finally a huge banking and currency crisis in 1981. A strong increase in income inequality also took place during this period.

The manufacturing industry was particularly affected by this policy setting, and a significant fall in industrial output and employment took place. However, while labor-intensive and knowledge-intensive activities were the most damaged, intermediate goods production—in which domestic conglomerates had a leading participation, often associated with military interests—were favored by industrial promotion policies and trade protection.

The 1981 crisis was soon followed by the foreign debt crisis, giving way to a huge recession and forcing another closure of the economy. All relevant economic indicators, except exports, showed a negative performance during the 1980s. The recessive and inflationary economic climate was hardly conducive for investment and productivity growth, and growing exports were to a large extent the outcome of investment projects designed during the late 1970s that found a much smaller domestic market than originally envisaged. The prevalence of high inflation rates and high macroeconomic volatility favored short-term speculative behavior and a strong preference for flexibility in economic agents. In turn, the dollar gradually replaced the peso as a store of value.

Return to democracy was the only good news in the 1980s—and naturally we cannot but highlight the enormous relevance of this fact in a country that for more than 50 years was periodically hit by military coups. Significant advances also took place in the enhancement of human rights protection, a field largely deteriorated by the illegal activities of the last military government. However, unfortunately, this neither led to a significant improvement in quality of the policymaking process nor to the end of political instability (as proven by the fact that President Alfonsín, the first president of the new democracy, had to resign some months before the end of his mandate).

After having gone through two hyperinflation crisis, price stabilization was finally attained in the early 1990s due to the adoption of the Convertibility Plan. At the same time, a far-reaching program of structural reforms, comprising trade liberalization (mild reforms on that direction had been adopted in late 1980s), privatizations, and market deregulation was implemented. FDI and technology transfer were completely liberalized—a task that had been initiated by the military government in 1976. Furthermore, Argentina aligned its domestic policies with international compromises assumed at the WTO, as well as with "best practices" norms as in the banking area (e.g., Basel regulations). The country also signed several investment treaties and joined Brazil, Paraguay, and Uruguay to create a (imperfect) customs union known as MERCOSUR.

The aims of this reforms package were to introduce a productivity shock in the Argentine economy as well as to gain reputation in the eye of foreign investors. Both objectives were attained. The growth spurt between 1991 and 1998 was led by TFP growth, although capital deepening also progressed at fast rates. FDI played a key role in this regard since it not only contributed to finance balance of payments—jointly with the more volatile portfolio inflows—but was also a key source of technology and productive modernization. Capital goods imports and technology transfer were also key channels for economic restructuring.

All major economic sectors grew during that period but nontradable activities performed better than tradable ones. Privatized services—including public utilities, energy, and fuels—showed substantial improvements in terms of productivity, quality, and increased supply, although often at the expense of high tariffs and weak regulations. Mining expanded as well due to a special incentives regime. The agricultural sector also boomed, due to the introduction of new technologies, including genetically modified organisms. However, many small farmers had to abandon production while the domestic contribution to technological modernization in agriculture was smaller than in previous stages—that is, most biological and mechanical innovations were largely imported.

As for the industrial sector, in the 1990s, it was more efficient but smaller and quite different from that of the ISI period. Product and process technologies were closer to the international frontier, but local innovative efforts, on average, were lower than in the ISI stage. Labor-intensive branches kept losing weight in the industrial structure, while resource processing and scale intensive sectors increased their share. Capital goods had a poor performance, especially after a 0 tariff for imports was adopted; the same happened with the few high tech activities that had survived after the ISI ended.

Whereas in the first growth spurt industrial labor productivity increased with growing occupation, this was not the case during the 1990s. Beyond a reduction in the number of manufacturing firms in the 1990s and the diffusion of subcontracting practices, this process of labor destruction was mainly due to the growing use of new labor-saving equipment and the implementation of organizational technologies that increased labor productivity, as well as to the output contraction in labor-intensive industries as a result of trade liberalization.

Labor destruction in manufacturing was not compensated by the growth of employment in services and in agriculture production, and in fact concurred with massive layoffs in the public sector as well as in privatized firms. This conjunction gave place to a substantial increase in the rate of unemployment, one of the key factors that contributed to gradually erode popular support to the reforms program.

Growing unemployment, poverty, and income inequality are surely the worst aspects of the 1990s legacy. Although structural reforms had a negative direct impact on those phenomena, their effects were amplified by the fact that low-income groups have often received poor quality education and have had low probabilities of getting higher educational qualifications.

In late 1998, GDP and TFP growth stopped. From then on until 2001 the economy entered into a recession that finally led to the biggest crisis in the country's history. As discussed in the previous chapter, the crisis was a combination of external and domestic factors. The crisis that affected East Asian countries, Russia, and Brazil were negative external shocks for the Argentine economy that affected exports earnings and led to a sudden stop in private financial flows. On the domestic side, there were large fiscal imbalances, high debt levels, and a lack of adjustment mechanisms derived from the existence of a currency board that was, at the same time, the core contractual device of economic and financial transactions. Hence, in this context exit costs from convertibility were perceived as too high even though an adjustment in the overvalued exchange rate was needed.

In this scenario, neither the increasingly weak De la Rua's government nor the IMF were able to prevent a systemic crisis that dissipated most of the growth in GDP per capita that had been achieved in 1991–1998. While it is obvious that the causes of the crisis were mainly macroeconomic and institutional, in our view the weaknesses of the microeconomic restructuring process induced by structural reforms also contributed to explain why the growth spurt of the 1990s was finally unsustainable.

The Microeconomics of the ISI and the 1990s: Similarities and Differences

We have just seen that the dynamics of the manufacturing industry was very different when one compares the two growth periods. This should not be a surprise in the light of dramatic changes that took place both in the domestic economic policy regime as well as in the international scenario. However, similarities—some of them perhaps unexpected—also arise. The main stylized facts regarding industrial firms' strategies and performance in both periods are highlighted below:

1. While industrial production was mainly oriented toward the domestic market, significant exports increases (mostly oriented toward Latin American countries) were attained in the second half of both growth spurts, as a result of the maturation of new investments and gradual productivity improvements.

However, productivity and competitiveness gains in both periods were not enough to produce a decisive transformation in the industrial sector and make it competitive at the world level, except for a handful of manufacturing plants in some natural resource and scale-intensive sectors.

2. In view of growing import penetration ratios, the degree of competition in manufacturing production in the 1990s was greater than during the ISI period, when import penetration was only significant in machinery and equipment. Nonetheless, the adoption of nontariff barriers and the lack of an effective antitrust legislation constrained the influence of imports as a competitive drive in several branches of the manufacturing sector.

3. A deep reduction in the degree of vertical integration of local production took place in the 1990s as compared with earlier periods, which allowed lower production costs. Firms were also able to achieve economies of specialization by reducing their product mix and complementing their local supply with imports of final products. This was at the cost of diminishing the intersectoral linkages that the industrial sector used to have in the past.

4. Foreign firms were key industrial restructuring actors during both growth spurts. In spite of domestic firms accounting for most of industrial production, TNCs affiliates dominated key branches, had higher productivity levels than domestic firms, and contributed to the bulk of investments in the manufacturing sector (in fact, during the 1990s their share in terms of sales, employment, and value added was substantially higher than in the ISI). In spite of the significant changes in the trade regime, most FDI in both periods was market-seeking. However, both export and import coefficients of TNCs affiliates increased during the 1990s, as a consequence of trade liberalization as well as of efficiency-seeking investments in some sectors.

5. Whereas in the first phase foreign firms made mostly greenfield investments (although sometimes with second-hand equipment), takeover of domestic firms were the predominant mode of entry for TNCs in the 1990s. Though these takeovers generally led to substantial productivity, quality, and export gains in acquired firms—naturally leading to improved business performance—this was at the cost of increasing industrial concentration and lower domestic linkages.

6. During the ISI period, FDI spillovers were mostly in the form of knowledge leakages coming from TNCs affiliates' introduction of technologies previously unknown in Argentina. In the 1990s—when the existence of rich databases allowed to perform this kind of analysis on the basis of econometric techniques—product innovation spillovers to domestic firms were found to be positive in the case of backward linkages. In contrast, no evidence on horizontal spillovers was found regarding variables such as productivity, trade, and innovation expenditures. Taken as a whole, these findings suggest that some positive FDI spillovers may arise when they also benefit

TNCs (as it is the case of backward spillovers, which indirectly benefit foreign affiliates insofar they allow higher technological capabilities in their suppliers).

7. Domestic conglomerates gradually increased their presence in the Argentine economy first in the ISI period and later on during the long recession between 1976 and 1990, when they acquired preeminence in industrial leadership. Reforms had a heterogeneous impact on these firms. While some of them disappeared or drastically shrank, others concentrated their business in their core activities to consolidate their positions in the domestic market. In some cases domestic groups also gained presence in foreign markets through exports as well as through FDI. In any case, they failed to play a role similar to that of the Japanese *keiretsu* or the Korean *chaebols* in the respective economic development processes of those countries.

8. The ISI environment was more favorable for SMEs development than the rules of game prevailing in the 1990s. While in both periods, on average, SMEs productivity, export, and innovative performance was weaker than that of large firms, and public policies often discriminated against them (in spite of some pro-SMEs initiatives launched in the 1990s), some key trends of the 1990s severely affected this group of firms. First, they were scarcely prepared for competition with imports as their technological, management, and marketing capabilities were weak. Second, in the 1990s, there was less room for technological imitation. Third, massive FDI inflows in a trade liberalization context resulted in lower linkages with domestic suppliers—especially affecting SMEs. Fourth, they had to adapt to new stringent requirements for market competition in areas such as quality and environmental management, without effective support from public policies. Fifth, adoption of stringent financial regulations and increasing presence of foreign banks reduced the already low possibilities of SMEs access to credit.

9. The main source of technological innovation and productivity improvements in both periods were inputs from abroad, in the form of imported capital goods, disembodied technologies transfer, and FDI. Imitation through "reverse engineering" and other means also took place, but it was seemingly more intense in the first growth period—to some extent, due to modifications in the intellectual property regime (e.g., acknowledgment of pharmaceutical patents), but also to changes in the domestic and international technological scenario.

10. Product and processes innovations in both stages were the outcome of firm level learning processes through which relevant tacit knowledge was acquired as well as of codified knowledge received from machinery suppliers, licensors, consulting firms, foreign partners, or from headquarters in the case of foreign firms. In contrast, linkages with local technology institutions were mostly absent in both periods.

11. The idiosyncratic technological efforts to adapt imported inputs and foreign products and to extend the life cycle of industrial machinery were quite important elements in the dynamics of innovation in the 1960s and early 1970s. These efforts, jointly with production and process engineering and labor organization improvements, were behind the productivity gains of that period. In the 1990s, in the context of domestic reforms and technology globalization in many sectors, there was less need of idiosyncratic efforts. At the same time, as mentioned earlier, there was less room for copying imported products.

12. However, substantial technological requirements arose from the modernization process that took place in the 1990s. They were related to the launching of new products, the adoption of modern production processes and organizational, advertising, and marketing techniques, the diffusion of quality improvements and the advances in environmental management. All these tasks implied human and financial resources allocated not only to acquire (mainly imported) knowledge but also to absorb and exploit it.

13. In this regard, it must be noted that performing innovation activities—in-house R&D and technology acquisition—enhanced the probability of becoming an innovator (i.e., of launching a new product of process). Continuous R&D efforts had a considerably larger impact on the probability of having an innovative output when compared to discontinuous expenditures. In turn, innovators performed better than noninnovators in terms of labor productivity.

On balance, shadows and lights are visible when analyzing the microeconomics of the ISI and that of the 1990s. During most of the ISI stage, the main objective of the industrial policy was to promote production without paying much attention to productivity, exports, or innovation (technology was considered something that could be "acquired" through FDI or capital goods imports). However, in spite of the lack of incentives from the public policy set and in a context of an excessively inward-oriented economic regime, a learning process took place that allowed significant productivity gains, growing exports of goods and technology, and the accumulation of innovation capabilities in many industrial sectors (even in some high-tech ones, such as pharmaceutical or electronics).

The limits of this process came mainly from the above mentioned features of the ISI: a set of public policies that stimulated production and investments without defining incentives for pursuit of productivity or quality gains and an industrialization strategy based on a much closed and relatively small domestic market. Furthermore, the lack of effective linkages between education and S&T policies, and the industrialization strategy was also an obstacle for building a competitive manufacturing sector.

During the 1990s, the economic policy setting supposedly aimed at efficiency and modernization. Trade liberalization jointly with access to state-of-the-art technology (through FDI, capital goods imports, technology licenses, and so on) would give both the incentives as well as the means to improve productivity and gain competitiveness. These processes effectively took place in the industrial sector, but favoring mostly large and/or foreign owned firms. In turn, SMEs had a very heterogeneous performance. While many of them shrank, went bankrupt or sold their businesses, others were able to survive and expand through innovation activities and the reaping of positive spillovers from FDI presence.

On balance, industrial sector restructuring was far from the expectations of reformers and led, among other negative consequences, to high levels of unemployment. The reasons behind this outcome are many, but in our view emphasis must be placed on three of them: (1) industrial firms had accumulated very different levels of productive, organizational and technological capabilities prior to the reforms and hence were not in the same position to face the challenge of modernization and restructuring; (2) in previous years firms had to survive in a scenario characterized by high levels of macroeconomic and institutional volatility and uncertainty; when reforms came they had to abruptly change their strategies and search for other package of assets—for example, new technologies, quality and environmental improvements— so as to survive and make progress in a new context in which previously accumulated capabilities and routines that were well fit with the rules of the game of the 1980s were no longer useful; (3) existing public policies addressed adequately neither the specific need to assist firms to adapt to the new rules of the game nor the existence of market and coordination failures in fields such as technology, human capital, and finance. The next section, among other issues, analyzes this policy failure.

The Role of Public Policies

A stable macroeconomic environment, avoiding sharp cyclical fluctuations, is an essential prerequisite for productivity improvements. Unfortunately, macroeconomic policies have often been unable to meet that goal in Argentina. Volatility and uncertainty, on the contrary, have been present during most of the period under analysis, hence negatively affecting productivity through their effects on the economic agents' behavior—that is, inducing a preference for short-term strategies and precluding long-term commitments.

A particularly relevant aspect of macroeconomic policy in a country like Argentina is exchange rate. Periodical devaluations leading to huge income redistributions marked the "stop and go" cycles that characterized the

Argentine economy during the ISI period. In 1976–1981, the exchange rate was used to contain inflation, failing to meet that objective and provoked a dramatic financial and economic crisis. In a context of very high inflation rates, exchange rate management was extremely difficult in the 1980s. The currency board in the 1990s was certainly a good instrument for eliminating inflation but proved at the end to be very difficult to sustain in a world of volatile capital flows and external shocks.

Beyond the determinant influence of the macroeconomic environment, trade and foreign investment regimes have been, by far, the policies that have contributed the most to shape the evolution of the Argentine growth and productivity record in the long run.

During the ISI period incentives coming from import competition were absent. This favored industrial expansion but at the cost of not providing enough stimuli for productivity growth and quality improvements. Since selectivity and temporality criteria were absent, and protection was granted without quid pro quo commitments by favored firms and sectors, it is no wonder to find many cases of "eternal" infant industries. The excessively inward-oriented policy of the time also precluded attaining scale economies needed to compete internationally and led to higher than desirable vertical integration levels. Although exports promotion regimes were available since late 1960s—as a means to mitigate the anti-export bias of the protectionist regime—no evidence is available on their effective impact on the growth of industrial exports observed at the time. Their lack of stability in the light of budget restrictions and frequent economic policy shifts surely helped to reduce their impact.

Industrial promotion regimes were the other "big policy" during the ISI stage. They undoubtedly favored massive—mainly foreign—investments during the "developmentalist" government and since then until late 1980s most large industrial investments in Argentina were undertaken under the auspices of some kind of special incentive regime. Beyond their often very high fiscal cost, these regimes were mostly aimed at promoting productive capacity enlargement, and they seldom established performance requirements commitments—that is, in terms of productivity, exports, technological development, and others. Productive and technology learning processes observed at the firm level were largely spontaneous events. Hence, although they played a positive role for investments in a scenario in which access to long-term finance was absent and institutional and macroeconomic uncertainty prevailed, they largely failed to build a competitive industrial sector (except in some natural resource intensive activities).

After 1976, a trade liberalization experiment took place. As it mixed proefficiency with anti-inflation goals, and was adopted in a context of overvalued peso, it was no wonder that it finally had negative consequences on the manufacturing sector. Later on, the economy was closed by macroeconomic reasons. However, contrary to what happened in the ISI period, protectionism went pari passu with a chaotic and recessive macro-economic environment, hence failing to provide any stimulus for industrial development.

In turn, various kinds of investment and export promotion regimes were available during most of the 1976–1990 period. Since their above mentioned weaknesses were far from being resolved, it comes as no surprise to find that the available evaluations on their impact are mostly negative.

In the 1990s, a deep and rapid trade liberalization process was implemented. Some of its key objectives were met. On one hand, greater competition in the local market due to the entry of imports competing with domestically produced goods was a major incentive for inducing productivity improvements in tradable sectors. On the other hand, capital goods imports were a major source of technology modernization. Trade liberalization was especially successful in helping the technological modernization of the agricultural sector, which boomed since mid-1990s.

However, trade liberalization had also negative consequences. First, it was implemented in a drastic way, in a scenario in which the industrial sector had gone through more than a decade of contraction and private firms had developed strategies and routines adapted to survive in a closed and volatile economy. Second, no complementary policies were adopted—or when they were, their real impact was marginal—to help industrial firms adapt to the new scenario. Hence, a sort of perverse Darwinian selection took place, which led to the closure of several—mainly small and medium—firms and to the contraction of high-tech and skilled and nonskilled labor-intensive industrial branches.

Naturally, manufacturing firms affected by trade liberalization often resorted to lobbying actions to obtain protection against imports. The proliferation of antidumping, safeguards, and other nontariff barriers illustrates how these pressures were successful in many cases. The special protection for the automotive sector is another example in the same direction. "Contamination" of tariff policy with macroeconomic objectives also contributed to distort signals coming from the trade liberalization process.

A number of WTO-compatible export promotion policies were in force during the 1990s. A relevant innovation in this area was the adoption of a so-called "mirror" criterion that equalized export reimbursements with tariffs paid by the same items. However, this instrument, jointly with others such as indirect taxes refunding, were often subject to changes and delays in their operation due mostly to fiscal restrictions and were not linked with other enterprise and technology policies in place during the same period.

MERCOSUR creation favored access to a huge market for Argentine exports making possible to attain scale and specialization economies that were hardly feasible in the domestic market. In fact, it was so successful in the trade arena that led to a high concentration of Argentine exports in the Brazilian market. However, the lack of macroeconomic coordination and the difficulties in making progress in the negotiation of nontariff barriers regimes, investment policies, and other "deep integration" issues turned MERCOSUR from a big opportunity to a source of conflicts, especially after the Brazilian devaluation in early 1999.

Depending on the level of economic activity in each country, real foreign exchange rate fluctuations and individual sectors competitiveness levels, integration with Brazil was sometimes an inducement for productivity gains and sometimes a source of problems that led to a variety of trade conflicts. Unfortunately, little progress was made to go beyond defensive trade policies to deal with these problems, since MERCOSUR never had regional instruments in the areas of industrial, export, technology, and enterprise policies.

Investment promotion regimes were almost completely eliminated in the 1990s. Following the terminology proposed by Oman (1999), a sort of "rules based competition" for investments was followed, through macroeconomic stability, privatizations, trade liberalization, and an "investor friendly" legal regime. No regulations on FDI entrance or on TNCs affiliates activities were put in place. Within the manufacturing industry, only in the automobile sector was there some kind of sectoral preference for investment attraction (privatizations, mining, and forestry regimes also led to sectoral biases in the investment attraction policy).

The automobile regime is a good example of failures in the design and implementation of public policies in Argentina. It contained a novel system for encouraging model specialization through increasing foreign trade flows, but aimed at the same time at keeping a balance between imports and exports. Later on a common trade regime was negotiated with Brazil. This regime was plagued by discussions on issues such as investment diversion, local content requirements and mechanisms to deal with the impact of changes in macroeconomic policies on bilateral trade. It also failed to design a strategy that could lead to a procompetitive restructuring of the MERCOSUR automobile industry as a whole. Furthermore, while the motor vehicles regime encouraged substantial investments by TNCs, it also led to excess capacity and induced investments that mostly aimed at taking advantage of the regime incentives without having real perspectives of surviving in a liberalized market—a similar picture arose soon after the first automobile regime was adopted in late 1950s. At the same time no attention was paid to strengthen backward linkages. The low magnitude of

R&D activities performed by affiliates in Argentina as a consequence of regional sectoral restructuring was not a matter of concern for the economic authorities. Furthermore, automobile firms did not always meet the assumed commitments, and although penalties were foreseen in such an event, in the end they were not made effective.

In fact, the lack of attention to issues such as the need of fostering domestic linkages and enhancing endogenous innovation capability was a common feature of most economic policies adopted at the time. This is no surprise since one of the cornerstones of the economic policy regime prevailing during this period was that the key inputs for technological modernization were to come from abroad—in the form of FDI, capital goods, or intangible technology transfer. The notable increases in these three channels testify that the aim of reformers was met, although this success was not enough as to bring forth a sustainable development path for the economy as a whole.

Nonetheless the above mentioned basic features of the economic policy regime of the 1990s, the difficulties experienced by many firms to adapt to the new rules of the game and the dramatic growth in unemployment led the government to launch a number of enterprise and technology policies mostly aimed at dealing with market failures in areas such as credit access, information, technology development, and others, as well as to facilitate access of SMEs to foreign markets and their linkages with domestic consultancy and technology services.

Although most of those initiatives had a sound theoretical rationale and were based on the imitation of best international practices, they seem to have failed in having a significant impact on its expected clientele performance. Hence, in spite of the existence of those initiatives, surviving and making progress during the 1990s was mostly dependant on each firms' capabilities to adapt to the new scenario. According to the available evidence, the main factors that led to this outcome include:

1. Enterprise and technology policies had no priority for the national government and were not part of a long-term strategy in which the public and private sectors engaged in a shared procompetitive restructuring policy process.
2. They were often based on a parallel bureaucracy financed through multilateral agencies programs. Programs' continuity over time was threatened by uncertainty about finance sources and risk of being eliminated and changed by new authorities with other priorities. Naturally, the policy learning process was impaired by these factors.
3. Lack of coordination among the several agencies in charge of them. This institutional fragmentation prevented from taking advantage of

synergies among the different programs led to duplicated bureaucratic structures and often precluded firms from getting a comprehensive diagnosis of their problems and the possible solutions.

4. Lack of evaluation mechanisms to learn about their effectiveness.
5. Excessive emphasis on horizontal policies and assistance to individual firms, while the importance of clusters type of support was acknowledged only after the crack of the Convertibility Plan.

In turn, old and new problems faced by the Argentine economy were not adequately resolved. Among the new problems, the environmental dimension of industrial restructuring was omitted by the government, as environmental regulations were not complemented or linked to existing enterprise and technology policies.

In the case of old problems, the lack of effective linkages between the S&T public institutions and the educational system with the requirements of productive and technological development in the private sector was far from being solved. Furthermore, the once acknowledged quality of Argentine education, which granted the country a privileged position among developing countries, has been eroding dramatically in recent decades and hence its negative contribution to productivity growth.

In the finance area, problems detected during the ISI period such as insufficient financial deepening, the absence of a well-developed domestic capital market and pervasive banking system market failures that prevented many viable firms and projects access to credit did not show signs of improvement in the 1990s. While large firms had access to international finance sources, SMEs were the most affected by these problems.

On balance, in our view the Argentine experience of the 1990s illustrates the benefits, costs, and limits of a mainly market-driven restructuring process. What would have happened in a scenario with more and better designed policies? Notwithstanding the fact that counterfactual analysis are always subject to controversy, available evidence on the "microeconomics" of the reforms suggests that policies aimed at enhancing absorption capabilities and removing obstacles for undertaking innovation activities in domestic firms would have allowed many more firms to survive and expand productivity during the 1990s—a fact that would probably translate into lower unemployment levels.

From the international experience we can also suggest that policies fostering more linkages and collaborative efforts among firms in the different value chains—as well as with organizations related with those chains such as S&T institutions, universities, and so on—would have led to better results than those applied in Argentina, which mostly aimed at helping individual firms. Other areas in which much could have been learned from international experience include environmental policies and finance. In the latter case, seed and venture capital systems are notably underdeveloped—and, in general, entrepreneurship promotion schemes hardly exist.

The lack of policies oriented toward promoting TNCs linkages with domestic suppliers, clients, and S&T organizations, inducing their affiliates to engage in R&D and other innovation activities and improving their export performance—as well as that of their suppliers and customers—are all missed opportunities that could have been better exploited in the wake of the FDI boom of the 1990s.

The Challenges in the PostCrisis Scenario

After the 2001–2002 crisis, the debt default and the megadevaluation, the main government priorities were to avoid hyperinflation, to assist the large number of people who had fallen into poverty, and to deal with the effects of the contractual breakdown that followed the end of the Convertibility scheme.

On the basis of a prudential fiscal and monetary policy, in combination with different measures aimed at controlling some key domestic prices, the danger of hyperinflation was avoided and inflation rates remained at relatively low levels after 2002. Growth was resumed in 2003 and has remained at very high levels since then. These objectives were attained without any financial assistance from the IMF—a key difference with other systemic crisis in emergent markets—and in fact, the Argentine government made net payments to the IMF in all years after the crisis until the entire debt with the organization was paid off at the beginning of 2006.

As for contractual breakdown, the government managed to arrange an agreement with most of the foreign debt holders that has reduced the burden of paying the debt services. In turn, on the domestic side, the worst consequences of the banking crisis have been mostly overcome. In contrast, price freezing in privatized firms is still an unsolved problem which has led to several suits against the Argentine government.

A massive plan of subsidies to poor families helped to deal with the immediate worst consequences of the crisis, and unemployment has been steadily falling thanks to economic growth. However, it still remains at high levels, while improvements in poverty and income inequality have been weak. These are very relevant problems that need to be addressed with more emphasis by the government.

In order to achieve sustained growth, the current policy of keeping a stable and high RER is perhaps a necessary condition, but it is not enough for promoting significant long run productivity gains in the productive sector, without which growth will ineluctably decelerate sooner than later.

The continuity of the current process of exports growth is also dependant on improvements in productivity and technology. The right set of public policies is required to attain those objectives.

After the end of the Convertibility Plan, import trade policy has not been very different from that of the 1990s, although the government is now more prone to adopt nontariff barriers in sector competing with imports (note must be taken that industry is more protected from imports than it was in the 1990s through the high exchange rate). While export promotion efforts seem more articulated than in the past, the lack of a capital market and the widespread presence of market failures in the financial system have not yet been effectively addressed. Some initiatives have been taken in the area of investment promotion, but with limited resources. SMEs policy is also mostly a continuation of initiatives that had been taken in the late 1990s.

Some good news has arisen in the area of education, where the government is currently more conscious of the need of allocating far more financial resources and to fostering more effective linkages between the educational system and the demands of the productive and technological development. The launching of a law fostering the software and information services sector through fiscal incentives linked to firms' commitments in terms of R&D, exports and quality, is also a step in the right direction. More generally, in the technology area there seems to be a more active approach, partly based on instruments introduced in the 1990s (now with more funds) but also on a more focused approach in sectoral terms. Nevertheless, no development strategy or long-term vision has emerged so far, a serious failure that cannot only be attributed to the short time that has passed since the last crisis.

In this scenario, a potentially valuable initiative has been launched in 2003. Several competitiveness fora were established in the Secretary of Industry, Trade and SMEs since that year, on the basis of a cluster approach, incorporating all relevant agents and organizations related with each value chain and paying attention to a wide set of specific issues relevant for each sector including human capital requirements, technological needs, and so on. Although most of these fora have limited human and financial resources, they are far from being at the top of the economic policy agenda and are not yet integrated in any strategic vision for the medium and long run; this is certainly good news. They could be one of the basis to revert what is certainly a historical bad record in terms of policy-making in Argentina (as it is shown by the experience of the software and information services forum).

Finally, the Argentine experience, as well as the lessons from the received international literature, suggests that without institutional building and macroeconomic stability, even the best designed public policy is probably doomed to failure, since policymaking is a learning process—by public authorities as well as by the private sector directly related with the respective instruments—that requires continuity in order to lead to positive outcomes. Argentina has much to improve in this area, as the institutional foundations of the policymaking process are still very weak and public policies largely lack credibility, stability, and coherence and are often poorly implemented. State capabilities also need to be dramatically enhanced, since the country is far from having a stable and efficient bureaucracy—a lack that is generally replaced with a temporal parallel staff whose term matches that of the public official who appointed them—and coherence and coordination among the different government areas are seldom attained.

In our judgment, State restructuring is then a top priority in the economic development agenda of Argentina, a task that unfortunately has not yet been addressed in the current economic recovery.

NOTES

Chapter 1 Introduction: The End of Panaceas; from the Postwar Consensus to the Post–Washington Consensus

1. Rosenstein-Rodan was one of the economists who along with Hirschman, Nurkse, Lewis, Myrdal, and others, contributed to the creation of the "high development theory" that emerged in the 1940s and 1950s. Some of those ideas have been formalized recently, as in the case of the "Big Push" hypothesis (Murphy, Shleifer, and Vishny, pp. 1003–1026, 1989). In Krugman's (1993) view, formalization allows modern economists to understand the arguments of the old "development theorists."

2. The Second Five Year Plan implemented in India (1951–1956) was probably the more comprehensive of the Five Year Plans. Self-reliant industrialization (including self-reliance in capital goods) was the key objective of the Indian plan.

3. Prebisch was the second executive secretary of the Economic Commission for Latin America and the Caribbean (ECLAC), which would become one of the leading centers of the "structuralist" approach.

4. As stated by Waterbury (1999), even the United States endorsed the need of an ISI strategy in developing countries and shared the "export pessimism" argument.

5. Oman and Wignaraja (1991) report that, as acknowledged by some ECLAC's members, the State itself did not constitute a subject of analysis at ECLAC during the ISI stage.

6. At the same time, the technical difficulties in implementing ambitious planning exercises soon proved to be enormous and led to the emergence of a literature on the "crisis in planning" (Little, 1982).

7. The proportion of people living in absolute poverty in developing countries had been falling in the previous two decades but since population grew the number of people in absolute poverty increased. The most striking advances have been observed in health—average life expectancy in low income countries had increased 15 years over the previous 3 decades—(World Bank, 1981).

8. "The point is not the same as saying that growth does not matter. It may matter a great deal, but, if it does, this is because of some associated benefits that are realized in the process of economic growth" (Sen, 1983, pp. 753).

9. Cárdenas, Ocampo, and Thorp (2000) argue that the term "ISI" is inappropriate. They suggest that "State-led industrialization" is more accurate and they also rightly stress that governments changed their policies during this period rather than following a constant model throughout.

10. In this context, it is not surprising that the leading Latin American countries were unable to become relevant players in the production of any significant segment within the emerging electronic and telecommunications technologies complex (with the possible exception of minicomputer production in Brazil, see Evans 1995) in sharp contrast to the "Asian Tigers."

11. The ISI model was also criticized by some of its early proponents (Hirschman, 1968), as well as by "dependency" theorists, who called for more State intervention and less integration within the world economy—in some cases they even advocated for an across-the-board rupture with capitalism—(Cardoso and Faletto, 1969; Frank, 1969). See also Hirschman (1981), Sen (1983), and Krugman (1993) for interesting assessments of the PWDC.

12. The neoclassical interpretation of the East Asian development experience was not only strongly criticized by Amsden (1989) in his book on South Korea but also by Wade (1990) in his book on Taiwan. It was also criticized by the World Bank staff in the book on the East Asian miracle (World Bank, 1993) in which the equalitarian pattern of the growth process was also duly acknowledged.

13. Another important factor in the triumph of the WC was the enormous influence of the professional economists trained in the top U.S. universities who, back in their countries of origin, attained important research (in think tanks and leading universities) and government positions. They considered the WC as conventional wisdom on what is to be done to put Latin American countries into a growth path (see Bouzas and Ffrench Davis, 2005).

14. The more popular use of the term "WC" is in its "neoliberal" sense, though as Williamson (2003) tries to explain, there are large differences between the WC and the kind of neoliberalism promoted by authors such as Friedman and Hayek. As rightly suggested by Naim (2002), there is much confusion in the use of the term WC, which has become something of a "damaged brand."

15. Chile, Bolivia, Argentina, and Peru are considered aggressive reformers while Mexico, Costa Rica, Jamaica, Colombia, and Brazil are classified as cautious reformers by Stallings and Peres (2000). The differences between the two groups were closely correlated with initial conditions (such as inflation rates, GDP growth, economic distortions, and institutional settings)—see Forteza and Tommasi (2005) for the stylized facts of the reform process in eight Latin American countries studied in a project of the Global Development Network.

16. The average growth rate in 1990–2003 was 2.6% a year, less than half the record for the ISI period—5.5% a year between 1950 and 1980—(Ocampo, 2004).

17. Point five of the WC recommendation states that developing countries need a unified exchange rate at a level sufficiently competitive to induce a rapid growth in nontraditional exports (Williamson, 1990).

18. "Mistaken macroeconomic policies—a fixed exchange rate to reduce inflation regardless of the loss of competitiveness this entailed, combined with relative freedom for capital inflows and financial deregulation without effective supervision—led to the disaster of the 1982 collapse" (Williamson, 2003, p. 307, referring to the Chilean crisis.).

19. Williamson not only acknowledges that the original WC did not emphasize crisis avoidance but it also recognizes that the WC "was indeed guilty of a reckless enthusiasm for capital account liberalization" (Williamson, 2003, p. 328).

20. See Roubini and Steter (2004) for a comprehensive analysis of the vulnerabilities in emerging economies that are the root of the crises analyzed here as well as of other crises (Ukrania, Pakistan, Turkey, Ecuador, and Uruguay). They also provide a good summary of the academic discussion on first, second, and third generation models of financial crises.

21. See the "A post-Washington Consensus? The End of Development Panaceas" section for a review of the debates on the link between institutions and development.

22. See Ocampo (2004) for a critique of this approach.

23. See Haussman et al. (2005), who show that the mix of goods that a country produces may have important implications for economic growth.

24. Acemoglu et al. (2001) devised a way to avoid this problem by using an instrumental variable approach, though this procedure has not been exempt of criticisms (see Albouy, 2004)

Chapter 2   Argentina's Economy in a
Long-Term View

*There are some important books devoted to the analysis of the Argentine economy in the nineteenth and twentieth centuries. The classic study by Díaz Alejandro (1975) is a key reference in this regard. See also Cortés Conde (1997) and Della Paolera and Taylor (2003).

1. According to Della Paolera and Taylor (2003), Argentina's per capita income had risen from about 67% of developed country levels (a weighted average of Western Europe, Western offshoots, and Japan) in 1870, to 90% in 1900, and 100% in 1913. For all practical purposes they considered Argentina an advanced country. In graph 2.1 a different sample of countries is used for the purpose of comparison, but the main trends are the same as those reported by Della Paolera and Taylor.

2. In order to avoid distortions in long-run comparisons, Gerchunoff and Llach (2003)—on whose data graph 2.2 is based—use exports and imports in the numerator and tradable production in the denominator. This allows them to eliminate the bias that could come from the inclusion of services, whose share in the Argentine economy has grown throughout the twentieth century.

3. Total population increased from 21.3 million in 1962 to 36.8 million in 2000.

4. Note must be taken that data on GDP in 1993 constant pesos for years before 1993 are unofficial and differ among sources (there was a change on the base year on which GDP data are estimated in 1993). Other sources show a small decline in GDP between 1975 and 1990.

5. See Chen (1997), Felipe (1999), Felipe and McCombie (2004), and Hulten (2000) for an analysis about the TFP concept and the difficulties faced when defining the best method to measure it.

6. Hopenhayn and Neumeyer (2003).

7. Rauch and Evans (2000) rank Argentina in the bottom 5 among 35 developing countries in terms of quality of bureaucracy as quoted in Spiller and Tommasi (2003).

Chapter 3   The Import-Substitution Industrialization, 1962–1974

1. In order to reduce the anti-export bias derived from the tariff structure, the drawback and temporary admission regimes were established in 1962–1963. During these years promotional credit lines for industrial exports were also implemented for the first time in the country's history.

2. Industrial promotion policies granted generous fiscal and credit subsidies as well as duty-free imports of capital goods.

3. The manufacturing sectors with the highest increases in exports were automobiles, machine tools, agricultural machinery, capital goods for the food industry, chemicals and petrochemicals, steel products, and calculation machines.

4. High transaction costs in a context of macroeconomic instability and import restrictions also contribute to explain why vertical integration levels were high.

5. The university enrollment was mainly oriented toward "liberal" professions— as it had occurred in earlier periods. Compared with other countries, Argentina showed low enrollment rates in careers related to pure and applied sciences—including noncivil engineering—and high rates in medicine and law (OECD, 1967). In turn, there was a lack of high-quality technical education at secondary level.

6. This ratio was obtained by dividing the total R&D expenditures by the total gross production value of the surveyed firms.

7. This ratio was estimated as explained in footnote 6.

8. There were also suspicions that payments for technology items could include disguised profit remittances between affiliates and their parent companies.

9. Local pharmaceutical firms spent proportionally more in R&D than TNC affiliates in the same sector (1.6 versus 1.1% in 1972). The pharmaceutical sector also spent the most in R&D in the manufacturing industry (Chudnovsky, 1976; Arce et al., 1968). In the 1970s, a group of national laboratories was vertically integrated into the production of active principles or pharmaceutical raw materials through small multipurpose plants in which they produced limited amounts for their own use in specialties under their

own trademarks (Burachik and Katz, 1997). An important technological capacity was developed in antibiotic fermentation and teams to develop process innovations at plant level were consolidated. As a result, productivity grew and the firms gradually started to export. This process was interrupted in the second half of the 1970s, when the acceleration of technological change at world level made it difficult for local producers to follow the innovation patterns of firms at international level. Even though this industry was born in the 1950s with production scales similar to the international ones, diseconomies of scale eventually appeared. Capital equipment obsolescence also emerged due, in part, to the high cost of imported capital goods. The lack of strong interaction among the different stakeholders in the knowledge base in this sector (private firms, universities, public laboratories) also explains the gradual slackening of the innovation path. Last but not the least, the liberalization process cum foreign currency undervaluation that started in 1977 meant the coup de grace for the most ambitious vertical integration and technology development strategies in this industry.

10. FATE's technological strategy was based on the avoidance of licenses and trademark payments and focused on finding and exploiting nonproprietary technological information. This included visits to other countries, and the training of its technicians in excellence centers, such as the Massachusetts Institute of Technology (MIT). The firm spent up to 7% of its sales in R&D. In turn, it was in contact with local Science and Technology (S&T) institutions such as the National Commission of Atomic Energy (CNEA), the National Institute of Industrial Technology (INTI), and the University of La Plata. The firm produced some microcomputers and the prototype of a medium-sized computer. However, there are discrepancies among analysts about the ability of this computer to be competitive in the market. Furthermore, software development and marketing activities were poor (Adler, 1987). In any event, the project was cancelled in 1976, due to problems internal to the firm and the unwillingness of the new government to support this kind of infant industry.

11. While the R&D/sales ratio in large firms in Argentine industry was around 20% of the same ratio in the U.S. industry, in the case of the aforementioned sectors that ratio did not exceed 13% (Katz, 1972).

12. To illustrate these efforts, it is worth quoting at some length a paper by Cimoli and Katz (2003). "Launching the Ford Taunus to the Argentine market, back in 1974, demanded some 300 thousand hours of domestic engineering efforts carried out by a local team of 120 professionals employed by Ford's Engineering Department. These people were responsible for generating a steady flow of incremental units of production organization and engineering knowledge required for the adaptation of the German-designed 'blue prints' to the local environment, to the available raw materials, to the idiosyncrasies of the Argentine plant—not bigger than 10% of Ford's production facilities in Germany—to the technological capabilities of domestic subcontractors producing parts and components for the referred vehicle, and so forth. One-and-a-half year of domestic engineering activities were

required in order to introduce changes and adaptations in the design of the vehicle, in production planning and organization routines, in the technologies employed by local subcontractors for the production of parts and components, and so on before the car could be brought to the market. Domestic content for such car was close to 90% of the total value of the vehicle. Nearly 400 subcontractors supplied parts and components under Ford's stringent specifications. Direct expenditure in the above-mentioned engineering efforts was in the order of U\$S6 million in activities that would normally classify as 'development' expenditure in contemporary R&D statistics."

13. Market-seeking investments are aimed at exploiting the host country's market—and, eventually, neighboring countries' markets—(Dunning, 1993).

14. In 1977, U.S. TNC affiliates in Argentina exported 15.4% of their sales (Kosacoff and Azpiazu, 1989). At the time, the average for all U.S. TNC affiliates in the world was 38% (data from the Bureau of Economic Analysis of the U.S. government).

15. For example, IBM exported its production to affiliates in Japan, Switzerland, and Canada, among other countries. Exports included, for example, printers, perforating machines, and card classifiers.

16. Among the several cases analyzed in the received literature, the learning experience of Turri, a producer of machine tools, is among the most interesting ones (see Castaño et al., 1981 for a detailed analysis).

17. These conglomerates usually had a high level of diversification, including not only industrial, but also agricultural and service activities. They also often owned banks or investment companies to help the finances of the whole group. This gave them a relevant differential advantage vis-à-vis other agents in a context in which the access to finance was restricted (Lewis, 1993).

18. The aforementioned experiences of FATE, along with that of the local pharmaceutical companies, are perhaps the main exceptions to this rule.

19. See López (1997) for a description of industrial promotion initiatives in the petrochemical sector, one of the most favored by this regime.

20. Even the name of the bank was changed to National Bank of Development (BANADE).

21. Between 1967 and 1976, BANADE had 11 presidents and none of the over 40 directors appointed during those years completed their 3-year term (Rougier, 2003).

22. In their influential account of the Argentine industrialization process, Katz and Kosacoff (1989) do not make a single mention about the role of INTI.

23. These groups, founded in 1960, were integrated by farmers from the west of the Buenos Aires province and their objective was to develop and diffuse better agricultural and livestock handling techniques.

24. According to Barsky et al. (1988), the expansion of agriculture between 1960 and 1973 was due to the diffusion of hybrids, as they allowed substantial production increases without demanding large investments or changes in the productive structure.

25. This process of technology modernization often required domestic research efforts. In soybean, for example, it was necessary to develop research activities

on the characteristics of the imported varieties to adapt them to different ecological zones.

26. It must be noted that, until the 1930s, agricultural yields in Argentina were similar to those in the United States.

Chapter 4   The Long Recession, 1975–1990

1. Law No. 21,382 guaranteed equal treatment of foreign and domestic investors and the free remittance of profits and principals.

2. It is important to mention that several sectors producing intermediate goods continued to be protected through nontariff measures and benefited from subsidies under the national industrial promotion law (see note 3). The Armed Forces had a direct influence on these sectors, both through the ownership of some industrial firms as well as through the control of regulatory schemes, a fact that could well explain why they were exempted from trade liberalization.

3. The program, adopted in December 1978, envisaged a progressive reduction in tariffs (and a reduction in their dispersion) up to an average level of 20% in 1984. However, in practice, the government modified the program accelerating the rate of reduction in tariffs. For example, the tariff for capital goods was reduced to 0% soon after liberalization was launched. Furthermore, the program was used as a short-term policy instrument, as the government was allowed to reduce tariffs in the presence of monopolistic practices that could have negative effects on inflation.

4. In this connection, it is important to mention that besides the payment of interests on the external debt (reduced to a half in successive renegotiations), the subsidies to the private sector from the industrial promotion schemes were another key component of the fiscal deficit. While debt servicing amounted to 5% of the GDP in the period 1985–1988 (Machinea, 1990), industrial promotion subsidies amounted to 2.6 of the GDP in 1986.

5. Overall unemployment stayed at low levels during this period due to employment absorption in other sectors (notably, services).

6. The main source of credit for acquiring capital goods during this decade were some special lines granted by foreign governments (see the following issues in this chapter).

7. In this connection, in late 1987, the government sent a project proposal to the Parliament in order to modify the industrial promotion schemes with the aim of increasing transparency and reducing the fiscal costs. The proposal was approved, with some changes, a year later.

8. Many new industrial plants, especially in the intermediate goods sectors, such as steel and petrochemicals, had to begin exporting because actual domestic demand was lower than that expected at the time when the respective investment decisions were taken.

9. Machine tools were one of the segments of the manufacturing industry in which Argentine firms did well in the preferential trade agreement with Brazil (Chudnovsky and Erber, 1999).

10. Interestingly, in this case, instead of leading to an anti-export bias, domestic market protection functioned, in a context of economic recession, as a nonplanned export-promotion tool.

Chapter 5   Structural Reforms and Complementary Policies during the 1990s

1. One of the pillars of the Convertibility Plan was the separation of the Central Bank from the nonfinancial public sector, establishing it as an independent monetary authority. The 1991 Convertibility Law created a money-creation rule that effectively limited monetary policy and Central Bank's financing of public sector deficits. In September 1992, a new law strengthened the Central Bank's autonomy and further restricted its ability to extend credit to the government.
2. See Gerchunoff and Torre (1996) for a good analysis of the political and economic conditions explaining the manner in which Menem's government launched the structural reforms in a country with such macroeconomic instability.
3. The 1989 State Reform Act (No. 23,696) set the legal framework to carry forward the privatization process. It presided over the transfer to the private sector of the vast majority of the public sector firms in areas as diverse as telecommunications, ports, energy, airlines, electricity generation and distribution, railways, and sanitation. The transfers were made either through sales or concession contracts.
4. While some analysts attributed State enterprise failures to the intrinsic inefficiency of State management, others stated that they had been weakened by lack of investment resources (due to fiscal restrictions) and the political influence on their tariff structures (which had been used as an anti-inflationary tool for many years).
5. Alfonsín's government had tried to partially privatize some State enterprises by finding private partners, but it found fierce opposition from the Peronist Party, which one or two years later was to approve the 1989 State Reform Act (No. 23,696).
6. Some privatizations, in fact, involved subsidies from the government in order to attract investors (passenger railways, for instance)—foreign firms seldom entered into this kind of privatization, which mostly attracted domestic companies.
7. Employment in former State enterprises decreased by approximately 40% after privatization. YPF, for instance, reduced its personnel from 36,935 to 9,350 employees.
8. A tax refund of 15% to the buyers of domestic capital goods was established to compensate local capital goods producers for trade liberalization in their sector, but its implementation suffered many delays and was very complex, which caused the regime to have limited real benefits for local firms (see Sirlin, 1997).

9. In spite of this compromise, in the following years the Argentine government introduced different regimes that established lower tariffs for imports of capital goods not produced in MERCOSUR and in 2001 the 0 rate for capital goods imports was adopted once again.

10. Even though the supposed aim of the statistical tax was to contribute to finance data collection on foreign trade, it is clear from its high levels that in practice it worked as a nontariff extra charge.

11. The main sectors involved in trade conflicts were dairy products, pigs and hogs, chicken, textiles, steel, wheat, and rice.

12. Patent applications in Argentina increased by 128% between 1990 and 2002. However, almost the entire increase was due to applications by foreign companies aiming to get protection for products already patented in other countries.

13. However, registration allows tax deductions, which is an incentive for firms to register their contracts.

14. Later on, the National Institute of Industrial Property (INPI) was granted this role after its creation in mid-1990s.

15. These figures were substantially higher than their counterparts during the ISI period. Between 1959 and 1963, FDI inflows to Argentina averaged US$464 million annually (measured in constant 2001 dollars). In the 1990s, the same figure was over US$6.76 billion. While in the first period FDI inflows amounted to around 0.3% of GDP, in the 1990s they were above 2% of GDP almost every year.

16. The oil industry, together with the mining sector, attracted mainly resource-seeking investments—resource-seeking FDI is motivated by the availability and/or cost of natural and human resources (Dunning, 1993).

17. While the remarkable growth in technology payments may have been due to a real increase in the amount of expertise transferred from abroad in the context of economic restructuring, it may also have been related to the strong presence of affiliates of TNCs in Argentina.

18. A recent study indicates that the number of manufacturing firms fell from 50,000 in 1995 to 45,000 in 2001. Whereas 3,500 enterprises collapsed, 2,500 firms were created annually on average during this period. Preliminary estimates suggest that the majority of companies that closed their doors predated 1995 (JICA-UNGS, 2003).

19. Besides the automobile and mining regimes, which will be discussed in the following sections of this chapter, a regime for promoting investments in the forestry was also established. It granted 30 years of fiscal stability and other tax incentives. Substantial investments were fostered by this incentives scheme.

20. It is important to mention that finished car exports from Argentina include a high share of imported parts and components from Brazil and elsewhere.

21. Investments made by TNC affiliates aimed at increasing the efficiency of their activities by integrating assets, production, and markets to better exploit economies of scale and scope are called "efficiency-seeking" (or "rationalized") investments (Dunning, 1993).

22. Naturally, the 2001 crisis was even more damaging for the sector: in 2002 and 2003, production was about one-third of that achieved in 1998. Production recovered in 2004 and 2005 but in this last year was only 70% of the 1998 record.

23. In recent years Argentine car makers have increased exports (though they are still exporting fewer units than in 1998) and have diversified export markets to reduce "Brazil-dependence." In 2004, the main destination for automotive exports was Mexico (44% of total exports) while in mid-1990s Brazil received more than 80% of the exports of the sector.

24. See Chudnovsky and López (2001).

25. Besides the aforementioned incentives, in 1999, in the face of the domestic market recession, the so-called *Plan Canje* was launched, by which consumers could change their old cars for new ones at a lower price than the market one—the discount was financed by a special tax reduction on cars sold under that regime.

26. While in 1991 there were no ISO 9000 certifications in the country, between 1992 and 1997, 251 certifications were granted. In July 1999, 869 firms/institutions had 1,112 certifications. At present, the number of valid certifications is around 2,600. Different subsidy mechanisms have been available both at national as well as at subnational government levels for firms wishing to attain ISO 9000 certifications.

27. In the past two or three years some initiatives have been taken aimed at changing the CONICET's traditional reluctance to engage in technological activities. Even if no information is available so far on the impact of these initiatives, they are in the right direction.

28. However, available evidence suggests that while in larger public universities linkages with the private sector are scarce, in smaller and newer universities there is more interest in entering into partnerships.

29. They include R&D expenditures plus others related to the diffusion of S&T activities, specialized libraries, and so on.

Chapter 6   Economic and Social Performance during Convertibility "High Growth" Years

1. It is important to mention that in 1992 Plan Brady was launched. Argentina officially recognized its debt (around US$21,000 million) jointly with US$8,300 million of unpaid accumulated interests. The total amount was converted into government bonds as new debt: the Brady bonds. This refinancing scheme contributed to reduce the country's risk premium for foreign investors.

2. Exports in 1996–2000 reached almost 11% of the GDP vis-à-vis less than 8% in 1991–1995. In the case of investments, the respective figures were 20% and 18% of the GDP.

3. This deterioration came about in spite of the reforms adopted by the government from 1991 onward, which were aimed at simplifying the revenues structure, eliminating "distorting" taxes and strengthening the tax collection agency. Massive layoffs in the federal bureaucracy also took place.

However, little progress was made on other fiscal issues, such as the distribution of revenues between the national government and the provinces— the revenue-sharing regime (*coparticipación federal*).

4. One of the objectives of the new system was to channel long-term financing to the private sector. However, the government had to allow the crowding-in effect by absorbing at least part of the drop in revenues that would go into the pension funds without raising borrowing requirements. To the extent that the implementation of the new system proved feasible over time, the public sector was indeed reducing future liabilities; however, these liabilities under the old regime were not contractually binding in definite amounts while the bonds that the government had to sell to finance the transition represented mostly dollar denominated fixed commitments. In this sense the reform hardened the government's intertemporal budget constrains and made it dependent on the evolution of the real exchange rate (Galiani, Heymann, and Tommasi, 2003).

5. In 2000, a law was passed decentralizing collective bargaining. Suspicions were raised that some legislators had been bribed to approve the law, a fact that led to the vice president's resignation and to the beginning of the end of the political coalition that had taken office in 1999. In fact, law dispositions were never put in practice.

6. The number of firms quoted on the stock exchange fell by 20% between 1989 and 1995 (Llach, 1997).

7. In the mid-1990s, only 58% of SMEs had access to banking credit, while another 25% did not even have any relationship whatsoever with banks (Llach, 1997).

8. It may be argued that small domestic banks had accumulated a relevant amount of knowledge about their SMEs clients, which allowed them to lend to those firms even if they did not meet the standards derived from strict norms of lending evaluation. This "knowledge capital" was lost when the banks were transferred to foreign owners.

9. A study found that firms that had gone through a M&A process in the 1990s showed a better performance in terms of sales growth than those firms that had remained in hands of their previous owners (Chudnovsky and López, 2000). More research would be needed, however, to learn if that was a consequence of improvements in management and technology in acquired firms, or if it only reflected the fact that buyers tended to acquire the most promising firms.

10. In this scenario, parliamentary discussions about a new antitrust regime began in 1997, but it was only in 1999 that the congress passed a new Law, which was enacted in September 1999. In fact, the complete takeover of the former State oil enterprise, YPF (Fiscal Petrol Fields, which had been sold to private investors in a public offering in 1993) by the Spanish TNC Repsol in the first months of 1999 accelerated the approval of the new Law.

11. Estimates based on information from the Household Permanent Survey— that are not exempt of problems themselves—suggest that industrial employment fell at an annual average rate of 1% between 1991 and 2000.

12. All manufacturing sectors experienced job losses between 1993 and 1998.

13. TNCs affiliates' share on the exports of the 500 Argentine leading firms passed from 67 to 85% between 1992 and 2003, while the respective figures in the case of imports were 76 and 85% (see Chudnovsky and López, 2006).

14. Soybean and its derivatives amounted to 20% of total exports in 2001.

15. Expansion in planted area came mainly from two sources: enlargement of the agricultural frontier and displacement of livestock. Moreover, a sort of "virtual" expansion also took place, since in many areas now it is possible to double crop wheat and soybean (see chapter 6).

16. Soybean productivity does not show a large improvement because estimated yields average yields from Pampas areas (which have increased significantly) with those from marginal areas where it is nowadays possible to plant soybean, but where yields are still relatively low.

17. Although Argentina has a long tradition in seed research, both in public and private organizations, multinational companies—as well as in many other countries—have taken the lead in the area of GMOs. One of the reasons that explains the minor role of local players in new seed releases is the huge amount of resources that are needed for R&D in agricultural biotechnology. However, it must be noted that, so far, private breeders have been able to keep their businesses through partnerships with TNC affiliates. These affiliates provide the transgenic genes that are combined with varieties well adapted to local conditions and owned by local breeders (Bisang, 2001).

18. See Trigo et al. (2002) for the details of this process.

19. At present, Monsanto has embarked on a battle to charge a royalty in Argentina on its genetically modified soybean seeds. Due to the failure to reach an agreement with associations representing agricultural producers, it has recently threatened to impose a US$15-per-metric-ton fee on soybean exports. If exporters decline to pay the fee, they will face the prospect of being sued in the courts of European countries that import Argentine soybeans. The Argentine government has deemed this an unacceptable threat.

20. No-tillage maintains a permanent or semipermanent organic soil cover (e.g., a growing crop or dead mulch) that protects the soil from sun, rain, and wind and allows soil microorganisms and fauna to take on the tasks of "tilling" and soil nutrient balancing. These are natural processes that are disturbed by mechanical tillage.

21. Differences in students' performance are observed when comparing private and public schools, but are also apparent within the public system.

22. These negative trends took place in spite of reforms that increased compulsory education from 7 to 10 years. The new educational system is now divided into four levels: preprimary school (from three to five years old—with only the last year compulsory), compulsory primary school (from 6 to 14 years), secondary school (from 15 to 17/18 years) and college level (universities and technical colleges).

23. A national evaluation program of university education was adopted in the 1990s. So far, no serious analysis exists on its impact, but a significant drawback is that the major Argentine University—the University of Buenos Aires— rejected evaluations made under that program, mainly for political reasons.

24. In contrast with these findings, Rozada and Menéndez (2002) find that unemployment accounted for a large part of the increase in inequality and poverty between 1991 and 1996, and 1998 and 2001, while returns to education played a minor role. As the unemployment rate fell between 1996 and 1998, it had a positive effect on both variables.

Chapter 7   The Microeconomics of Industrial Restructuring during the Convertibility Era

1. For instance, the privatization program in the steel sector reduced the number of workers from 32,148 in 1989 to 16,220 in 1994 (Etchemendy, 2001). This, together with an increase in the level of use of the installed capacity, increased labor productivity from 120 tons of steel per worker in 1989 to 204 tons in 1994 (Bisang and Chidiak 1995). The privatization program in the petrochemicals industry showed an improvement in management techniques, a reduction in employment (from 12,500 in 1990 to nearly 9,000 in 1994), increased labor productivity, and enhanced quality control systems (López and Chidiak 1995).

2. It must be noted that the strategies of TNC affiliates regarding R&D activities are far from being homogenous across countries that have gone through similar reform processes. On the basis of data from the U.S. Bureau of Economic Analysis, it is evident that the R&D to sales ratio of U.S. TNC affiliates in Argentina shifted from 0.21% to 0.11% between 1991 and 1999, while in Brazil it increased from 0.45% to 0.51%. Considering only the manufacturing industry, the differences are more striking: from 0.29% to 0.15% in Argentina, and from 0.56 to 0.80 in Brazil. These findings suggest that the creation of MERCOSUR, by allowing the deployment of efficiency-seeking strategies by TNC affiliates, may have led to a diversion of some innovative activities in Argentina for the national market to Brazilian affiliates, which now have regional and in some cases even global responsibilities in R&D activities.

3. Foreign firms in Argentina are largely fully or majority owned by nonresident investors.

4. Comparisons with the trading performance of TNCs during the ISI period are available only for U.S. affiliates. According to data from surveys undertaken by the U.S. Bureau of Economic Analysis, export/sales ratios for U.S. affiliates in Argentina in the manufacturing industry increased from an average of 12% in 1983 to 21% in 1999. Although it is clear that U.S. affiliates are much more export-oriented than in the past, it is also true that their export propensity is lower than that of other regions (all U.S. affiliates in the world exported, on average, 41% of their sales in 1999).

5. For instance, domestic conglomerates had a dominant position in the petrochemical industry in the 1980s. However, by 2000, they were almost no longer present, being replaced by TNC affiliates, which gained the lead by takeovers of public and private firms in the industry, as well as through substantial new investments.

6. In fact, in some cases domestic conglomerates abandoned their business in R&D-intensive sectors (that is the case of Pérez Companc, for instance, which had a partnership with NEC to manufacture telecommunications equipment—Pérez Companc sold their share to NEC in the mid-1990s).

7. Around 8,000 firms were exporting between 2000 and 2002, of which 7,500 were SMEs. However, the latter accounted for less than 9% of total exports during those years (CEP, 2003).

8. OECD (1997) and RICYT (2001), respectively.

9. These firms accounted for 29% of sales, 27% of employment and 24% of exports of the manufacturing sector in 1992–1996. For 1998–2001, the figures were 27%, 20%, and 19% respectively.

10. An important feature of the Argentine innovation surveys is that, as opposed to the European Community Innovation Services (CIS), both innovators and noninnovators were required to answer the whole questionnaire—in particular, to report innovation expenditures. This avoids the selectivity problem in CIS surveys acknowledged in Crepon, Duguet, and Mairesse (1998).

11. The classification of sectors into R&D, scale, labor, and natural resources intensive was developed by Pavitt (1984) and later adapted by Guerrieri and Milana (1989).

12. No information is available in the Innovation Surveys on the stock of capital to be able to measure total factor productivity.

13. While it may be understandable that studies for developed countries do not take into account (embodied and disembodied) technology acquisition when measuring innovative expenditures, this should not be the case when analyzing the innovative behavior of the firms in developing countries, where external sources of technology are in general more significant than in-house innovation activities.

14. In our study, a firm is considered an innovator during 1992–1996 (or 1998–2001) if it introduced new or radically modified products and/or processes during that period. In other words, a firm is defined as an innovator depending on the outcome (or *output*) of its innovation process and not on whether it has undertaken innovation activities—which are *inputs* to this process. In fact, not every innovator reported innovation expenditures, and vice versa (see below). It is important to take note that, according to the definition of the innovation surveys, the innovation of a firm can be new to either the market or the firm. The issue is discussed several paragraphs below.

15. Hence, although labor productivity increased approximately at the same rate in both groups, it seems that this result was mainly attained by market expansion among innovators, while noninnovators resorted to labor force reductions.

16. Although the data do not allow us to identify the reasons behind this fact, we can suggest two explanations: (1) innovations may have been the result of expenditures in previous years, which were discontinued during the period when the introduction of these innovations occurred; (2) innovations may have been the result of informal innovation activities not properly captured by the survey questionnaire.

17. Tentative explanations for this fact are: (1) the existence of lags between the investment in innovation and its yield; (2) the possibility that innovation expenditures were directed to objectives other than introducing new products or processes, such as reduction of costs or minor adaptations of existing products and processes.

18. The estimated increase in the probability of engaging in innovation activities originated by a doubling of the number of employees in the median firm in the data set (from 104 to 208 employees) during 1998–2001 is 22.6% (from 38.7% to 61.3%).

19. In order to interpret the meaning of the reported findings correctly, it is important to bear in mind that the sample of firms on which the study worked might have performed better than the national average. Under such circumstances, the conclusion that, for example, innovation in products and processes has a positive impact on productivity might be valid for this subgroup of best performing firms, while we do not know what could have happened with those firms that bankrupted during the period under analysis (and were not covered by the innovation surveys).

20. Labor productivity is, on average, 14.1% higher in innovators than in non-innovators, *ceteris paribus*.

21. Surveys of the literature on spillovers from FDI can be found in Gorg and Strobl (2001), Gorg and Greenaway (2004), and in Chudnovsky et al. (2004).

22. In a previous study, based on a less rich data set, similar findings had been reached, that is, TNCs affiliates had higher export and import propensities than domestic firms (see Chudnovsky, López et al., 2002).

23. It is important to take into account that the evidence discussed in this section is only related to environmental management activities, while no data are available on the environmental performance of manufacturing firms.

24. The "end-of-pipe" approach is based on the identification, processing, and disposal of discharges or waste. It is thus a corrective approach, which tries to control the pollution after it has occurred.

25. On the basis of EMA items in table 7.8, complex clean production management comprises firms that undertook at least one of the items 5, 6, 7, and 8; simple clean production management includes firms that undertook at least one of items 3 or 4 but did not undertake complex CP management activities. "End-of-pipe" management comprises firms that undertook at least one of the items 1, 2, and 9 but did not undertake any other activity mentioned in table 7.8.

26. In order to measure absorption capabilities, following Yoguel and Rabetino (2002), an index was elaborated, including different factors, as follows: (1) quantitative variables: the ratio of R&D employees relative to total employment, the ratio between expenditures in consultancy and sales, the payments for technology licenses relative to sales, the expenditures in capital goods related to new process or new products relative to sales and the ratio between innovation activities (including not only expenditures in formal R&D but also in adaptive and incremental innovation activities, project engineering, and so on) and sales; (2) qualitative variables: the degree of

formalization of R&D activities (i.e., whether the firm has or does not have a R&D department), the use of modern organizational techniques, the importance assigned to product innovation in firms' strategies, the use of information technology in the relationships with customers and suppliers and the importance of tacit and codified sources of technological information; (3) qualitative-quantitative variables: whether the firm undertook training activities and, if so, the expenditures in training relative to sales.

27. The finding that technology acquisition expenditures (that were composed mostly of imported inputs) enhance EMA—while R&D outlays do not—may be explained taking into account that environmental problems may be dealt with technology already available at international level.

28. Access to credit was mentioned as an obstacle for innovation by 74% of small firms—the corresponding figure for medium-sized firms was 59% and for large firms 45%.

Chapter 8   From Crisis to Recovery, 1998–2006

1. The flows of foreign portfolio investment, which were on average US$11 billion per year in the 1996–1998 period, became negative since 1999. From 1999 to 2001, US$16 billion left the country according to balance of payment figures.

2. For a detailed study on this subject, see Perry and Serven (2002).

3. The REER is the RER weighted by the share in exports and imports from the main trading partners.

4. Nofal (2002), Mussa (2002), Krueger (2002), and Teijeiro (2001) also highlight the increase in public wages and pensions.

5. Argentina signed a stand-by loan for US$7.2 billion in January 2000 and received more funds in that year and in 2001 (see below).

6. Though the population surely agreed on adjustments in areas that meant a privilege to public officials or which were perceived to be associated with state corruption.

7. All through 2000 and 2001, the IMF strongly insisted on the need to reduce fiscal deficits of the provinces. The federal administration entered into agreements with the provinces on several occasions so as to achieve that goal but the negotiations were long and tough and in the end did not fulfill the expectations of the IMF.

8. Despite the nonfulfillment of the fiscal targets for 2000, a loan of almost US$40 billion was announced in December 2000. The parties involved in the loan, along with the international institutions such as the IMF (US$13.7 billion), the World Bank (US$2.5 billion), and the Inter American Development Bank (US$2.5 billion), were the Government of Spain (US$1 billion), a group of Argentine commercial banks and the private pension funds. Only a bit more than a quarter of those funds was received in 2001. Financial assistance was conditioned to the fulfillment of fiscal targets and the execution of specific structural reforms. Funds were basically used

to finance public spending given the difficulty to obtain private external funds. Unfortunately, a large proportion of the received funds contributed to finance the capital flight in 2001.

9. This dispute resulted in the resignation of the president of the Central Bank in April, 2001.

10. Neither was the announcement made by Cavallo of a future introduction of the euro in the Convertibility regime a measure welcomed by "the markets."

11. The purpose of the *mega-canje* was to reschedule the short- and medium-term debt to more extended periods (between 2002 and 2005). The debt swap succeeded in raising to almost three years the bonds' average life (the debt service decrease US$16 billion until 2005), but at the expense of higher interest rates and an increase in the debt nominal value (of about US$2 billion). Even though the *mega-canje* enabled the government "to buy time" while it waited for a possible recovery in the level of activity, it validated interest rates on the public debt that turned its dynamic hardly sustainable.

12. After the last agreement signed with the IMF, the government tried to organize, between September and December 2001, a new "ordered" debt restructuring. This time, the government intended to make creditors accept a lower interest rate, compromising—with the parliament agreement—to guarantee bond payments by means of affecting the collection of the financial transfer tax (which had been introduced by Cavallo at the beginning of his tenure). The operation was announced at the beginning of November 2001 and it established a 7% (or lower) annual interest rate, which would have reduced substantially the consolidated public sector interest payments in the next years. The restructuring was projected in two phases: a local one with mainly banks and the private pension funds (that ended at the beginning of December 2001) and an external phase (that did not even start).

13. After tough deliberations among Argentine authorities, the IMF and the U.S. government and between the latter parties, the IMF announced that it would increase the available credit funds for Argentina. Staff members first declared that the total amount agreed in the *blindaje* loan between Argentina and the IMF would be increased by US$8 billion. The IMF insisted in the need to guarantee somehow the achievement of "zero-deficit" both in national government and provinces accounts and stated that the Argentine authorities were studying a new debt restructuring that the institution would support. It is worth pointing out that, at that moment, the IMF and the U.S. Treasury positions with regard to Argentina case were not homogeneous. While Horst Köhler, on behalf of the former, supported the approval of a new credit line, Paul O'Neill, on behalf of the latter, opposed to the idea of a new "life saving" without a debt restructuring. This restructuring, according to O'Neill, should incorporate the private sector and take the Argentine economy to a sustainable situation through time.

14. According to Damill et al. (2005) the main source of the new public debt after the default came from the government intervention in the financial system that involved a US$14.4 billion rise. It was aimed both at reducing the

wealth transfer from debtors to creditors and at avoiding the collapse that would have resulted from the fulfilling of contracts set in foreign currency.

15. Other issues that worried the IMF during 2002 and that delayed the signature of an agreement were: (1) to assure the fiscal sustainability of the economic program; (2) to limit the money emission targets; (3) to begin the financial system restructuring, including a reform and partial privatization of public banks; (4) to take up again the negotiations with external creditors; (5) to unfreeze public services tariffs; (6) to reduce provincial fiscal deficits and to rescue the so-called quasi-currencies (which were a sort of monies that had been issued by the provincial governments in order to deal with their deficits amidst the financial crisis).

16. After Remes Lenicov's resignation, and given the difficulties that had arisen in coming to an agreement with the IMF and the scarce disposition of developed countries' governments to help beyond an agreement with the IMF, a dispute regarding the possibility of adopting a radical change in the economic policy strategy arose inside the national government. Therefore, part of the Executive Branch—including President Duhalde—began evaluating the possibility of adopting a "self-centered" strategy based on the breaking up with multilateral organisms. Such turn found a serious opposition within the Executive Branch as well as in part of the parliament and provincial governments, and it finally did not succeed.

17. In this game of pressures, the Argentine government fell in a temporary default with multilateral organisms, although they always promised that payments would be reestablished as soon as the IMF agreement was achieved, posing as justification that there was no space for allocating reserves to multilateral institutions debt payments.

18. Export taxes, which had been abandoned during Convertibility, were reintroduced in 2002. From the point of view of the government, export taxes had a double objective: they were a noninflationary source of financing and, given that the country is a net commodity exporter (mainly those related with the consumption goods basket and oil), they made domestic prices to remain below international ones (and hence had a double benefit, to reduce inflation pressures and to avoid further deterioration in poverty rates).

19. By June 2005, Argentina was the country with more suits in the ICSID (40 over a total of 183).

BIBLIOGRAPHY

Acemoglu, D., S. Johnson, and J. Robinson. (2001). "The Colonial Origins of Comparative Development: An Empirical Investigation," *American Economic Review*, Vol. 91, No. 5, pp. 1369–1401.

―――. (2005). "Institutions as the Fundamental Cause of Long-Run Growth," in *Handbook of Economic Growth*. P. Aghion and S. Durlauf, eds., pp. 385–472 (Amsterdam: North Holland).

Acuña, C. and M. Tommasi. (1999). "Some Reflections on the Institutional Reforms Required for Latin America," *Centro de Estudios para el Desarrollo Institucional*, working paper no. 20.

Adler, E. (1987). *The Power of Ideology. The Quest for Technological Autonomy in Argentina and Brazil*. (Berkeley: University of California Press).

Aitken, B. and A. Harrison. (1999). "Do Domestic Firms Benefit from Direct Foreign Investment? Evidence from Venezuela," *American Economic Review*, Vol. 89, No. 3, pp. 605–618.

Albornoz M., L. Luchilo, G. Arber, R. Barrere, and J. Raffo. (2002a). "El Talento que se Pierde. Aproximación al Estudio de la Emigración de Profesionales, Investigadores y Tecnólogos Argentinos," mimeo [unpublished], *Centro de Estudios sobre Ciencia, Desarrollo y Educación Superior, REDES*, Buenos Aires.

Albornoz M., E. Fernández Polcuch, and C. Alfaraz. (2002b). "Hacia una nueva estimación de la Fuga de Cerebros," *Centro Redes*, working paper no. 1, Buenos Aires.

Albouy, D. (2004). *The Colonial Origins of Comparative Development: A Reexamination Based on Improved Settler Mortality Data*. (Berkeley: University of California).

Amsden, A. (1989). *Asia's New Giant: South Korea and Late Industrialization*. (New York: Oxford University Press).

Angelelli, P., C. Guaipatín, and C. Suaznabar. (2004). "La colaboración público-privada en el apoyo a la pequeña empresa: siete estudios de caso en América Latina," working report, Inter-American Development Bank.

Arce, H., P. Skupch, and C. Pozzo. (1968). "Una Estimación de los Gastos en Investigación y del Número de Investigadores en la República Argentina. 1961–1966," *Reunión de Centros de Investigación Económica*, Bahía Blanca, November.

Archibugi, D. and G. Sirilli. (2000). "The Direct Measurement of Technological Innovation in Business in Innovation and Enterprise Creation: Statistics and Indicators," Proceedings of the Conference held at Sophia Antipolis, November.

Aron, J. (2000). "Growth and Institutions: A Review of the Evidence," *The World Bank Research Observer*, February, Vol. 15, No. 1, pp. 99–135.

Azpiazu, D., A. Vispo, and M. Fuchs. (1993). "La Inversión en la Industria Argentina. El Comportamiento Heterogéneo de las Principales Empresas en una Etapa de Incertidumbre Macroeconómica, 1983–1988," ECLAC, working paper no. 49, Buenos Aires.

Balassa, B. (1971). *The Structure of Protection in Developing Countries.* (Baltimore: Johns Hopkins University Press).

Balassa, B. and Associates. (1982). *Development Strategies in Semi-industrial Economies.* (Baltimore: Johns Hopkins University Press).

Barsky, O. (1993). "La Evolución de las Políticas Agrarias en Argentina," in *La Problemática Agraria. Nuevas Aproximaciones—III.* M. Bonaudo and A. Pucciarelli, comps, eds., pp. 51–88. (Buenos Aires: Centro Editor de América Latina).

———. (1994). "Análisis del Sistema Argentino de Ofertas de Posgrado," Final Report, Project Reform of Superior Education, Ministry of Culture and Education, Buenos Aires.

Barsky, O., F. Cirio, J. C. del Bello, M. Gutiérrez, N. Huici, E. Jacobs, I. Llovet, R. Martínez Nogueira, M. Mumis, E. de Obschatko, and M. Piñeiro. (1988). *La Agricultura Pampeana. Transformaciones Productivas y Sociales.* (Buenos Aires: FCE/IIIC/CISEA).

Barsky, O., M. Posada, and A. Barsky. (1992). *El Pensamiento Agrario Argentino.* (Buenos Aires: Centro Editor de América Latina).

Bastos Tigre, P., M. Laplane, G. Lugones, F. Porta, and F. Sarti. (1999). "Impacto del MERCOSUR en la Dinámica del Sector Automotor," in *Impacto Sectorial de la Integración en el MERCOSUR.* J. J. Taccone and L. J. Garay, eds. (Buenos Aires: INTAL).

Bates, R., H. A. Greif, M. Levi, J. L. Rosenthal, and B. N. Weingast. (1998). *Analytic Narratives.* (Princeton: Princeton University Press).

Bebczuk, R. and L. Gasparini. (2001). "Globalisation and Inequality. The Case of Argentina," Universidad Nacional de La Plata, working paper no. 32, La Plata.

Becerra, N., C. Baldatti, and R. Pedace. (1997). *Un Análisis Sistémico de Políticas Tecnológicas. Estudio de Caso: El Agro Pampeano Argentino 1943–1990.* (Buenos Aires: CEA/CBC, Universidad de Buenos Aires).

Berlinski, J. (2003). "International Trade and Commercial Policy," in *A New Economic History of Argentina* Della Paolera, G. and A. Taylor, eds., pp. 197–232 (Cambridge: Cambridge University Press).

———. (2004). *Los Impactos de la Política Comercial: Argentina y Brasil. 1988–1997.* (Buenos Aires: Instituto Di Tella/Siglo Veintiuno de Argentina Editores).

Berlinski, J. and D. Schidlowsky. (1982). "Argentina," in *Development Strategies in Semi-Industrial Economies.* B. Balassa, ed., pp. 83–114 (Baltimore: Johns Hopkins University Press).

Bisang, R. (1990). "Sistemas de Promoción a las Exportaciones Industriales. La Experiencia Argentina en la Última Década," *ECLAC*, working paper no. 35, Buenos Aires.

———. (1998). "Apertura, Reestructuración Industrial y Conglomerados Económicos," *Desarrollo Económico*, Vol. 38, Special Edition, pp. 143–176, Buenos Aires.

———. (2001). "Shock Tecnológico y Cambio en la Organización de la Producción. La Aplicación de Biotecnología en la Producción Agropecuaria

Argentina," mimeo [unpublished], Instituto de Industria, Universidad Nacional de General Sarmiento, Buenos Aires.

———. (2003). "Apertura Económica, Innovación y Estructura Productiva: La Aplicación de Biotecnología en la Producción Agrícola Pampeana Argentina," *Desarrollo Económico*, Vol. 43, No. 171, pp. 413–442, Buenos Aires.

Bisang, R., C. Bonvecchi, B. Kosacoff, and A. Ramos. (1996). "La Transformación Industrial en los Noventa. Un Proceso con un Final Abierto," *Desarrollo Económico*, Vol. 36, Special Edition, Summer, pp. 187–222, Buenos Aires.

Bisang, R. and M. Chidiak. (1995). "Apertura Económica, Reestructuración Productiva y Medio Ambiente. La Siderurgia Argentina en los 90," working paper no. 19, Fundación CENIT, Buenos Aires.

Bisang, R. and B. Kosacoff. (1995). "Tres Etapas en la Búsqueda de una Especialización Sustentable. Exportaciones Industriales Argentinas 1974–93," in *Hacia una Nueva Estrategia Exportadora. La Experiencia Argentina, el Marco Regional y las Reglas Multilaterales*. B. Kosacoff, ed., pp. 23–94 (Buenos Aires: Universidad Nacional de Quilmes).

Borghesi, S. (1999). "The Environmental Kuznets Curve: A Survey of the Literature," working report, European University Institute, Florence.

Bouzas, R. and D. Chudnovsky. (2004). " 'Foreign Direct Investment and Sustainable Development: The Recent Argentine Experience," working paper no. 47, Universidad de San Andrés, Buenos Aires.

Bouzas, R. and R. Ffrench-Davis. (2005). "Globalización y Políticas Nacionales: ¿cerrando el círculo?" *Desarrollo Económico*, Vol. 45, No. 179, pp. 323–348, Buenos Aires.

Bouzas, R. and E. Pagnotta. (2003). *Dilemas de la Política Comercial Externa Argentina*. (Buenos Aires: Universidad de San Andrés/Fundación OSDE).

Braun, O. and L. Joy. (1968). "A Model of Economic Stagnation. A Case Study of the Argentine Economy," *The Economic Journal*, Vol. 78, No. 312, pp. 868–887.

Burachik, G. and J. Katz. (1997). "La Industria Farmacéutica y Farmoquímica Argentina en los Años 90," in *Apertura Económica y Desregulación en el Mercado de los Medicamentos*. J. Katz, G. Burachik, J. Brodovsky, and S. Queiróz, eds. (Buenos Aires: ECLAC/IDRC Alianza).

Calvo, G. and E. Mendoza. (1996). "Mexico Balance of Payments Crises: A Chronicle of a Death Foretold," *Journal of International Economics*, Vol. 41, No. 3–4, pp. 235–264.

Calvo, G. A., A. Izquierdo, and E. Talvi. (2002). "Sudden Stops, the Real Exchange Rate and Fiscal Sustainability: Argentina's Lessons," Research Department, Inter-American Development Bank, June.

Campos, J. (1998). "Argentina: Government Policies to Attract FDI," mimeo [unpublished], OECD, Buenos Aires.

Canitrot, A. (1994). "Crisis and Transformation of the Argentine State (1978–1992)," in *Democracy, Markets, and Structural Reform in Latin America: Argentina, Bolivia, Brazil, Chile and Mexico*. W. C. Smith, C. H. Acuña, and E. A. Gamarra, eds. (North-South Center: University of Miami).

Cárdenas, E., J. A. Ocampo, and R. Thorp. (2000). "Industrialization and the State in Latin America: The Postwar Years," in *An Economic History of Twentieth-Century*

Latin America, Vol. 3. E. Cárdenas, J. A. Ocampo, and R. Thorp, eds. (Oxford: Palgrave/St. Antony's College).

Cardoso, F. and E. Faletto. (1969). *Dependencia y Desarrollo en América Latina*. (México: Siglo XXI).

Carullo, J., F. Peirano, G. Lugones, M. Lugones, and A. Di Franco. (2003). "Programa de Consejerías Tecnológicas. Evaluación y Recomendaciones. Informe final," prepared for the Science and Technology Secretariat, Argentina.

Castelar Pinheiro, A., R. Bonelli, and B. Ross Schneider. (2004). "Pragmatism and the Political Economy of Market Reform in Brazil," Global Development Network, mimeo [unpublished].

CEP (Centro de Estudios para la Producción). (1999). "El Empleo en la Industria," *Reporte industrial*.

————. (2003). "Una radiografía de la performance de los pequeños exportadores en el 2002: hay algo nuevo en el horizonte?" *Síntesis de la Economía Real*, No. 40, Mayo, Buenos Aires.

Cepeda, H. and G. Yoguel. (1993). "Las PyMEs Frente a la Apertura Externa y el Proceso de Integración Subregional: Un Desafío de Reacomodamiento Competitivo," working paper no. 13, IDI, FUIA.

Chen, E. (1977). "Factor Inputs, Total Factor Productivity, and Economic Growth: The Asian Case," *The Developing Economies*, Vol. 15, No. 1, pp. 121–143.

Chenery, H., M. Ahluwalia, C. Bell, J. Duloy, and R. Jolly. (1974). *Redistribution with Growth*. (Oxford: Oxford University Press).

Chudnovsky, D. (1976). *Dependencia Tecnológica y Estructura Industrial. El Caso Argentino*, mimeo [unpublished], FLACSO.

————. (1999). "Las Nuevas Políticas de Ciencia y Tecnología en la Argentina y el Enfoque del Sistema Nacional de Innovación," *ECLAC Review*, No. 67, pp. 153–171, Santiago de Chile.

Chudnovsky, D. and F. Erber. (1999). "Impacto del Mercosur sobre la Dinámica del Sector de Máquinas y Herramientas," *Integration & Trade*, Vol. 3, No. 7/8, pp. 197–234.

Chudnovsky, D. and A. López. (2000). "Industrial Restructuring through Mergers and Acquisitions: The Case of Argentina in the 1990s," *Transnational Corporations*, Vol. 9, No. 3, pp. 33–62.

————. (2001). *La Transnacionalización de la Economía Argentina*. (Buenos Aires: Eudeba).

————, coords. (2002). "Integración Regional e Inversión Extranjera Directa. El caso del MERCOSUR," Serie REDINT, INTAL/IADB.

————. (2006). "Inversión Extranjera Directa y Desarrollo: la Experiencia del MERCOSUR," in J. Berlinski, F. E. Pires de Souza, D. Cundnovsky y A. Lopéz coords., *15 Años del MERCOSUR*. (Buenos Aires: Siglo XXI/Red MERCOSUR).

Chudnovsky, D. and G. Pupato. (2005). "Environmental Management and Innovation in the Argentine Industry: Determinants and Policy Implications," mimeo [unpublished], prepared for the Trade Knowledge Network, Winnipeg, Canada.

Chudnovsky, D., E. Lerner, A. Makuc, M. I. Pietragalla, and R. Monsegur. (1974). "Aspectos Económicos de la Importación de Tecnología en la Argentina en 1972," *Trabajos del INTI*, Buenos Aires.

Chudnovsky, D., S. Rubin, E. Cap, and E. Trigo. (1999). "Comercio Internacional y Desarrollo Sustentable. La Expansión de las Exportaciones Argentinas en los Años '90 y sus Consecuencias Ambientales," working paper no. 25, Fundación CENIT, Buenos Aires.

Chudnovsky, D., A. López, and V. Freylejer. (2000). "The Diffusion of Pollution Prevention Measures in LDCs: Environmental Management in Argentine Industry," in *Industry and Environment in Latin America*. R. Jenkins, ed., pp. 66–88 (London: Routledge).

Chudnovsky, D., A. López, and G. Pupato. (2004a). "Research, Development and Innovation Activities in Argentina: Changing Roles of the Public and Private Sectors and Policy Issues," prepared for the Research on Knowledge Systems (RoKS) program/IDRC, Buenos Aires.

————. (2004b). "Innovation and Productivity: A Study of Argentine Manufacturing Firms' Behavior (1992–2001)," working paper no. 70, Universidad de San Andrés, Buenos Aires.

Chudnovsky, D., A. López, and G. Rossi. (2004c). "Foreign Direct Investment Spillovers and the Absorption Capabilities of Domestic Firms in the Argentine Manufacturing Sector (1992–2001)," working paper no. 74, Universidad de San Andrés, Buenos Aires.

Chudnovsky, D., A. López, M. Rossi, and D. Ubfal. (2006a). "Evaluating a Program of Public Funding of Private Innovation Activity. An Econometric Study of FONTAR in Argentina," prepared for the Inter American Development Bank (IADB), Buenos Aires.

Chudnovsky, D., A López, and G. Pupato. (2006b). "Innovation and Productivity in Developing Countries: A Study of Argentine Manufacturing Firms' Behavior," *Research Policy*, Vol. 35, No 2, pp. 266–288.

Chudnovsky, D., A. López, and E. Orlicki. (2006c). "Innovation and Export Performance in Argentine Manufacturing Firms," in *Inovacao nas Firmas Industriais Brasileiras e Argentinas*. J. De Negri y L. Turchi, organizers. (Rio de Janeiro: IPEA).

————. (2006d). "Impact of Foreign Direct Investment on Employment, Productivity, Trade, Innovation, Wage Inequality and Poverty: A study of Argentina 1992–2001," Final Report for the Global Development Network Project on the Impact of Rich Country Policies on Poor Countries, mimeo [unpublished].

Cimoli, M. and J. Katz. (2003). "Structural Reforms, Technological Gaps and Economic Development: A Latin American Perspective," *Industrial and Corporate Change*, Vol. 12, No. 2, pp. 387–411.

Cornia Giovanni, A. (2004). "Globalization and the Distribution of Income between and within Countries," in *Rethinking Development Economics*. Ha-Joon Chang, ed., pp. 423–450 (London: Anthem Press).

Cortés Conde, R. (1997). *La Economía Argentina en el Largo Plazo*. (Buenos Aires: Sudamericana/Universidad de San Andrés).

Crepon B., E. Duguet, and J. Mairesse. (1998). "Research, Innovation and Productivity: An Econometric Analysis at the Firm Level," working paper no. 6696, NBER.

Damill, M., J. M. Fanelli, R. Frenkel, and G. Rozenwurcel. (1989). *Déficit Fiscal, Deuda Externa y Desequilibrio Financiero*. (Buenos Aires: Editorial Tesis).

Damill, M., R. Frenkel, and M. Rapetti. (2005). "La Deuda Argentina: Historia, Default y Reestructuración," Nuevos Documentos CEDES No. 16, CEDES, Buenos Aires.

Decibe, S. and S. Canela. (2003). "Educación y Sociedad del Conocimiento," study requested by the Secretariat of Economy Policy, Ministry of Economy and Production, Argentina.

De la Torre, A., E. Levy Yeyati, and S. Schmukler. (2002). "Beyond the Bipolar View: The Rise and Fall of Argentina's Currency Board," paper presented at NBER conference on Argentina, July, Cambridge, MA.

Del Bello, J. C. (2002). "Desafíos de la Política de la Educación Superior en América Latina: Reflexiones a partir del Caso Argentino con Énfasis sobre la Evaluación para el Mejoramiento de la Calidad," LCSHD Paper Series No. 70, World Bank, Washington, DC.

Della Paolera, G. and A. Taylor. (2003). "Introduction," in *A New Economic History of Argentina*. Della Paolera, G. and A. Taylor, eds., pp. 1–18 (New York: Cambridge University Press).

Díaz Alejandro, C. (1975). *Ensayos sobre la Historia Económica Argentina*. (Buenos Aires: Amorrortu).

Dosi, G., C. Freeman, R. Nelson, G. Silverberg, and L. Soete. (1988). *Technical Change and Economic Theory*. (London: Pinter).

Dunning, J. (1993). *Multinational Enterprises and the Global Economy*. (Harlow: Addison Wesley).

Easterly, W. (2001). *The Elusive Quest for Growth. Economists' Adventures and Misadventures in the Tropics*. (Massachusetts: MIT Press).

Echart, M. (1999). "Educación y Distribución del Ingreso," *La Distribución del Ingreso en la Argentina*. FIEL, pp. 373–412 (Buenos Aires: Manantial).

ECLAC (Economic Commission for Latin America and the Caribbean) (1958). *El Desarrollo Económico de la Argentina*. (Santiago de Chile: UNCTAD).

Edquist, C. (1997). "Systems of Innovation Approaches. Their Emergence and Characteristics," in *Systems of Innovation: Technologies, Institutions and Organizations*. C. Edquist, ed., pp. 1–35 (London: Pinter).

Etchemendy, S. (2001). "Construir Coaliciones Reformistas: La Política de las Compensaciones en el Camino Argentino hacia la Liberalización Económica," *Desarrollo Económico*, Vol. 40, No. 16, pp. 675–706, Buenos Aires.

Evans, P. (1995). *Embedded Autonomy. State and Industrial Transformation*. (New Jersey: Princeton University Press).

Fagerberg, J., D. Mowery, and R. Nelson. (2005). *The Oxford Handbook of Innovation*. (Oxford: Oxford University Press).

Fanelli, J. M. (2002). "Growth, Instability and the Convertibility Crisis in Argentina," *ECLAC Review*, No. 77, pp. 25–43, Santiago de Chile.

———. (2004) "Desarrollo Financiero, Volatilidad e Instituciones. Reflexiones Sobre la Experiencia Argentina," working paper no. 3, Fundación PENT, Buenos Aires.

Fanelli, J. M. and R. Frenkel. (1996). "Estabilidad y Estructura: Interacciones en el Crecimiento Económico," in *Estabilización macroeconómica, reforma estructural y comportamiento industrial. Estructura y funcionamiento del sector manufacturero latinoamericano en los años 90*. J. Katz, ed., pp. 21–80 (Santiago de Chile: CEPAL/IDRC–Alianza Editorial).

Fanelli, J. M. and J. L. Machinea. (1995). "Capital Movements in Argentina," in *Coping with Capital Surges: The Return of Finance to Latin America*. R. Ffrench-Davis and S. Griffith-Jones, eds., pp. 145–188 (Boulder: Lynne Rienner).

Fanelli, J. M. and G. McMahon, eds. (2006). *Understanding Market Reforms*, chapter 1, Vol. 2. (New York: Palgrave-Macmillan).

Felipe, J. (1999). "Total Factor Productivity Growth in East Asia: A Critical Survey," *The Journal Of Development Studies*, Vol. 36, No. 4, pp. 1–41.

Felipe, J. and S. McCombie. (2004). "Is a Theory of Total Factor Productivity really Needed?" CAMA working papers No. 12, Centre for Applied Macroeconomic Analysis, Australian National University.

FIEL (Fundación de Investigaciones Económicas Latinoamericanas) (2002). *Productividad, Competitividad y Empresas. Los Engranajes del Crecimiento*. (Buenos Aires: FIEL).

Fishlow, A. (1972). "Brazilian Size Distribution of Income," *American Economic Review*, Vol. 62, No. 2, pp. 391–402.

Forteza, A. and M. Tommasi. (2005). "Understanding Reform in Latin America," working paper no. 2205, Department of Economics, UDELAR.

Frank, A. G. (1969). *Capitalism and Underdevelopment in Latin America: Historical Studies of Chile and Brazil*. (New York: Monthly Review Press).

Frenkel, R. (2003). "Deuda Externa, Crecimiento y Sostenibilidad," *Desarrollo Económico*, Vol. 42, No. 168, pp. 545–562, Buenos Aires.

Fuchs, M. (1990). "Los Programas de Capitalización de la Deuda Externa," mimeo [unpublished], ECLAC, Buenos Aires.

———. (1994). "Calificación de los Recursos Humanos e Industrialización El Desafío Argentino de los Años Ochenta," working paper no. 57, ECLAC, Buenos Aires.

Galiani, S. and P. Gerchunoff. (2003). "The Labor Market," in *A New Economic History of Argentina*. G. Della Paolera and A. Taylor, eds., pp. 122–169 (Cambridge: Cambridge University Press).

Galiani, S., P. Gertler, E. Schargrodsky, and F. Sturzenegger. (2001). "The Benefits and Costs of Privatization in Argentina: A Microeconomic Analysis," in *Privatization in Latin America*. A. Chong and F. López de Silanes, eds., (Stanford University Press).

Galiani, S., D. Heymann, and M. Tommasi. (2003). "Great Expectations and Hard Times: The Argentine Convertibility Plan," *Economia, The Journal of the Latin American and Caribbean Economic Association*, Vol. 3, No.2, pp. 109–160.

Galiani, S. and P. Sanguinetti. (2003). "The Impact of Trade Liberalization on Wage Inequality: Evidence from Argentina," *Journal of Development Economics*, Vol. 72, No. 72, pp. 497–513.

Galiani, S. and E. Schargrodsky. (2002). "Evaluating the Impact of School Decentralization on Educational Quality," *Economia, The Journal of the Latin American and Caribbean Economic Association*, Vol. 2, No. 2, pp. 275–314.

Gasparini, L. (1999). "Un Análisis de la Distribución del Ingreso en la Argentina sobre la Base de Descomposiciones," in *La distribución del ingreso en la Argentina*. FIEL. (Buenos Aires: Manantial).

Gasparini, L., M. Marchionni, and W. Sosa Escudero. (2004). "Characterization of Inequality Changes through Microeconometric Decompositions. The case of Greater Buenos Aires," in *The Microeconomics of Income Distribution Dynamics in East Asia and Latin America*. N. Lustig, F. Bourguignon y F. Ferreira, eds., pp. 47–82 (Washington DC: World Bank-Oxford University Press).

Gatto, F. and G. Yoguel. (1993). "Las PyMEs Argentinas en una Etapa de Transición Productiva y Tecnológica," in *El Desafío de la Competitividad. La Industria Argentina en Transformación*. B. Kosacoff, ed., pp. 183–248 (Buenos Aires: ECLAC/Alianza).

Gerchunoff, P., E. Greco, and D. Bondorevsky. (2003). "Comienzos Diversos, Distintas Trayectorias y Final Abierto: Más de una Década de Privatizaciones en Argentina, 1990–2002," *Gestión Pública Series*, ILPES, ECLAC, Santiago de Chile.

Gerchunoff, P. and J. Llach. (1975). "Capitalismo Industrial, Desarrollo Asociado y Distribución del Ingreso entre los dos Gobiernos Peronistas: 1950–1972," *Desarrollo Económico*, Vol. 15, No. 57, pp. 3–54, Buenos Aires.

Gerchunoff, P. and L. Llach. (2003). "Ved el Trono a la Noble Igualdad. Crecimiento, Equidad y Política Económica en la Argentina, 1880–2003," mimeo [unpublished], Fundación PENT, Buenos Aires.

Gerchunoff, P. and J. C. Torre. (1996). "La Política de Liberalización Económica en la Administración de Menem," *Desarrollo Económico*, Vol. 36, No. 143, pp. 733–68.

Gorg, H. and D. Greenaway. (2004). "Much Ado about Nothing? Do Domestic Firms really Benefit from Foreign Direct Investment," *The World Bank Research Observer*, Vol. 19, No. 2, pp. 171–197.

Görg, H. and E. Strobl. (2001). "Multinational Companies and Productivity Spillovers: A Meta-Analysis," *Economic Journal*, Vol. 111, No. 475, pp. 723–739.

Guerrieri, P. and C. Milana. (1989). *L'industria Italiana nel Commercio Mondiale.* (Bologna: Ed. Il Mulino).

Halac, M. and S. Schmukler (2003), "Distributional Effects of Crisis: The Role of Financial Transfers", mimeo [unpublished].

Hallak, J. C. and J. Levinsohn. (2004). "Fooling Ourselves: Evaluating the Globalization and Growth Debate," working paper no. 10244, NBER.

Hausmann, R., J. Hwang, and D. Rodrik. (2005). "What You Export Matters," working paper no. 11905, NBER.

Hausmann, R. and A. Velasco. (2002). "Hard Money's Soft Underbelly: Understanding de Argentine Crisis," mimeo [unpublished], Kennedy School of Government, Harvard University.

Helpman, E. (2004). *The Mystery of Economic Growth.* (Cambridge: Belknap Harvard).

Hirschman, A. (1958) *The Strategy of Economic Development.* (New Haven: Yale University Press).

———. (1968). "The Political Economy of Import-Substituting Industrialization in Latin America," *Quarterly Journal of Economics*, Vol. 82, No. 1, pp. 1–32.

———. (1981). *The Rise and Decline of Development Economics in Essays in Trespassing. Economics to Politics and beyond.* (Cambridge: Cambridge University Press).

Holm-Nielsen, L. and T. N. Hansen. (2003). "Education and Skills in Argentina. Assessing Argentina's Stock of Human Capital," mimeo [unpublished], LCSHD, the World Bank.

Hopenhayn, H. and P. Neumeyer. (2003). "The Argentine Great Depression (1975–1990)," mimeo [unpublished], the Global Development Network and Agencia de Promoción Científica y Tecnológica, Buenos Aires.

Hulten, C. (2000). "Total Factor Productivity: A Short Biography," working paper no. W7471, NBER.

INDEC-SECYT. (1998). "Encuesta Nacional de Innovación y Conducta Tecnológica de las Empresas Industriales Argentinas," Estudios 31, INDEC, Buenos Aires.

INDEC-SECYT-CEPAL. (2003). "Segunda Encuesta Nacional de Innovación y Conducta Tecnológica de las Empresas Industriales Argentinas," Estudios 38, INDEC, Buenos Aires.

INTA. (2003). "El INTA ante la Preocupación por la Sustentabilidad de la Producción Agropecuaria Argentina," INTA, Buenos Aires.

Javorcik, B. S. (2004). "Does Foreign Direct Investment Increase the Productivity of Domestic Firms? In Search of Spillovers through Backward Linkages," American Economic Review, Vol. 94, No. 3, pp. 605–627.

JICA-UNGS. (2003). "La Creación de Empresas en la Argentina y su Entorno Institucional," Final Report, mimeo [unpublished], Buenos Aires.

Kantis, H., P. Angelelli, and F. Gatto. (2000). "Nuevos Emprendimientos y Emprendedores en Argentina: de qué Depende su Creación y Supervivencia?" mimeo [unpublished], Universidad Nacional de General Sarmiento, Buenos Aires.

Katz, J. (1969). "Una Interpretación de Largo Plazo del Crecimiento Industrial Argentino," Desarrollo Económico, Vol. 8, No. 32, pp. 511–642, Buenos Aires.

―――. (1972). "Importación de Tecnología, Aprendizaje Local e Industrialización Dependiente," mimeo [unpublished], Instituto Torcuato Di Tella, Buenos Aires.

―――. (1987). Technology Generation in Latin American Manufacturing Industries. (London: The Macmillan Press).

―――. (1998). "Aprendizaje Tecnológico, Ayer y Hoy," ECLAC Review, Special Edition, pp. 63–75, Santiago de Chile.

―――. (1999a). "Reformas Estructurales y Comportamiento Tecnológico: Reflexiones en Torno a la Naturaleza y Fuentes del Cambio Tecnológico en América Latina en los Años Noventa," Economic Reforms Series, No. 13, ECLAC, Santiago de Chile.

―――. (1999b). "Cambios en la Estructura y Comportamiento del Aparato Productivo Latinoamericano en los Años '90: Después del Consenso de Washington, qué?" prepared for the International Seminary: Políticas para Fortalecer el Sistema Nacional de Ciencia, Tecnología e Innovación: La Experiencia Internacional y el Camino Emprendido por la Argentina, SECYT, Buenos Aires.

Katz, J. and E. Ablin. (1977). "Tecnología y Exportaciones Industriales: Un Análisis Microeconómico de la Experiencia Argentina Reciente," Desarrollo Económico, Vol. 17, No. 65, pp. 89–132, Buenos Aires.

―――. (1985). "De la Industria Incipiente a la Exportación de Tecnología: La Experiencia Argentina en la Venta Internacional de Plantas Industriales y Obras de Ingeniería," in Internacionalización de Empresas y Tecnologías de Origen Argentino. E. Ablin, F. Gatto, J. Katz, B. Kosacoff, R. Soifer, eds. (Buenos Aires: ECLAC/EUDEBA).

Katz, J. and B. Kosacoff. (1983). "Multinationals from Argentina," in *The New Multinationals: The Spread of Third World Enterprises*. S. Lall, ed., pp. 137–219 (London: Wiley/IRM).

———. (1989). *El Proceso de Industrialización en la Argentina: Evolución, Retroceso y Prospectiva*. (Buenos Aires: CEAL).

———. (1998). "Aprendizaje Tecnológico, Desarrollo Institucional y la Microeconomía de la Sustitución de Importaciones," *Desarrollo Económico*, Vol. 37, No. 148, pp. 483–502, Buenos Aires. Translated in English in *An Economic History of Twentieth-Century Latin America. Vol. 3: Industrialization and the State in Latin Amercia: The Postwar Years*. E. Cárdenas, J. A. Ocampo, and R. Thorp, eds. (Wiltshire: St. Antony's College and Antony Rowe Ltd.).

———. (2000). "Import-Substituting Industrialization in Argentina, 1940–80. Its Achievements and Shortcomings," in *An Economic History of Twentieth-Century Latin America, Vol. 3: Industrialization and the State in Latin America. The Postwar Years*. E. Cárdenas, J. A. Ocampo, and R. Thorp, eds. (Oxford: St. Antony's Series, Palgrave).

Kharas, H., B. Pinto, and S. Ulatov. (2001). "An Analysis of Russia's 1998 Meltdown: Fundamentals and Market Signals," *Brookings Papers on Economic Activity*, No. 1, pp. 1–68.

Kim, L. and R. Nelson, eds. (2000). *Technology, Learning and Innovation*. (Cambridge: Cambridge University Press).

Kline, S. and N. Rosenberg. (1986). "An Overview of Innovation," in *The Positive Sum Strategy. Harnessing Technology for Economic Growth*. R. Landau and N. Rosenberg, eds., pp. 275–306 (Washington, DC: National Academy Press).

Kosacoff, B., ed. (1998). *Estrategias Empresariales en Tiempos de Cambio*. (Buenos Aires: ECLAC/Universidad Nacional de Quilmes).

———, coord. (1999a). 'Hacia un Mejor Entorno Competitivo de la Producción Automotriz en Argentina,' working paper no. 82, ECLAC, Buenos Aires.

———. (1999b) "El Caso Argentino," in *Las Multinacionales Latinoamericanas. Sus Estrategias en un Mundo Globalizado*. D. Chudnovsky, B. Kosacoff, and A. López, eds., pp. 65–164 (Buenos Aires: Fondo de Cultura Económica).

———. (2000). *Corporate Strategies under Structural Adjustment in Argentina. Responses by Industrial Firms to a New Set of Uncertainties*. (Wiltshire: St. Antony's College and Antony Rowe Ltd.).

Kosacoff, B. and D. Aspiazu. (1989). *La Industria Argentina: Desarrollo y Cambios Estructurales*. (Buenos Aires: CEAL/ECLAC).

Kosacoff, B. and G. Bezchinsky. (1993). "De la Sustitución de Importaciones a la Globalización. Las Empresas Transnacionales en la Industria Argentina," in *El Desafío de la Competitividad. La Industria Argentina en Transición*. B. Kosacoff, ed., pp. 249–302 (Buenos Aires: ECLAC/Alianza).

Krueger, A. (1974). "The Political Economy of the Rent–Seeking Society," *American Economic Review*, Vol. 64, No. 3, pp. 291–303.

———. (1990) "Government Failures in Development," *Journal of Economic Perspectives*, Vol. 4, No. 3, pp. 9–23.

———. (2002) "Why Crony Capitalism Is Bad for Economic Growth," in *Crony Capitalism and Economic Growth in Latin America: Theory and Evidence*. S. Haber, ed. (Stanford: Hoover Institution Press).

Krugman, P. (1993). "Toward a Counter-Revolution in Development Theory," proceedings of the World Bank Annual Conference on Development Economics, (Washington, DC: Banco Mundial).

Kugler, M. (2000). "The Diffusion of Externalities from Foreign Direct Investment: Theory Ahead of Measurement," Discussion Papers in Economics and Econometrics, University of Southampton.

Kuznets, S. (1955). "Economic Growth and Income Inequality," *American Economic Review*, Vol. 45, No. 1, pp. 1–28.

Lall, S. (2000). "Technological Change and Industrialization in the Asian Newly Industrializing Economies. Achievements and Challenges," in *Technology, Learning and Innovation*. L. Kim and R. Nelson, eds., pp. 13–68 (Cambridge: Cambridge University Press).

Lall, S. and M. Teubal. (1998). "Market-Stimulating Technology Policies in Developing Countries: A Framework with Examples from East Asia," *World Development*, Vol. 26, No. 8, pp. 1369–1385.

Lewis, P. (1993). *La Crisis del Capitalismo Argentino*. (Buenos Aires: Fondo de Cultura Económica).

Lindauer, D. and L. Pritchett. (2002). "What's the Big Idea? Three Generations of Development Advice," *Economia*, Vol. 3, No. 1, pp. 1–39.

Little, I. (1982). *Economic Development*. (New York: Basic Books).

Little, I., T. Scitovsky, and M. Scott. (1970). *Industry and Trade in Some Developing Countries*. (London: Oxford University Press).

Llach, J. (1997). *Otro Siglo, otra Argentina. Una Estrategia para el Desarrollo Económico y Social Nacida de la Convertibilidad y de su Historia*. (Buenos Aires: Ariel).

———. (2002). "La Industria (1945–1983)," in *Nueva Historia de la Nación Argentina Tomo 9: La Argentina del Siglo XX*, pp. 85–116 (Buenos Aires: Planeta).

Llach, J. and E. Kritz. (1997). *Un Trabajo para Todos. Empleo y Desempleo en la Argentina*. (Buenos Aires: Consejo Empresario Argentino).

Llach, J., S. Montoya, and F. Roldán. (1999). *Educación para Todos*. (Córdoba: IERAL).

Llach, J., P. Sierra, and G. Lugones. (1997). "La Industria Automotriz Argentina. Evolución en la Década del Noventa, Perspectivas Futuras y Consecuencias para la Industria Siderúrgica," mimeo [unpublished], Buenos Aires.

Loayza, N., P. Fajnzylber, and C. Calderón. (2005). *Economic Growth in Latin America and the Caribbean. Stylized Facts, Explanations and Forecasts*. (Washington, DC: The World Bank).

López, A. (1997). "Desarrollo y Reestructuración de la Petroquímica Argentina," in *Auge y Ocaso del Capitalismo Asistido. La Industria Petroquímica Latinoamericana*. D. Chudnovsky and A. López, eds. (Buenos Aires: ECLAC/IDRC, Alianza Editorial).

———. (2006). *Empresarios, Instituciones y Desarrollo Económico: El Caso*. (Buenos Aires: CEPAL).

López, A. and M. Chidiak. (1995). "Reestructuración Productiva y Gestión Ambiental en la Petroquímica Argentina," working paper no. 18, Fundación CENIT, Buenos Aires.

Lora, E., U. Panizza, and M. Quispe-Agnoli. (2004). "Reform Fatigue: Symptoms, Reasons and Implications," *Economic Review*, Vol. 89, No. 2, pp. 1–28.

Maddison, A. (1995). *Monitoring the World Economy 1820–1992*. (Paris: OECD).

———. (2001). *The World Economy. A Millennial Perspective*. (Paris: OECD).

———. (2003). *The World Economy. Historical Statistics*. (Paris: OECD).

Maia, J. L. and M. Kweitel. (2003). "Argentina: Sustainable Output Growth after the Collapse," Dirección Nacional de Políticas Macroeconómicas, Ministry of Economy and Production, Argentina.

Moran, T., E. Graham, and M. Blomstrom, eds. (2005). *Does Foreign Direct Investment Promote Development?* (Washington, DC: Institute for International Economics).

Morley, S. (2000). "The Effects of Growth and Economic Reform on Income Distribution in Latin America," *ECLAC Review*, No. 71, pp. 23–40, Santiago de Chile.

Mortimore M., S. Vergara, and J. Katz. (2001). "La Competitividad Internacional y el Desarrollo Nacional: Implicancias para la Política de Inversión Extranjera Directa (IED) en América Latina," *Desarrollo Productivo Series*, No. 107, ECLAC, Santiago de Chile.

Murphy, K., A. Shleifer, and R. Vishny. (1989). "Industrialization and the Big Push," *Journal of Political Economy*, Vol. 97, No. 5, pp. 1003–1026.

Mussa, M. (2002). *Argentina y el FMI: del Triunfo a la tragedia*. (Buenos Aires: Planeta).

Myrdal, G. (1972). *The Challenge of World Poverty*. (London: Penguin).

Naim, M. (1994). "Latin America: The Second Stage of Reform," *Journal of Democracy*, Vol. 5, No. 4, pp. 33–48.

———. (2002). "The Washington Consensus: A Damaged Brand," *The Financial Times*, October 28.

(NCES) National Center for Education Statistics. (2003). *The Condition of Education 2003*, NCES 2003–067. (Washington, DC: U.S. Government Printing Office).

Nef, J. (2003). "Structural Correlates of Government Corruption in Latin America: Explaining and Understanding Empirical Findings," in *Governance in Southern Africa and beyond*. D. Olowu and R. Mukwena, eds. (Namibia: McMillan-Granberg).

Nelson, R. (2005). *Technology, Institutions, and Economic Growth*. (Cambridge, MA: Harvard University Press).

Nochteff, H. (1994a). "Patrones de Crecimiento y Políticas Tecnológicas en el Siglo XX," *Ciclos*, Vol. 4, No. 6, pp. 43–72.

———. (1994b) "Los Senderos Perdidos del Desarrollo. Elite Económica y Restricciones al Desarrollo en la Argentina," in *El Desarrollo Ausente. Restricciones al Desarrollo, Neoconservadorismo y Elite Económica en la Argentina*. D. Azpiazu and H. Nochteff, eds., pp. 21–156 (Buenos Aires: FLACSO/Tesis-Norma).

Nofal, B. (2002). "Las Causas de la Crisis de la Argentina," *Boletín Informativo Techint*, No. 310, May–August.

Nogués, J. (1986). "The Nature of Argentina's Policy Reforms during 1976–81," World Bank Staff Working Papers No. 765, World Bank.

North, D. (1990). *Institutions, Institutional Change and Economic Performance*. (Cambridge: Cambridge University Press).

Nurkse, R. (1952). "Some International Aspects of the Problem of Economic Development," *American Economic Review*, Vol. 42, No 2, pp. 571–583, May.

Obschatko, E. and J. C. Del Bello. (1986). "Tendencias Productivas y Estrategia Tecnológica para la Agricultura Pampeana," document no. 20, CISEA/ Proagro, Buenos Aires.

Obschatko, E., F. Sola, M. Piñeiro, and G. Bordelois. (1984). "Transformaciones en la Agricultura Pampeana: Algunas Hipótesis Interpretativas," document no. 3, prepared for the project *Alternativas de Política Agropecuaria*, CISEA, Buenos Aires.

Ocampo, J. A. (2004). "Beyond the Washington Consensus: What Do We Mean?" *Journal of Post Keynesian Economics*, Vol. 27, No. 2, pp. 293–314.

OECD. (1967). *Education, Human Resources and Development in Argentina*. (Paris: OECD).

———. (1994). *Managing the Environment. The role of Economic Instruments*. (Paris: OECD).

———. (1997). *National Innovation Systems*. (Paris: OECD).

———. (2001). *Encouraging Environmental Management in Industry, Business and Industry Policy Forum Series, Science, Technology and Industry Directorate*. (Paris: OECD).

OECD/UNESCO. (2003). *Literacy Skills for the World of Tomorrow. Further Results from PISA 2000*. (Paris: OECD).

Oman, C. (1999). *Policy Competition and Foreign Direct Investment. A Study on Competition among Governments to Attract FDI*. (Paris: OECD Development Centre).

Oman, C. P. and G. Wignaraja. (1991). *The Postwar Evolution of Development Thinking*. (London: OECD Development Centre/Macmillan).

OTA. (1994). "Industry, Technology and the Environment: Competitive Challenges and Business Opportunities," Congress of the United States, Washington, DC.

Pavitt, K. (1984). "Sectoral Patterns of Technical Change: Towards a Taxonomy and a Theory," *Research Policy*, Vol. 13, No. 6, pp. 343–373.

Perry, G. and L. Serven. (2002). "La Anatomía de una Crisis Múltiple: ¿qué tenía Argentina de Especial y qué Podemos Aprender de ella?" *Desarrollo Económico*, Vol. 42, No. 167, pp. 323–375.

Petrei, H. and J. de Melo. (1985). "Adjustments by Industrial Firms in Argentina during 1976–81," in *Scrambling for Survival: How Firms Adjusted to the Recent Reforms in Argentina, Chile and Uruguay*. V. Corbo and J. de Melo, eds. (Washington, DC: The World Bank).

Porter M. E. and C. Van der Linde (1995). "Toward a New Conception of the Environment-Competitiveness Relationship," *Journal of Economic Perspectives*, Vol. 9, No. 4, pp. 97–118.

Prebisch, R. (1950). "Crecimiento, Desequilibrio y Disparidades: Interpretación del Proceso de Desarrollo," *Estudio Económico de América Latina 1949*, United Nations, New York.

Rauch, J. and P. Evans. (2000). "Bureaucratic Structure and Bureaucratic Performance in Less Developed Countries," *Journal of Public Economics*, Vol. 75, No. 1, pp. 49–71.

Ray, D. (1998). *Economía del Desarrollo*. (Barcelona: Antoni Bosch).

RICYT. (2001). *Standardization of Indicators of Technological Innovation in Latin American and Caribbean Countries* [Bogotá Manual] (LUGAR: RICYT).

Rodríguez, C. (1988). "Estabilización versus Cambio Estructural: La Experiencia Argentina," working paper no. 62, CEMA, Buenos Aires.

Rodríguez, H. (2004). "Análisis de la Balanza de Pagos Tecnológica Argentina," SECYT, Buenos Aires.

Rodriguez F. and D. Rodrik (2000). "Trade Policy and Economic Growth: A Skeptic's Guide to the Cross-National Evidence," in *NBER Macroeconomics Annual 2000*. B.Bernanke and K. Rogoff, eds. (Cambridge, MA: MIT Press).

Rodrik, D. (2003). *In Search of Prosperity: Analytic Narratives on Economic Growth*. (Princeton, NJ: Princeton University Press).

———. (2005). "Why We Learn Nothing from Regressing Economic Growth on Policies," mimeo [unpublished], Kennedy School, Harvard.

———. (2006). "Goodbye Washington Consensus, Hello Washington Confusion?", *Journal of Economic Literature*, Vol. 44, No. 4.

Romero, L. A. (2002). *A History of Argentina in the Twentieth Century*. (Pennsylvania: State University Press).

Ros, J. (2001). "Del Auge de Capitales a la Crisis Financiera y más allá: México en los Noventa," in *Crisis Financieras en Países 'Exitosos'*. Ffrench Davis Ricardo, comp. (Santiago de Chile: ECLAC/McGraw Hill).

Rosenstein-Rodan, P. (1943). "Problems of Industrialization of Eastern and South-Eastern Europe," *Economic Journal*, Vol. 53, pp. 202–211.

Roubini, N. and B. Setser. (2004). *Bailouts or Bail-Ins? Responding to Financial. Crises in Emerging Markets*. (Washington, DC: Institute for International Economics).

Rougier, M. (2003). "Estado de Empresas y Crédito en la Argentina. El Banco Nacional de Desarrollo (1967–1976)," Universidad de San Andrés' PhD. thesis, Buenos Aires.

———. (2004) "Estado, Empresas y Crédito en la Argentina. Los Orígenes del Banco Nacional de Desarrollo, 1967–1973," *Desarrollo Económico*, Vol. 43, No. 172, pp. 515–544.

Rozada, M. and A. Menéndez. (2002). "Why Has Poverty Income Inequality Increased so Much? Argentina 1991–2002," mimeo [unpublished], Global Development Network (GDN).

Sábato, J. F. (1988). *La Clase Dominante en la Argentina Moderna*. (Buenos Aires: CISEA/GEL).

Sachs, J. D. and S. Radelet. (1998). "The East Asian Financial Crisis: Diagnosis, Remedies, Prospects," *Brookings papers on Economic Activity*, No. 1, pp. 1–74.

Sachs, J. D., A. Tornell, and A. Velasco. (1996). "The Mexican Peso Crisis: Sudden Death or Death Foretold," *Journal of International Economics*, Vol. 41, No 3–4, pp. 235–264.

Sanguinetti, P. (2005). "Innovation and R&D Expenditures in Argentina: Evidence from a Firm Level Survey," mimeo [unpublished], UTDT.

Schvarzer, J. (1996). *La Industria que Supimos Conseguir. Una Historia Político–Social de la Industria Argentina*. (Buenos Aires: Planeta).

Seers, D. (1969). "The Meaning of Development," XI World Conference of the Society for Internacional Development, Nueva Delhi.

Sen, A. (1983). "Development. Which Way Now?" *Economic Journal*, Vol. 93, No. 372, pp. 745–762.

———. (1999) *Development as Freedom*. (Oxford: Oxford University Press).

Shirley, M. (2005). "Institutions and Development," in *Handbook of New Institutional Economics*. C. Ménard and M. Shirley, eds., pp. 611–638 (Dordrecht: Springer).

Sikkink, K. (1993). "Las Capacidades y la Autonomía del Estado en Brasil y la Argentina: Un Enfoque Neoinstitucionalista," *Desarrollo Económico*, Vol. 32, No. 128, pp. 161–204.

Singer, H. W. (1950). "The Distribution of Gains between Investing and Borrowing Countries," *American Economic Review*, Vol. 40, No. 2, pp. 473–485.

———. (1997). "Editorial: The Golden Age of the Keynesian Consensus—The Pendulum Swings Back," *World Development*, Vol. 25. No. 3, pp. 293–295.

Sirlin, P. (1997). "An Appraisal of Capital Goods Policy in Argentina," *ECLAC Review*, No. 61, 149–165, Santiago de Chile.

Smith, W. C. (1991). *Authoritarianism and the Crisis of the Argentine Political Economy*. (Stanford: Stanford University Press).

Solá, F. (1986). "Empresas Agrícolas, Diferenciación, rentabilidad e Impactos de Políticas Alternativas," document no. 12, prepared for the project *Alternativas de Política Agropecuaria*, CISEA, Buenos Aires.

Sonnet, F. (1999). "La Reforma Económica y los Efectos sobre el Sector Agropecuario en Argentina (1989–1998)," *Anales de la XXXIV Reunión Anual de la Asociación Argentina de Economía Política*, Rosario.

Sourrouille, J., B. Kosacoff, and J. Lucangeli. (1985). *Transnacionalización y Política Económica en la Argentina*. (Buenos Aires: CEAL/CET).

Spiller, P., E. Stein, and M. Tommasi (2003). "Political Institutions, Policymaking Processes and Policy Outcomes. An Intertemporal Transactions Framework." Report for the Latin American Research Network, Inter-American Development Bank.

Spiller, P. and M. Tommasi. (2003). "The Institutional Foundations of Public Policy: A Transactions Approach with Application to Argentina," *Journal of Law, Economics, and Organization*, Vol. 19, No. 2, pp. 281–306.

Stallings, B. and W. Peres. (2000). *Crecimiento, Empleo y Equidad. El Impacto de las Reformas Económicas en América Latina y el Caribe*. (Santiago de Chile: ECLAC).

Stern, D., M. Common, and E. Barbier. (1996). "Economic Growth and Environmental Degradation: The Environmental Kuznets Curve and Sustainable Development," *World Development*, Vol. 24, No. 7, pp. 1151–1160.

Stiglitz, J. E. (1998). "Más Instrumentos y Metas más Amplias para el Desarrollo. Hacia el Consenso Post-Washington," *Desarrollo Económico*, Vol. 38, No. 151, pp. 691–721.

———. (2002). *El malestar de la globalización*. (Madrid: Taurus).

Streeten, P., S. J. Burki, M. ul Haq, N. Hicks, and F. Stewart (1981). *First Things First: Meeting Basic Human Needs in the Developing Countries*. (New York: Oxford University Press).

Teijeiro, M. 2001. "Una vez más, la Política Fiscal . . .," Centro de Estudios Públicos, Buenos Aires.

Trigo, E., D. Chudnovsky, E. Cap, and A. López. (2002). *Los Transgénicos en la Agricultura Argentina: Una Historia con Final Abierto.* (Buenos Aires: Libros del Zorzal/IICA).

UNDP. (1999). *Human Development Report 1999. Globalization with a Human Face.* (New York: UNDP-Oxford University Press).

UNESCO. (1998). *First International Comparative Study of Language, Mathematics, and Associated Factors for Students in the Third and Fourth Years of Primary School.* (Santiago de Chile: OREALC/UNESCO).

Veganzones, M. A. and C. Winograd. (1997). *Argentina in the 20th Century: An Account of Long-Awaited Growth.* (Paris: OECD).

Ventura, J. P. (2001). "Política de Apoyo a las Pequeñas y Medianas Empresas: Análisis del Programa de Reconversión Empresarial para las Exportaciones," *Estudios y Perspectivas Series*, No. 1, ECLAC, Buenos Aires.

Wade, R. (1990). *Governing the Market: Economic Theory and the Role of Government in East Asian Industrialization.* (Princeton: Princeton University Press).

Waterbury, J. (1999). "The Long Gestation and Brief Triumph of Import-Substituting Industrialization," *World Development*, Vol. 27, No. 2, pp. 323–341.

Williamson, J. (1990). *Latin American Adjustment. How Much Has Happened?* (Washington, DC: Institute for International Economics).

———. (1997) "The Washington Consensus Revisited," in *Economic and Social Development into the XXI Century*. L. Emmerij, ed., pp. 48–61 (Washington, DC: Banco Interamericano de Desarrollo).

———. (1999) "The Impact of Globalization on Pre–Industrial, Technologically Quiescent Economies: Real Wages, Relative Factor Prices and Commodity Price Convergence in the Third World before 1940," working paper, no. 7146, NBER.

———. (2003). "Appendix. Our Agenda and the Washington Consensus," in *After the Washington Consensus. Restarting Growth and Reform in Latin America*. P. Kuczynski and J. Williamson, eds., pp. 323–331 (Washington, DC: Institute for International Economics).

Winkler, D. (1990). "Higher Education in Latin America. Issues of Efficiency and Equity," discussion paper no. 77, (Washington, DC: World Bank).

World Bank. (1981). *World Development Report.* (Washington, DC: Oxford University Press).

———. (1993). *The East Asian Miracle: Economic Growth and Public Policy.* (Washington, DC: Oxford University Press).

———. (1998). "Project Appraisal Document on a Proposed Loan in the Amount of US$ 119.0 Million to Province of Buenos Aires with the Guarantee of the Argentine Republic for a Third Secondary Education Project," Report No. 17498, World Bank.

———. (2000). *World Development Report 2000/2001 Attacking Poverty.* (Washington, DC: Oxford University Press).

———. (2004). *Inequality in Latin America and the Caribbean Breaking with History.* (Washington, DC: Oxford University Press).

———. (2006). *Virtuous Circles of Poverty Reduction and Growth.* (Washington: Oxford University Press).

Yoguel, G. (1998). "El Ajuste Empresarial Frente a la Apertura: La Heterogeneidad de las Respuestas de las PyMEs," *Desarrollo Económico*, Vol. 38, Special Edition, Autumn, pp. 177–198, Buenos Aires.

——. (1999) "El Aislamiento de las Firmas y el Rol del Ambiente de Negocios," in *Los Problemas del Entorno de Negocios. El Desarrollo Competitivo de las PyMEs Argentinas*. G. Yoguel and V. Moori Koenig, coords., pp. 151–166 (Buenos Aires: UNGS/Fundes/Miño and Davila Editores).

Yoguel, G. and V. Moori Koenig, coords. (1999). *Los problemas del entorno de negocios. El desarrollo competitivo de las PyMEs argentinas*. (Buenos Aires: FUNDES Argentina/UNGS/Edición Ciepp Miño Dávila).

Yoguel, G., V. Moori Koenig, and F. Boscherini. (1998). *Nuevos Enfoques de la Política Industrial de Apoyo a la PyME*. (Buenos Aires: SOCMA).

Yoguel, G. and R. Rabetino. (2002). "La Incorporación de Tecnología en la Industria Manufacturera Argentina en los Noventa: los Factores Determinantes," in *Apertura e Innovación en la Argentina. Para Desconcertar a Vernon, Schumpeter and Freeman*. R. Bisang, G. Lugones y G. Yoguel, eds., pp. 135–158 (Buenos Aires: Editorial Miño y Dávila).

INDEX